Cultural Adaptation and
Resistance on St. John

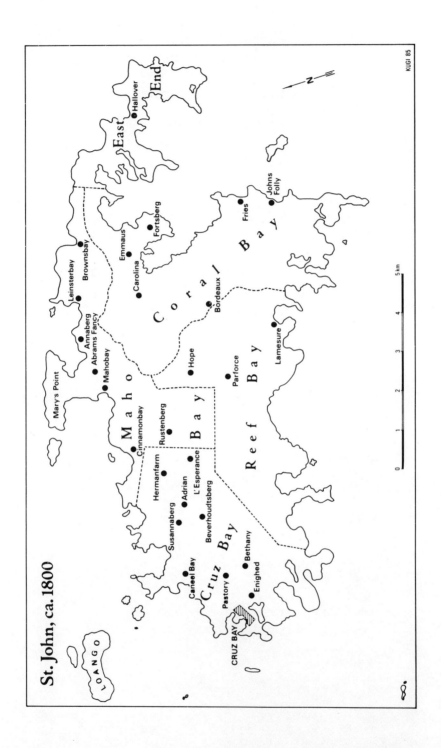

St. John, ca. 1800

LOANGO

Mary's Point

Leinsterbay
Brownsbay
Annaberg
Abrams Fancy
Mahobay

East End

Hallover

Emmaus
Fortsberg
Carolina

Coral Bay

Fries
Johns Folly

Maho Bay

Cinnamonbay
Rustenberg
Hope
Bordeaux
Parforce
Lamesure

Reef Bay

Hermanfarm
Adrian
L'Esperance
Beverhoudtsberg
Susannaberg

Cruz Bay

Caneel Bay
Bethany
Pastory
Enighed

CRUZ BAY

N

0   1   2   3   4   5 km

KUGI 85

Cultural Adaptation and Resistance on St. John

Three Centuries of Afro-Caribbean Life

Karen Fog Olwig

UNIVERSITY PRESSES OF FLORIDA
University of Florida Press / Gainesville

UNIVERSITY PRESSES OF FLORIDA is the central agency for scholarly publishing of the State of Florida's university system, producing books selected for publication by the faculty editorial committees of Florida's nine public universities: Florida A&M University (Tallahassee), Florida Atlantic University (Boca Raton), Florida International University (Miami), Florida State University (Tallahassee), University of Central Florida (Orlando), University of Florida (Gainesville), University of North Florida (Jacksonville), University of South Florida (Tampa), University of West Florida (Pensacola).

Orders for books published by all member presses of UNIVERSITY PRESSES OF FLORIDA should be addressed to University Presses of Florida, 15 NW 15th Street, Gainesville, FL 32603.

2nd printing, 1987

Library of Congress Cataloging in Publication Data

Olwig, Karen Fog, 1948–
    Cultural adaptation and resistance on St. John.

    Bibliography: p.
    Includes index.
    1. Slavery—Virgin Islands of the United States—Saint John—History.   2. Saint John (V.I.) —Race relations.   3. Plantation life—Virgin Islands of the United States—Saint John.   I. Title.
    HT1071.O43   1985   306'.097297'22   85-13414
    ISBN 0-8130-0818-2

Contents

Tables and Figures

Tables

Figures

Carolina Estate in Coral Bay, owned by the Schimmelmann family; the Moravian Mission, Emmaus, can be seen to the right. Watercolor by Fr. v. Scholten, 1833, Handels -og Søfartsmuseet, Kronborg, Elsinore.

Preface

THE ISLAND of St. John was colonized as a plantation society in the early eighteenth century; it became a peasant society in the latter part of the nineteenth century and developed into a society serving tourism in the mid-1950s. On the basis of archival records, printed sources, and field research data, this book describes the complex ways in which the local Afro-Caribbean culture developed in relation to these very different social and economic patterns. This community is *not* one of well-established formal institutions, ancient customs and traditions, or publicly sanctioned values that support the official social and economic order. Rather, it consists of wide-ranging and loosely structured networks of social and economic relations, changing social practices and forms, and a belief system that in many ways runs counter to the larger social and economic structure. Cultural development on St. John has had a double character, constantly oscillating between strategies of adaptation and strategies of resistance to the conditions of life presented to the population.

St. Johnian culture is more, however, than a long series of ever-changing responses to forces beyond control. Behind the many different cultural and social forms that have surfaced throughout the history of the island, an enduring system by which interpersonal relations are regulated can be discerned. It is a system of exchange involving a large network of relatives and friends who share and redistribute favors, goods, land usage, and children, as the need and the desire arise. This exchange network functions both as a means of subsistence and as a means of forming an autonomous identity. It can be traced back to the early period of slavery, and its very beginning can be seen as a coming together of more or less articulated needs to create a basis for Afro-Caribbean economic, social, and cultural autonomy within the oppressive plantation society. Exchange is therefore basic to the character of the local community and culture and sets it apart from externally imposed social structures. To the extent that St. Johnians are aware of this and have clung to their own ways, the exchange system has become an ideology that has played an active role in the history of the island. To the extent that St. Johnians are doing what they have always done, though their exchange relations have undergone certain modifications in appearance, they are simply functioning within their own particular cultural framework.

Theoretical considerations

In orienting my work to the cultural history of St. John, I am departing from established anthropological practice. Anthropological research on Afro-Caribbean cultures has been characterized by two interrelated concerns. On the one hand, it has been motivated by an academic interest in applying and redefining theory developed in studies of other areas of the world characterized largely by tribal and peasant societies. The Caribbean, one of the main areas of African settlement in the Americas, has thus been an important testing ground, often challenging established notions in the field. On the other hand, research has been guided by the need to clarify issues involving people of African origin in the Americas in general that are of popular interest and are points of controversy in Western societies. These issues spring from social values and problems that are not specific to Afro-Americans. The result has been that the efforts of researchers have tended to be directed by concerns external to the study of Afro-American history and culture per se. The many family studies provide a good case in point.

Social and academic interests have converged, to a remarkable extent, in studies of Afro-American family structure (R. T. Smith 1982). When anthropological research among Afro-Americans became an established subfield within the discipline, there was already a strong tradition of research on kinship and family structure. Much of this had focused on corporate kin groups or relatively permanent household structures. The fluid households found among Afro-Americans, often headed by women, and the relative lack of legally recognized marriages were therefore puzzling. Confronted with an unusual family type, anthropologists reacted by treating it as a special case, the "matrifocal family" (R. T. Smith 1973). Coincidentally, governmental and religious authorities were expressing concerns about family impermanence or instability. The "unusual" Afro-American family has been viewed in these contexts as contributing to, if not causing, social and economic problems common among Afro-Americans; it has also been regarded as evidence of loose morals. A solution to the "family problem" has been seen as a necessary step toward improving the conditions of the Afro-Americans (M. G. Smith 1966). The many studies of the matrifocal family therefore may not derive from theoretical interest alone but also from the social perception of the family as problematic (see, for example, Gonzalez's discussion of the concept of "matrifocality" [1970] and Shifflett 1975).

Contrary to established anthropological methodology, much of the research on Afro-American social structure in the Caribbean has not been holistic in character. With few exceptions (R. T. Smith 1978a, 1978b), there has been little discussion of kinship structure as such, much less of the larger sociocultural systems (Olwig 1981a). Despite the fact that a great number of case studies have been completed in Afro-Caribbean communities, they have resulted in few works on the culture of these communities (exceptions include Mintz 1974 and Wilson 1973). Instead, a long series of publications on Afro-Caribbean family structure has emerged (see, for example, Marks and Römer 1978). The lack of a sociocultural framework has been even more apparent in historians' work on the Afro-Caribbean family; in recent years they have tested anthropological hypotheses about the family largely by computing statistical tables of household and mating relationships among slaves. There has been little sense of the family being part of an Afro-American culture developed in the Caribbean (Olwig 1981b).

My attempt at reconstructing the development of a culture among a people of Afro-American descent represents a return to the study of fundamental social relations and cultural categories. Although it does not address the family as a separate institution for social research, it nevertheless deals with family relations and the role they have had in the network of exchange that forms the basis of St. Johnian life. From this vantage point there is much to interpret and understand, and perhaps not so much to explain. The conclusions that I draw on the basis of this case study are specifically valid for St. John; however, since the historical background of St. Johnians is similar to that of other Afro-American people, the study provides an example of the more general development of some important features of Afro-American culture, including the family.

Acknowledgments

The research upon which this work is based has taken place over a ten-year period beginning in 1972. Fieldwork was conducted on St. John in July 1972, April 1974–May 1975, December 1977–March 1978, December 1979–January 1980. This research was funded by the Department of Anthropology of the University of Minnesota, the Danish Research Council of the Humanities, and the Institute of Ethnology and Anthropology at the University of Copenhagen. Research in the Danish West Indian Archives in Copenhagen was conducted intermittently from 1973 to 1982, primarily September 1973–March 1974, June–August 1975, September–November 1978, and February–June 1981; all translations are mine unless otherwise noted. Research in the National Archives in Washington, D.C., took place in June 1978. Archival research was funded by the University of Copenhagen and the Carlsberg Foundation. I thank the above agencies for the support I have received.

The staff at the National Archives in Copenhagen and Washington and at the Enid M. Baa Library and Archives on St. Thomas provided me with invaluable assistance in my archival research. I owe a great debt to the people of St. John, in particular the elderly; without their help, this book would not have been possible. I thank Enid M. Baa, Lito Valls, and Noble Samuel for helping me enter into this community. I am also grateful to Stephen Gudeman, John Modell, Richard Price, Charles Carnegie, Susan Whyte, Michael Whyte, Jonathan Friedman, Steven Sampson, and Kenneth Olwig, who read and commented on the manuscript at various stages of its development, and Lise Steiness and Birthe Andersen, who helped with its preparation.

1

The Historical Anthropology
of St. John

THROUGHOUT its less than 300-year history, St. John has undergone a number of abrupt changes, which might be supposed to have precluded any continuity in the development of an Afro-Caribbean culture. The mountainous island of less than twenty square miles was settled in 1717 by Danish colonists to develop plantation cultivation. Visitors to the island in the eighteenth and early nineteenth centuries saw a plantation society in full force and could not have failed to be impressed with the overwhelming presence of the plantations and the way they seemingly permeated all relationships on the island. The whole political and economic structure of the island was organized around the plantations and geared exclusively toward advancing the interests of their owners. Virtually all the arable land was held by large estate owners and staked out in fields of sugarcane and cotton. The majority of the St. Johnian population had been imported from Africa to work on the plantations. Most of the time, the slaves tended the crops or operated the mills and sugar works. The island society was administered by Danish colonial officials, who were closely aligned with the planters' interests; several were planters themselves.

A visitor to St. John in the late nineteenth century, a few decades after the emancipation of the slaves in 1848, met an entirely different society. Gone were the large plantations with their vast fields of sugarcane and cotton. Most of the mills, sugar works, and great houses, which had towered above the cultivated landscape, had been abandoned for some time and were being covered by tangles of vine and bush gradually enveloping the island. Some of the old sugarcane fields had been converted into pastures, where cattle were kept by the estate owners who lived on the island. Most of these owners were not descendants of the former planters but were latecomers from Europe and other West Indian islands (some of the latter of partly African descent) who had purchased faltering sugar plantations at low prices. In place of the former plantation society had emerged a peasantry. The descendants of the slaves made their living from small farming, fishing, and charcoal burning. They lived in their own settlements scattered about in the bush on small plots of land that the emancipated slaves had purchased from their former owners, but most of them depended upon access to additional land owned by the cattle estates. Still they lived a rather undisturbed life; in fact, the colonial government had all but lost interest in this small peasant backwater, which appeared to be an isolated rural idyll.

A century later, St. John presents to the visitor a completely different aspect, a vacation paradise for tourists from North America and Europe. Most of the former cattle estates have been turned into a "nature park" covering more than half of the island. Within the boundaries of the park are housing facilities for tourists, including a luxury hotel, holiday homes, and campgrounds. The park land can be used only for recreation, and very little farming is now done on the island. The old peasant settlements have been abandoned or turned into lots on which modern concrete block houses are being built primarily for outsiders. Most of the native Afro-Caribbean population, called St. Johnians, have moved to Cruz Bay, the main town on the island, which has grown from a hamlet of a few dozen houses to a settlement of almost a thousand persons. St. Johnians nowadays make their living as wage laborers in either the tourism industry or governmental employment. In the past, visitors to the island were few and infrequent; today, St. John is visited every year by tens of thousands of people eager to enjoy its pleasant climate and beautiful scenery.

St. Johnian society has undergone dramatic changes in less than a hundred and fifty years. From a slave-labor-based plantation society cultivating export crops for the benefit primarily of European economic interests it changed to a peasant society based on a subsistence economy functioning without much interference from the colonial system and more recently to a tourism society based on providing services to vacationers from far away and an economy developed with capital from the United States. It

would be easy to conclude that St. John has undergone such tre-
mendous transformations that the sequence of three distinct societies on the island have little connection with one another.
While this interpretation might be reasonable from a political-
economic standpoint, from a social and cultural standpoint the
three systems appear merely to have provided the external framework for the life of the St. Johnians and thus for the development
of their culture and society.

The emergence of a culture

The St. Johnians may seem to have been an active force in the
history of St. John only during the peasant period (after the Danish and American colonial system left the stage open to them). In
fact this is not true; their active role as a quasi-independent
peasantry began under slavery. As has been suggested by Sidney
Mintz, Caribbean peasantries can be regarded as "reconstituted
peasantries, having begun other than as peasants—in slavery, as
deserters or runaways, as plantation laborers, or whatever—and
becoming peasants in some kind of resistant response to an externally imposed regimen" (1974: 132). This occurred because of
inherent contradictions in both the system of slavery and the
plantation system as it took form in the West Indies.

Scholars have documented the extreme subjugation experienced by African slaves. Economically, they were reduced to
being property, a part of the owner's capital on a par with for example, machinery and livestock (Hindness and Hirst 1975: 128).
Indeed, the slave has been defined as "one who owns or controls
neither his own labor-power nor the means of production" and
who receives only "as the direct means of his or her livelihood
that portion which is the product of 'necessary labor'" (Padgug
1976: 4). Legally or morally, it has been noted that "two qualities
set the slave apart from other forms of compulsory labour. One is
the totality of his subjection; the slave is powerless and rightless
in all respects, forever (unless he is freed by his master as a personal act of indulgence). The other is his being an outsider" (Finley 1980: 256).

Theoretically, these observations may be correct; however,
they describe a conception of slave status only in its pure form
unmodified by the social and economic environment in which

slavery actually exists. In reality, it is doubtful whether this ideal slave status ever has existed anywhere except perhaps in the minds of the slaveholders. And even this is questionable. The history of the West Indies certainly shows that the reality of the plantation system of which the slaves were a part precluded their being entirely denied the use of their "own labor-power or the means of production."

To be sure, the plantation owners kept slaves in order to use their labor-power in plantation cultivation. In order to have a continuous supply of laborers, it was not enough to own some number of slaves. For slave labor to produce crops or goods, it had to physically revitalize or "reproduce" its labor power on a daily basis, just as it had to reproduce itself on a generational basis. Furthermore, this daily and generational reproduction took place in a social context. "Social reproduction" thus became integral to labor reproduction.[1] As long as the transatlantic slave trade continued, slave owners could import replacement slaves from Africa. After the cessation of the slave trade, however, masters were forced to rely on the slaves' own procreation for the replenishment of the slave population. For the slaves' daily subsistence, the planters could provide either imported or locally cultivated foodstuffs. By importing foodstuffs, plantation owners could concentrate on cash crop production. This was particularly desirable where there was little marginal land and conditions for sugar production were ideal. It was much cheaper and more dependable, however, to grow the foodstuffs on the estates, sometimes under the planters' supervision in the normal work hours and on fields otherwise devoted to export crops. But on many estates a great amount of marginal land unsuitable for large-scale plantation cultivation could be used for smaller-scale farming as provision grounds. On such estates, slaves customarily cultivated their own subsistence crops without supervision in their spare time by whatever methods they chose to use, as long as they did not interfere with the plantation routine (Mintz and Hall 1960).

Despite the constraints of slavery and of the plantation society, the slave population was provided with an opportunity of developing its own system of daily and generational reproduction. The word "reproduction" is used in this book to mean (1) the production and distribution of the means of living, and (2) procreation and the rearing of children. While the masters thought of this system, at least initially, as a convenient and inexpensive way of reproducing the slave labor force, the slaves saw it quite differently. As Rubin has observed (1975: 165), every system of human reproduction is "shaped by human, social intervention and satisfied in a conventional manner, no matter how bizarre some of the conventions may be." The slaves, having human emotional and intellectual resources, changed the reproduction system from purely a matter of reproducing labor power to one of reproducing the particular social and economic relations that emerged in the course of the development of the reproductive system. On St. John, as on many other West Indian islands, these relations came to revolve around a peasantlike culture. When plantation cultivation on St. John ended in the latter part of the nineteenth century, the emancipated slaves already had a long tradition of a peasantlike culture dating well back into the period of slavery.

While the slaves' system of social reproduction may be regarded as a means of accommodating to the plantation system and its demand for labor-power, it can also be regarded as a form of resistance, which became the basis for the development of a culture that was largely controlled by the slaves. As Africans, or people of African descent, they were "outsiders" in the European colonial society. Their cultural background was therefore not understood, perhaps not even always recognized by the master class. This cultural isolation, combined with the fact that slaves were thought of by many as subhuman beings, provided the environment for the relatively unrecognized growth of a culture that had strong elements of resistance to the proprietors. It is thus possible to interpret the Caribbean peasantries as representing both "*a mode of response* to the plantation system and its connotations, and *a mode of resistance* to imposed styles of life" (Mintz 1974: 132–33).

The nature and relative importance of the elements of response and resistance have varied depending on the character of the local manifestation of the larger colonial framework. In the case of St. John, this framework, as already noted, has changed a great deal. Until the latter part of the nineteenth century, colonial power was tied to a European plantocracy, which had a great need for cheap, unskilled labor and used slavery as a means of acquiring and controlling this labor. In the face of this oppression, St. Johnian culture contained strong elements of both response and resistance, the former providing the basis for sheer physical survival of the slaves and the latter raising the slaves above complete subjugation and creating a socioeconomic system that, in the long run, outlived the plantation society. From the mid-nineteenth to the mid-twentieth century, there emerged a new class of estate owners who, though they owned most of the land on the island, were relatively poor and powerless in the larger colonial context. They had only limited need for laborers and cultivated a rather small portion of their land. Free St. Johnians were thus presented with the possibility of developing their own peasant society. In this period, the St. Johnian culture responded by making great efforts to elaborate on social and economic relations that would enable St. Johnians to sustain their own society in the face of their limited economic resources.

Since the mid-twentieth century, a powerful external economic framework has once more become visible on St. John. It is now composed of a large, amorphous network of primarily American economic interests seeking to take advantage of investment possibilities generated by tourism. In this period, St. Johnians have been displaced from their traditional economically insecure peasant mode of subsistence to become wage laborers. They have in turn, however, lost the measure of social and economic autonomy they once possessed. Their present culture is most important, therefore, as a means of resistance to the social and economic dominance of the new master class.

In spite of the long history of the Afro-Caribbean culture, it has been little understood by representatives of the external rule. The planters welcomed the slaves' subsistence farming and appreciated the economic benefits they themselves might derive from it. The planters also saw the value that the slaves attached to their provision grounds and regarded it as a means of making them a more reliable and stable plantation labor force. Characteristically, the planters did not envision the economic independence that the slaves would acquire through their provision farming nor did they realize the full ramifications of the slaves' social and economic relationships that surrounded this farming. The planters discovered too late that the provision grounds provided an excellent support for marooning (running away and living in hiding) and that the social relations associated with the system of production provided an important organizational framework for protest and rebellion (Mathurin 1975; Craton 1979). Similarly, planters and colonial officials showed an almost complete lack of understanding of the slaves' system of kinship and family (cf. Craton 1978c: 166). After the abolition of the transatlantic slave trade, certain concessions were granted to pregnant women and mothers of infants to help them bear and rear children who could be future laborers. The cultural background of the representatives of the external framework, however, was so much at variance with that of the St. Johnians that the former could see only a chaos of immoral relationships. While the planters recognized the slaves' provision farming as an advantage to the plantations, i.e., as an adaptation to the plantation system, they viewed the slave family (or rather what they considered perhaps to be the lack thereof) as a great liability to the plantations, working against the planters' interest in acquiring a stable number of laborers. As will be seen, however, the slave family, like subsistence farming, contained elements of adaptation as well as resistance to the plantation system. This lack of understanding of the St. Johnian system of generational reproduction has continued to characterize the relationship between the St. Johnians and representatives of external social and economic interests since the abolition of slavery.

The reconstruction of the history of the St. Johnian community involves not just an account of the Afro-Caribbean past but also the delineation of the external colonial and neocolonial framework within which it has evolved. This approach to the development of St. Johnian community and culture is confronted with a paradoxical situation. On the one hand, since the earliest colonization of the island St. Johnian culture has undergone continuous change as the demands of the external colonial framework have changed and the St. Johnians have responded to and resisted these demands. On the other hand, this very interplay between the external framework and the St. Johnian community has sustained a situation of response and resistance to oppression that has been more or less constant throughout the history of the island. Viewed in this way, the character of St. Johnian community and culture has persisted. In creating and developing their community and culture, St. Johnians have employed the resources that have been available to them, drawing on elements of European as well as African origin. The origin of these elements, in this context, is less significant than the use to which they were put and the way in which they were combined to form a culture with both practical and symbolic importance.

Empirical and methodological
bases of the study

When anthropologists began to study West Indian peoples, field-work was already established as the basic research method of a discipline that largely saw itself as studying "nonhistoric" peoples. Therefore anthropologists relied almost exclusively upon fieldwork data, despite the fact that in their theoretical work they pointed to the importance of the past in the formation of present-day Afro-Caribbean culture and often made specu-lative assertions regarding its development. Most anthropolo-gists have shied away from supporting their interpretations through historical research. The available historical sources present serious difficulties in that most of the descriptions of the slaves were written by planters, colonial officials, and visitors from Europe. These accounts are distorted by a misunderstand-ing of and negative attitudes toward people of African descent. Though the sources are biased, they can be useful in revealing the impressions and feelings that representatives of the planter class had for the Afro-Caribbeans (see Olwig 1985). But to de-lineate the development of the Afro-Caribbean culture itself, it is necessary to turn to other types of sources.

The slaves themselves were, by the nature of the institution of slavery, virtually barred from writing down their experiences and feelings and their reactions toward the situation in which they had been placed within the plantation society. Fortunately, historical research is not confined to dealing with descriptive sources. Marc Bloch, in a discussion of historical evidence (1953: 61–65), has distinguished between "narrative sources" that are "consciously intended to inform their readers" and "the evidence of witnesses in spite of themselves," sources never intended to be part of the historical record. As examples of such witnesses, he mentions inscriptions, material objects, and administrative records, which, when brought together and cross-examined against each other, contain implicit information about the society that produced them.

Handler and Lange's work on plantation slavery in Barbados is an example of an approach using such unintentional witnesses. In this case, archaeological records from the Newton Plantation and material objects unearthed through archaeological excava-tions provided the main sources. Though their archaeological research was made difficult because of prior disturbances in the sites by farming activities, their study nevertheless produced important insights into the early development of Afro-Caribbean culture, especially with reference to mortuary practices (Handler and Lange 1978).

In my research on the development of Afro-Caribbean culture on St. John, I have primarily employed archival records and data collected in anthropological fieldwork. The government of the Danish West Indies was very hierarchical and centralized, conforming with the structure of the absolute monarchy that ruled the mother country. In the Danish West Indies, the governor general was the representative of the king; he deferred major decisions and all legislative acts to the king and his councillors in Denmark. Only after a free constitution had been enacted in Denmark in 1849 were colonial councils established in the Danish West Indies, in 1852 (see Olsen 1980). On St. John almost all governmental functions were gathered in the office of the *landfoged*; he was judge in the lower court, bailiff, policemaster, public notary, administrator of auctions and the probate court, postmaster, and customs officer (ibid.: 75). His superiors were the St. Thomas governor and the governor-general on St. Croix.

The archives of the *landfoged* contain extensive records reporting in great detail on many aspects of life on St. John to which his duties pertained. In plantation societies where the planters were resident on their estates and maintained close supervision over their slaves, most of the encounters between the governmental administration and the slaves were channeled through the planters. In such societies, the government archives may contain few references to the slaves, and research on slavery in these societies is dependent upon the survival of contemporaneous plantation archives. On St. John, however, most of the owners of the large plantations, which held the vast majority of the slaves, lived outside the island; therefore the daily administration of the plantations was passed on to temporary overseers or, in some cases, even to slaves (head drivers). As plantation authority in these instances was relatively weak, there were many direct encounters between the colonial administration, represented by the *landfoged*, and the slaves. The archives of the *landfoged* are rich in testimony from the slaves, describing the inner workings of the plantations and the system of slavery.

In addition to the records of the office of the *landfoged*, there are tax lists and census returns, completed by order of the colonial administration, and church records kept by missionaries on the island. The tax records contain yearly accounts of the acreage under cultivation on the estates, the number of slaves held by the different plantations, the amount of taxes due, and the owners' names. Thus they indicate the major trends in the plantation economy and provide figures on the size of the slave population. Toward the end of the eighteenth century, at the time of the ban of the slave trade, the annual tax rolls also recorded the slave population by age and sex. Census returns were the result of population counts begun toward the middle of the nineteenth century. Three censuses were completed during slavery (1835, 1841, and 1846) and nine during the remainder of the Danish period (1850, 1855, 1857, 1860, 1870, 1880, 1890, 1901, 1911). Unfortunately, only a few lists were salvaged from the 1835 census, and all the returns were lost from the 1890 census. During slavery, men were enumerated first, according to age, occupation, religion, and marital status, then women, according to the same criteria plus the number of their living children. The 1850 census follows the same pattern as far as the newly freed are concerned; but beginning with the 1855 census, all St. Johnians are listed according to household, and the residents' relationship to the head of the household is specified.

The Moravians kept records of their missionary activities, and the Emmaus Church books, which date back to 1833 and cover the largest of the two Moravian parishes on the island at this period, have been particularly useful. They include lists of baptized children and their parents, married couples, and burials, as well as records of the communicants. The listings of parentage are most important because they provide a record of the slaves' sexual relationships when the unions resulted in the birth of a child. Some records have survived from the work of the Lutheran Church on the island. A church book dating from 1822 has been preserved; however, it was not before 1859 that this church became important among the Afro-Caribbeans on the island.

Historian Barry Higman, one of the foremost authorities on the slave family, has pointed to some of the limitations and methodological problems generated by basing one's research on such records. The documents that deal most directly with the slaves and their family system are the population censuses and church records. Higman notes that, while these records can map out households and kin groups, the meaning of these groups remains unclear due to the lack of data describing their social and economic function. It is rather dubious, argues Higman (1977), whether it is justifiable to equate a household consisting of a man, woman, and children with the "nuclear family," an entity that has a specific structure and function in Western society.

Since archival records were never intended to describe the slaves' family life, historians may have expected too much if they have searched for explicit descriptions of family life in these records. Regarded as unintentional witnesses of Afro-Caribbean life as it is reflected in encounters between the colonial administration and the Afro-Caribbean community existing within a plantation society, the documents can yield a great deal of evidence. The questions addressed to the historical sources must be informed by theoretical considerations of the nature of the plantation system and its associated system of slavery. Many of the *landfoged* documents deal with the plantations' problems with a view to helping solve them. Because these problems often revolved around conflicts that emerged in connection with the slaves' development of their own system of reproduction, many of the records, in fact, focus on this important nexus of Afro-Caribbean culture. In many respects, the records are thus unintentional witnesses of the emergence of Afro-Caribbean culture.

While the plantation society and the earliest development of its subsumed Afro-Caribbean culture can be reconstructed only from historical materials, particularly archival sources, the more recent peasant society can be investigated through more various kinds of evidence. Apart from the Danish archival documents, transcripts from the American administrator on St. John are available, though not uniformly preserved. The American population censuses are not accessible, unfortunately, for research purposes. The shortcomings of the archival data are compensated for by information on the peasant society collected from older residents of St. John during a year's fieldwork on the island. This research centered on life history interviews, collection of genealogies, and general interviews on the history of the island community.

Fieldwork has been even more important as a means of obtaining data about the present tourism society on the island. Little archival material is available because the record keepers have sought to protect the individuals' right of privacy. My analysis of

this period is therefore based on field notes grounded in partici-
pant observation, interviews, and questionnaires I administered
to selected households.

In this study of the development of Afro-Caribbean culture on
St. John, I therefore had to deal with two completely different
types of data for the first and third phases of the history. I have
attempted to solve this problem by cross-checking the data collected from archival and fieldwork research against each other
in the analysis of the peasant period, for which both kinds of
records were available. This approach should help avoid the un-
fortunate tendency to interpret such archival data from what
R. T. Smith, in a review of West Indian family studies, has termed
"a common-sense European point of view" (1978a: 339). The
method has helped me generate, on the basis of the fieldwork,
statistical data comparable to those of the archival data. "Historical anthropology" is a relatively new discipline, particularly in
the Caribbean, where it is in a state of theoretical and methodological flux. This study should contribute not only to the understanding of St. Johnian and Afro-Caribbean society but also to
clarification of the discipline.

2

The Plantation Society

AFRO-AMERICAN history was initially framed by the experience of the plantation societies in the New World. The position that Afro-Americans attained was defined by the plantations' demands for labor combined with their owners' need to control a large population enslaved against its will. On St. John, as elsewhere, the requirement for labor involved, on the one hand, the extraction of all the toil that could be forced from the slaves, and, on the other, the contrary need to encourage their creative and independent action. The need to control the slaves led to their definition as chattels. Under ideal circumstances, it would have been most profitable for the slaves to be fed imported foodstuffs and for their numbers to be replenished by imported African slaves. In practice, however, the plantation owners came to depend on the slaves' ability to provide food for themselves and to maintain their numbers within a self-supporting social framework.

This dependency led to conflicts that could not be resolved by the persistent attempts of plantation owners to dehumanize the slaves in order to control them. The history of the plantation society became one of self-contradictions, of conflicts between planters and slaves mediated by colonial authorities. The plantation society was under constant pressure from the contradictions inherent in the system of slavery, and that pressure transformed the system of slavery itself.

The establishment of a plantation society

St. John was colonized in 1718, when plantation cultivation in the West Indies, particularly of sugarcane and cotton, was becoming increasingly profitable. The island of nineteen square miles, a small group of mountaintops and deep valleys that plunge into the sea, has little arable land and was not regarded as well suited to plantation agriculture. Only on a small plateau in the middle of the island and in a few of the valleys are there patches of level land of more than a hundred acres fertile enough for intensive sugarcane cultivation. In 1718, however, St. John was the island most accessible for expansion by the St. Thomas–based Danish colonial administration. A group consisting of one colonial representative, twenty planters from St. Thomas, five soldiers, and twelve slaves raised the Danish flag on the island, fired a few gunshots, drank to the health and prosperity of the Danish king and the West Indian Company (which governed St. Thomas until 1755, when the Danish state took direct control), and decided on a site where a fort was to be located (Bro-Jørgensen 1966: 216–18). Despite protests from the British governor of the Leeward Islands, St. John remained Danish, and soon a plantation society grew out of the wilderness encountered by the Danish colonization party.

In 1733, when the Danes purchased the larger island of St. Croix from the French, 109 plantations had already been staked out on St. John. Only 21 of them were sugar plantations; the rest were either cotton plantations or smaller estates producing staples. Sugar production became dominant toward the end of the century, much as it did in the British Leeward Islands (Goveia 1969: 103–4). By 1800, St. John had become a full-fledged plantation society based on sugar production (*VRR* 1755–1800; Sveistrup 1942: 125). The slave population, a little more than 1,000 in 1733, had been increased to more than 2,500 by the end of the century to meet the needs of this labor-intensive production (see Table 1). Almost 90 percent of the slaves lived and worked on the sugar plantations, which in 1805 used, on the average, 103 slaves to cultivate 110 acres, 85 of which were in sugarcane (Bro-Jørgensen 1966: 220–22; Green-Pedersen 1978: 21; *VRR* 1755–1810).

If St. John had been its only West Indian possession, Denmark probably soon would have lost interest in this economically marginal colony. The political framework of the Danish West Indies, within which St. John was developed as a plantation economy, included the two larger islands of St. Thomas and St. Croix. Like St. John, St. Thomas was not geographically well suited for sugar production. It had a large natural harbor, however, which became a major entrepôt for the northeastern area of the Caribbean Sea, and the harbor city of Charlotte Amalie quickly became the main economic base of the island's economy. St. Croix, with its flat topography and fertile soil, offered the best prospects for sugarcane cultivation, and the most significant plantation interests soon concentrated on that island.

St. John thus existed in the shadow of its two sister islands. Sugar production was only profitable on St. John when conditions were optimal; when sugar prices fell or the weather was bad, the plantations lost money and could not maintain their slave populations (cf. Goveia 1969: 126). To a certain extent, the St. Johnian plantation operators benefited from the great pressure that the Crucian planters applied to the colonial government to ensure that the slave laws during the eighteenth century were entirely in favor of the planters. Since it was administered under St. Thomas, where an urban economy predominated, St. John remained largely outside the interest of the colonial administration; the island was supervised by one official only, the *landfoged*—but until the nineteenth century he was closely identified with the planter class. Consequently the planters on St. John during the eighteenth century received legal sanction from the colonial government to exploit the slave labor force as they wished. With plantation cultivation only marginally profitable, the slaves sometimes fared miserably and eventually their numbers diminished. Not until the decimation of the labor force threatened to curtail plantation production and thus to weaken the island's economy did the colonial government, prompted also by developments on the larger plantation island of St. Croix, begin to take a more serious interest in the well-being of the slaves.

The slave labor force: Carolina Plantation

From the planters' point of view, the slaves were an expensive investment that had to be used as efficiently as possible. A lost hour of work represented a loss of profit (G. Hall 1971: 17). A Carolina Plantation journal covering the year 1766–67 gives an indication of how the slave labor force was utilized (*SAA* 62). Carolina's 1,687 acres of land made it the largest sugar plantation on St. John. Most of this land was mountainous, however, and could not be used in plantation cultivation. A watercolor of the estate from the 1830s shows a deep valley surrounded by

Table 1. Slave Population of St. John, 1718–1846, according to Tax Rolls (*Matrikler*)

Year	Number	Year	Number	Year	Number	Year	Number	Year	Number	Year	Number
1718	0	1767	—	1783	2,229	1799	2,503	1815	2,445	1831	2,063
1733	1,087	1768	2,303	1784	2,306	1800	2,430	1816	2,317	1832	1,955
1739	1,414	1769	2,215	1785	2,258	1801	2,435	1817	2,322	1833	1,988
1745	ca.1,650	1770	2,302	1786	2,322	1802	2,531	1818	2,402	1834	1,921
1755	2,031	1771	2,432	1787	2,293	1803	2,430	1819	2,316	1835[b]	1,809
1756	2,041	1772	2,431	1788	2,289	1804	2,604	1820	2,310	1836	2,004
1757	1,991	1773	2,324	1789	2,200	1805	2,541	1821	2,273	1837	1,973
1758	2,077	1774	2,293	1790	1,994	1806	—	1822	2,269	1838	2,007
1759	1,983	1775	2,355	1791	1,864	1807	2,598	1823	2,221	1839	2,003
1760	1,991	1776	2,398	1792	1,917	1808	2,588	1824	2,237	1840	1,923
1761	2,020	1777	2,482	1793	2,004	1809	—	1825	2,255	1841[c]	1,999
1762	1,969	1778	2,426	1794	2,008	1810	2,420	1826	2,259	1842	1,965
1763	1,986	1779	2,497	1795	2,006	1811	—	1827	2,207	1843	1,913
1764	1,974	1780	2,285	1796	2,109	1812	2,404	1828	2,108	1844	1,779
1765	2,024	1781	2,388	1797	2,145	1813	2,402	1829	2,131	1845	1,746
1766	2,164	1782	2,371	1798	2,247	1814[a]		1830	2,021	1846[d]	1,775

a. This tax roll is incomplete. The tax rolls in general offer only a fair indication of the overall developmental trends in the slave population and are not an entirely accurate account of the slave group. Furthermore, the categories are somewhat ambiguous, leading to different interpretations of total numbers. For example, Johansen (1981: 3) lists 1,845 slaves for 1791, 2,492 for 1802; Green-Pedersen (1978: 20) lists 1,864 for 1791, 2,531 for 1802 (see also *VRR* 1755–1848; Green-Pedersen 1976:351).

b. 1835 census, 1,943.

c. 1841 census, 2,001.

d. 1846 census, 1,767.

mountains on three sides and bordered by the sea on the fourth, a prospect similar to that of most other sugar plantations on St. John. The plantation grounds, with the windmill (until 1768 only a horse mill), sugar works, cattle pens, and slave quarters, were situated at the foot of a small hill in the valley. Atop the hill was the great house, inhabited by an overseer, who ran Carolina Plantation for the absentee owners. The planter owners on most of the St. Johnian plantations lived either on St. Thomas, the British Virgin Islands, or in Europe (as did Carolina's owner). For 1766, the estate held 125 slaves. The records do not state how much land was cultivated; judging from later tax records, however, it can be estimated that these slaves cultivated a little more than 100 acres of sugarcane and kept about 35 acres in pasture and other cultivation (*VRR* 1805), not much more than was cultivated on several smaller sugar estates. Of the 125 slaves, approximately 50 belonged to the "big gang," which did the hard physical labor, usually in the fields; during harvesttime ten to twelve of these slaves were occupied in the sugar works. There were 2–5 artisan slaves (carpenters, masons, and coopers); 2–5 watchmen; 5 house slaves; 1–2 stockkeepers; 1 attended the sick slaves and 1–3 dug potatoes. Between 33 and 38 slaves were listed as boys, girls, and children. Slave children worked as soon as they were able to do light chores on the estate (Oldendorp 1786: 356). From later records, it is apparent that children below 6–7 years old did not work, but children above that age carried water to the field slaves, looked after calves, and cared for smaller children (*LA* 88: February 25, 1845; August 20, 1845). At various times throughout the year, between 7 and 21 slaves were listed as sick, 1–8 as maroons (runaways), and ten to eleven as manqueroons (disabled and incapable of doing hard physical work [*G* 2: vol. 3]). Thus the plantation's slave population at any given time consisted of approximately 90 adult workers, at least 20 of whom were either disabled, sick, or fugitives. In other words, more than 50 of the total population, or at least 40 percent, were of limited or no use in plantation cultivation.

Slaves able to work were overworked. In the eighteenth century, slaves on the Danish West Indian islands had a workday of ten to eleven hours. They started at daybreak before 6:00 A.M. and continued to dusk, after 6:00 P.M. Between 7:00 and 8:00 A.M. they had a break of about half an hour to eat a meal and at noon they had a one- to two-hour lunch break. During the "noon" and after they had finished the fieldwork in the evening, they had to fetch grass for the cattle on the estate (Carstens 1981 [1740s]: 83–87; Haagensen 1758a: 53; Oldendorp 1786: 354–55; West 1793: 71).

The slaves' work centered almost exclusively on the production of sugar. The year could be divided into two main periods (see Figure 1): one in which sugarcane was planted and weeded (from mid-July to the end of January), and one in which it was harvested and processed (from the beginning of February to mid-July).

During the planting and weeding season, the slaves also cultivated estate provisions, which formed the basis of their food supplies during the strenuous harvest season; compared to sugarcane cultivation, these activities consumed little time and were often performed by only a few members of the field gang. In January and February, several days were spent cutting wood to be used as fuel in the boiling house during the sugarcane harvest; later, when the sugar had been processed, a few days were set aside for carting the sugar to the bay, where boats arrived to pick it up. During October and December some time was spent repairing the estate's roads, which were used to reach other estates and the sea.

The slaves usually worked six days a week for the estate, but outside the harvest season they were allowed the afternoon off on Saturdays in order to work on their own provision grounds. Furthermore, the slaves did not work for the plantation on New Year's Day, Easter Monday, Whitmonday, or on the first and second days of Christmas. Due to heavy seasonal rains, they worked only a few hours or not at all for a few days in the period from October to January.

Control of the slaves through dehumanization

The planter class apparently did not consider the demands they placed on the slaves to be excessive. Richard Haagensen, a planter on St. Croix who had formerly been an official in the West Indian Company, wrote in 1758 that the slaves were "as made for slavery, they know of nothing but steady work and therefore do it with pleasure, yes, even singing and in great spirits, as if they were the happiest creatures, most of them do not know of days of rest, and for this reason they don't find it difficult" (Haagensen

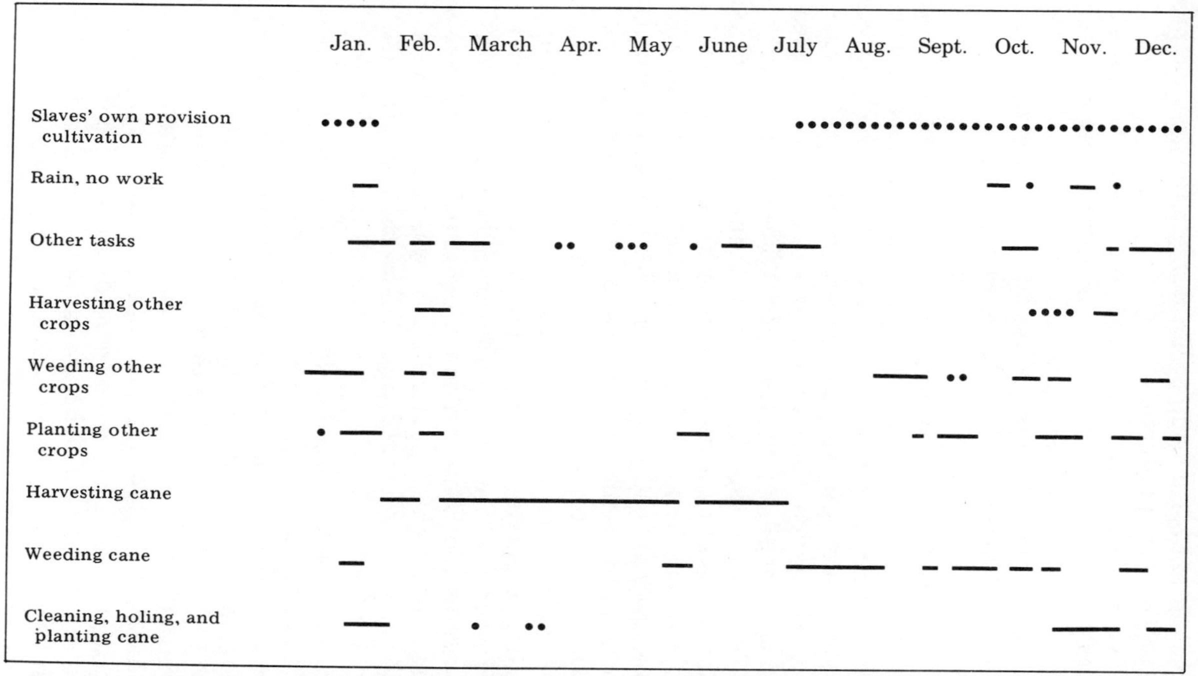

Figure 1. The yearly work cycle on Carolina Estate, 1766–67 (based on plantation journal, October 1, 1766–September 27, 1767). Source: SAA 62.

1758a: 51). The planter's main concern was to get as much work as possible out of his slaves in order to attain the greatest profit from the total estate production.

The slaves constituted a significant part of the planter's tangible property; when a plantation was appraised, they were listed along with the other property, usually with the animals. Men's names were listed first, in order by value, followed by women's names similarly ordered. (The slaves were accorded names, but on some plantations so were the animals: when Little Reefbay was appraised in 1841, for example, all slaves, cows, and horses were listed by name, the children, calves, and foals appearing with their mothers [*LA* 117: February 4, 1841]). The high value placed on the slaves is revealed by the yearly taxes levied on slave property, which were several times greater than taxes on other kinds of tangible property (*VRR* 1755–1848).

The relegation of the slaves to a subhuman status excluded close personal contact with them by whites. Members of the planter class who broke this unwritten law in public were socially ostracized at best, severely punished at worst, particularly in the eighteenth century when the planter class was consolidating its power, as is revealed in the following case brought before the *landfoged*. On one of the plantations, the planter family had held a party. Lieutenant Stürup showed up uninvited and was totally ignored because he had been seen dancing in one of the slave houses on the estate. When the ladies refused to dance with him, he started a fight and later fled. He was not to be found anywhere when the case was brought before the court (*LA* 67: November 28, 1778).

Sexual intercourse with the slaves was also frowned upon, at least publicly. Certain Marchée was knocked down by Mr. Johnston when he went into the Johnston house at night to visit one of the slave women. Mr. Johnston explained that he did not want Marchée to "turn his house into a whore house." Marchée excused himself by saying that he had often visited the slave women in the Johnston house at night, implying that this was tacitly accepted as long as it was done discreetly (*LA* 69: May 19, 1786). In another episode with sexual overtones, Mr. Conner denied that he was beaten up by his slave woman Maria. According to the witnesses, Maria threw Mr. Conner out of her room so that he fell, after which she held him by the throat, "choked him, and took her shoe off the foot and beat him with it on his body." When Mr. Connor got up again, Maria knocked him down again (*LA* 72:

August 17, 1802). The social disapproval of sexual relationships between white and black was most apparent when it involved white women. When Anna DeKoonigh, the daughter of a planter, had a child who was obviously racially mixed, she was deported from the colony, disinherited, and denied all of her possessions (*LA* 64: February 14, June 19, 1758).

The slave laws of the Danish West Indies (see Olsen 1983), as on other West Indian islands, did not reflect the actual treatment of the slaves; however, they were "important as an index of changing conditions and attitudes" (Knight 1970: 76). Until the 1830s, the official slave laws consisted of two codes promulgated in 1733 and 1755. In the 1733 code, the status of the slave as an element in the planters' private property was validated. The slave had no rights but was regarded "as property, consigned to servitude by the Almighty, and petrified in dumb superstition by his ignorance" (N. Hall 1977: 175). The code described a number of the slave's obligations to the master and set down punishments for his failing to meet them.

The slaves were thus given—implicitly—a status above that of private property, simply because, unlike the sugar mill or the cattle, they could have obligations and incur punishment. The list of possible crimes that slaves might commit included marooning, leaving the country, making menacing gestures or using insulting words, using "Negro instruments" in connection with parties or funeral rites, and practicing *obeah* (witchcraft). Punishments ranged from whipping to being pinched by glowing iron tongs, having an ear, arm, or leg cut off, or a combination of the above, followed by hanging or being beheaded (ibid.). Although punishments of this sort were meted out on several occasions to slaves on St. John for offenses such as marooning, theft, or murder, the grossest mutilations were not carried out and apparently the tools for such mutilations were not even kept on the island (*LA* 65: April 22, 1969), perhaps through a combination of humanitarian gesture and unwillingness to damage property.

Whereas the 1733 slave code had concerned itself only with the master's rights over the slave, the 1755 code defined the slaves' rights. The masters had no right to exploit the slaves sexually. The slaves were to be provided with certain minimum allowances of food and clothing, and they had no obligation to work on Sundays or on the major religious holidays of the Lutheran church. They were to receive religious instruction if they wished, and all slave children were to be baptized. They had permission to marry, but not polygamously. The code also elaborated on what was considered criminal behavior on the part of the slaves. Slaves from one estate could not assemble with those from another. They were not allowed to carry any produce to the market without a special permit. Evidence from a slave was not to be used as the basis for court decisions. Punishments were similar to (if not more severe than) those set out in the 1733 code (N. Hall 1977: 176–78).

Unlike the 1733 code, the 1755 code was never published in the Danish West Indies; the governor was allowed to administer the law as he saw fit, and this seems to have meant not administering it at all. The notion of slaves' rights was not yet acceptable in the colony, and throughout the eighteenth century the slaves officially retained the status of chattels. A number of governmental decrees were published later in the century further regulating and restricting slave life.

Production by and for the
slave labor force

The failure to publish the 1755 code and later restrictions on slave behavior were indications that there were problems in managing the slaves as a labor force. Some of these problems surfaced when the slaves began to grow their own foodstuffs. While small quantities of provision crops were cultivated on some estates in the normal work hours, these were not sufficient to feed the entire slave population. The Carolina Plantation journal shows that the estate's potato crop was intended primarily for slaves who worked extra hours, such as the slaves at the sugar works during the harvest season. The other slaves were given a long noon break, Sunday, and (outside the harvest season) Saturday afternoon in order to cultivate their own provisions. Some plantations expected the slaves to provide for themselves entirely. J. L. Carstens, who was a planter on both St. John and St. Thomas, wrote in the 1740s that "the slaves receive nothing from their master neither in the form of food nor clothing, except alone a little piece of land, which the master lets each of them stake out on the most distant outskirts of his plantation" (1981 [1740s]: 88).

The plantation economy on St. John did not allow for much of the normal labor on the estates to be diverted to subsistence activities, nor did it allow for importation of a great deal of foodstuffs. During the height of sugarcane cultivation on the island, in the late eighteenth and early nineteenth centuries, less than 10 percent of the island was planted in sugarcane. The extensive wasteland acreage, which could not be used in large-scale plantation cultivation, was useful for provision farming by the slaves on a small scale. The availability of land for small provision grounds and the high cost of importing foodstuffs therefore combined to make provision farming an attractive means of feeding the slaves, a common practice throughout the West Indies wherever marginally productive land was plentiful (Mintz and Hall 1960).

As long as slaves had sufficient free time to work on the provision grounds and the weather was favorable, they were able to provide food for themselves. Some produced a surplus, which they sold for cash (ibid.). This happened a great deal in the Danish West Indies (see, for example, Carstens 1981 [1740s]: 90; N. Hall 1980, 1983). The Danish colonial government had not anticipated that provision cropping would yield a surplus. The 1755 code and later governmental decrees placed restrictions on the slaves' marketing. These measures were attempts to control activities seen as incompatible with the slaves' status as chattels and therefore threatening to the planters' suzerainty over them. Nonetheless, the selling or trading of surplus crops could not be stopped. "What might have begun as a conveniently casual system of industrial feeding," writes Mintz, "had become a tradition with which it would have been profitless and dangerous to interfere" (1974: 194). Having let the slaves organize their own provision farming, the planters had irrevocably opened the door for the development of a larger exchange system.

While the slaves' provision farming posed a potential threat when it prospered, it caused a more immediate danger when it failed to provide the slaves with necessary foodstuffs, as in periods of drought. Planters operating marginally successful plantations could not afford to import foodstuffs for the slaves; they just let the slaves fend for themselves. Even when the owners could afford foodstuffs and tried to supply them (some did not), they were sometimes difficult to purchase on short notice. The resulting severe food shortages often led the slaves to flee, which in one celebrated case led to an island-wide uprising.

In 1733, fifteen years after the colonization of St. John, the island experienced a prolonged drought that made provision farming impossible. Little or no foodstuffs were purchased by the planters to feed the slaves, and by the middle of the year many slaves had left the plantations, preferring to eke out a living in the bush to working and starving on the plantations. The 1733 slave code, with its harsh punishment for marooning, was largely a response to this chaotic situation. Ironically, the law, which was intended to help control the slaves, actually helped to convince them that the only solution to their impossible situation was a revolt. In November 1733 the slaves staged an uprising and succeeded in taking over most of the island and killing the white population in the island's eastern section. The Danish West Indian colonial government needed help from French troops on Martinique to quell the revolt, and it was not until May 1734 that the planter class regained the upper hand on the island (Martfeld n.d.; Paludan 1894; Caron and Highfield 1983).

The stipulations concerning the feeding of the slaves contained in the 1755 code can be seen as a failed attempt to regulate this problematic aspect of the relationship between the master and his slaves. The history of St. John shows many instances of slave marooning provoked by starvation. In 1779, sixty slaves on Carolina Plantation ran away and could not be forced to return before a representative of the planter family, who was on St. Croix at the time, arranged for the importation of foodstuffs (Degn 1974: 85–87).

In addition to food shortages, the difficult working conditions of the plantation regime encouraged marooning. The field slaves, comprising most of the slave labor force, were made to work in long rows from before sunrise until after sunset under the close supervision of a driver, recruited from the slaves, who was free to punish them for even the slightest mistakes or signs of weariness (see, for example, Carsten 1981 [1740s]: 85–87; Haagensen 1758b: 291). Knowing that they could provide for themselves in the bush without much difficulty, the slaves often ran away. The planters and their overseers regularly organized hunting parties to track down maroons, but with limited success; the colonial government recognized the problem but felt powerless to do anything about it. In 1748, an African slave was brought to the *land-foged* on St. John after having been a maroon for fourteen months. The *landfoged* noted that, according to the slave, the owner had caused the marooning himself by being much too harsh in his treatment of the slaves, even to the point of having killed one of them. The *landfoged* believed that the slave's statement contained "the greatest truth," but a slave's word was not legally acceptable as evidence (*LA* 86: June 10, 1748).

In the course of the eighteenth century, the planters received help in controlling and domesticating the slaves from an unexpected quarter. Just before the 1733 slave revolt on St. John, missionaries from the Moravian church arrived in the Danish West Indies in order to work with the slaves, and in the 1740s they established their first missionary station on St. John. In the beginning the planters disliked these religious activities among the slaves. The missionaries' contact with the slaves and the notion that the slaves were worthy of religious instruction were totally contrary to the publicly accepted image of the slave, and the planters also feared that the missionaries would conspire with the slaves against them. However, much to the planters' relief, the Moravians were concerned with introducing the slaves only to Christianity, not freedom. The position of the master vis-à-vis the slave was compared with that of Jesus, and the slaves were told to serve their masters with the same faithfulness and obedience they showed their Redeemer (Oldendorp 1786: 360; see also Lawaetz 1902; Ramløv 1968). The Moravians had a significant impact on St. John as far as attendance at the two missionary stations on the island was concerned; statistics from 1806 indicate that more than half of the slaves had been converted to Christianity (*G* 1 1806). But the fact that marooning and other forms of resistance remained common makes it doubtful that most slaves accepted the idea of complete submission to their masters. It is likely, on the other hand, that the Moravians provided a warm and humane environment for the slaves in which they could find release for some of the worst emotional tension engendered by slavery. In this way, the church may have helped prevent this tension from erupting into more violent confrontations with the planter class.

Perhaps because of the efforts of the Moravians, slave resistance was expressed primarily in petty marooning during the latter part of the eighteenth century. But it was so frequent that it was a serious economic matter to the planter class on St. John, as revealed in the statement of an attorney in a court case involving a slave named Fortuna, who had been a maroon for a long time:

[Marooning] is so much greater and more strongly felt on St. John than on the other Danish islands, as it is permanent and without cease; also the island is covered with a big forest, so that the Negroes always have a safe refuge and know themselves safe from being caught, unless they occasionally make a mistake; it is therefore much too burdensome for the owners first to get into debt to purchase Negroes, later to pay interest on the capital, feed and educate the Negroes, until they can speak the language and have gotten to know the country, and then, finally, to lose both the money and the work by the Negroes' marooning. . . . [It] occurs daily, so that the fort here is never free of such arrestants, even though not even a twentieth of them are caught. (*LA* 70: April 26, 1789)

The attorney suggested that using the punishments for marooning stipulated in the 1733 code might scare the slaves into submission, and that therefore Fortuna should be beheaded and his head placed on a stake (ibid.).

Incipient breakdown of the plantation society

The economic hardships of the planters caused by marooning gradually forced the colonial government to regulate the operation of the plantations and the treatment of slaves. As noted by the attorney in the Fortuna case, the planters took out loans to purchase slaves; many of these loans were from the Danish king (i.e., the state). If mismanagement caused the slaves to die or provoked them to run away in great numbers, the colonial government was required to investigate in order to certify that there was collateral for the loan. The year before the Fortuna case, the governor-general had investigated one of the planters on St. John who had allegedly tortured nine slaves to death, causing the remainder to run away. Plantation cultivation had ceased, and the planter had been unable to repay his debt to the king. The governor-general demanded that an overseer be placed on the plantation to run it and that all punishment of the slaves be carried out at the courthouse under the direction of the *landfoged* (*LA* 70: June 5, 7, 1787, August 20, 1789).

   In another case, a planter had failed to make his loan payment and blamed a drought for his cash shortage. He assured the *landfoged* that "as long as God gave the country rain and the crops were fair, he had willingly paid every year, as much as the regulations required." God's failure to provide rain caused twelve of his thirty-nine slaves to die, representing the loss of much of his capital (*LA* 89: August 5, 1791). Cases such as these led the *landfoged* to conclude that "as the king has first mortgage in the plantation it is most certainly the *landfoged*'s duty to examine the conditions on the plantation. Besides, the slaves who are arrested and examined and punished must not have cause to complain about a lack of care on the part of the court" (*LA* 70: August 25, 1788). This interest in the condition of the plantations and the slaves was limited; generally, the *landfoged* did not seem to be well acquainted with the plantations and rarely inspected them. For example, when he went to collect taxes due on Rendezvous Estate, he was surprised to find that, after he "with great effort and difficulty, partly by horse, and partly by foot, had arrived at the aforementioned plantation, there were no buildings to be found, and therefore also no people who could be asked for the remaining taxes due to St. John's treasury" (*LA* 87: August 15, 1797).

During years of drought, when the slaves could not grow enough food crops to sustain themselves, slave mortality increased sharply. Carolina Plantation records indicate a severe drought in the year 1779, and the tax rolls show that in 1780 the slave population had declined by more than 200, a large decrease probably caused by widespread starvation among the slaves. The cases brought to the *landfoged* show that around 1790 there was also a period of drought, and coincidentally the slave population, nearly 2,300 in 1788, was less than than 1,900 by 1791.

Procreation

Even when the slaves were able to sustain themselves through provision farming, they were unable to maintain their numbers through biological reproduction. On the basis of statistics from the ten-year period 1793–1802, it has been calculated that the slave population on St. John showed a negative annual growth rate of 0.3 percent (Green-Pedersen 1979: 18). The plantations were dependent upon the transatlantic slave trade for the maintenance of the number of slaves. The availability of African slaves made it possible to make up for the negative replacement rate as well as more drastic reductions in population, such as those caused by starvation following upon drought. Furthermore, the slave trade made it possible to deal harshly with slaves who were becoming too independent and were therefore a threat to the plantation system. The planters could keep the system going by force as long as newly imported African slaves were available to replace casualties. This was an expensive strategy, however, and the result was often failure to repay loans and the collapse of ill-managed plantations.

Other West Indian islands also depended upon the slave trade for the maintenance of their labor force. St. Croix displayed a negative annual growth rate of 1.1 percent from 1780 to 1804, whereas the larger British sugar-producing island of Jamaica had an excess mortality rate of approximately 2 percent from 1776 to 1800. On Barbados, it was apparently even higher (Green-Pedersen 1978: 8–9). Particularly in Great Britain, but also in France, the economic as well as the moral aspects of the slave trade were criticized, and there was pressure to abolish it (Knap 1983). Influenced by the British, the Danish government formed a committee in 1791 to investigate the Danish slave trade. It concluded that the trade in general presented moral problems and was deleterious to the people of Africa; the Danish trade in particular was not profitable, and with improved conditions the slave population in the Danish West Indies would be able to reproduce itself without further supplies of African slaves. The slave population was not believed to be large enough; the committee stated that 30,000–45,000 slaves were needed on the island of St. Croix alone, where there were fewer than 22,000 slaves in the early 1790s (Green-Pederson 1979). As a result of the committee's report, in March 1792 a law was passed abolishing the slave trade after a ten-year transitional period in which the West Indian planters were to stock up on slaves. The law allowed ships from all foreign nations to send slaves to the Danish islands and gave the planters permission to sell a certain amount of sugar directly to foreign ships—thus at a higher price—within a year after the purchase of a slave. By opening the trade to foreign merchant houses and allowing the planters to sell sugar to them, the Danish government hoped that a greater supply of slaves would be imported to the islands and that the planters would be financially able to buy all the slaves they needed. To increase the number of female slaves, thus to encourage the reproduction of the slave population, import duties on female slaves and the yearly taxes on female field slaves were removed. Finally, the export of slaves from the Danish West Indies was prohibited (ibid.: 404–8).

Shortly before the ban on the slave trade was to be instituted, the Danish king received a petition from West Indian planters asking him to extend the trade. The king requested information on the slave population in order to determine whether there were sufficient slaves to maintain the labor force. When this information was received in 1806, Great Britain was just about to enact its own prohibition of the slave trade. The Danish government decreed its ban before the British, though the Danish ban did not actually go into effect until 1808 (ibid.: 408–18).

The planters on St. John availed themselves of the opportunity to replenish the slave population during the transitional period. The record low number of 1,864 slaves in 1791, just before the law on the slave trade was passed, increased to 2,006 by 1795; 2,430 in 1800, and 2,604 in 1804—an increase of 740, or 40 percent. St. John seems to have been saturated with slaves by 1804, and the population leveled off around the 2,500 mark. Statistics on sugarcane cultivation show that after the prohibition of the slave trade, the plantations maintained, at times even increased, the acreage in sugarcane attained in 1803 when the slave population peaked. Immediately before the 1792 slave trade law was passed, the number of slaves on St. John had been quite low, perhaps due to the serious drought that made provision farming impossible. The legally favorable conditions for the import of slaves may have enabled the St. Johnian planters to acquire new slaves at a time when the plantation economy and the slave labor force had been declining.

The introduction of slave rights

The law to end the slave trade may have helped the St. Johnian planters briefly, but in the long run it presented new problems that made the system of plantation cultivation by slaves even more fragile than it had been before. Providing new slaves to replace those who had been "used up" now became the responsibility of the slaves themselves, through their bearing and rearing of children. The reproduction of the slave labor force came wholly under the slaves' control.

During the slave trade, the colonial authorities had not inter-
fered significantly with the way in which the slaves were treated
and the plantations were run so long as the planters repaid their
loans and remitted their yearly taxes. After the cessation of the
slave trade, the colonial government had to make sure that the
slave population was not depleted, since the revenues that could
be extracted from the plantations and the ability of the planters
to repay their loans depended on the availability of a labor force.
In the nineteenth century the government therefore took an increasing interest in the conditions under which the slaves lived
and worked.

About twelve years after the slave trade was stopped, it became apparent that the slaves were not maintaining their numbers. The slave population on St. John was slightly below 2,500
in 1815, but by 1820 it had declined to 2,310, and the downward
trend continued so that by 1835 the population was close to
1,809, lower than it had been in 1791 (*VRR* 1 1805–35). On
the much larger and economically more significant island of
St. Croix, the slave population decrease was even greater; the
population of more than 27,000 that had been attained by the
end of the slave trade was approaching 24,000 by 1815, and in
1826 it was close to 21,000 (Johansen 1981: 3). The government
reacted to this decline by enforcing regulations on slave rights
for the first time. In 1817 the governor-general invoked the part
of the 1755 code that dealt with the slaves' food and clothing allowances. It stipulated that each slave above ten years of age was
to receive six quarts of cornmeal and two pounds of salt beef or
three pounds of fish per week. Children below ten were to receive
half of this allowance. Twice a year, on January 1 and June 1, a
shirt and a pair of pants were to be given to the men, a jacket and
a petticoat to the women. On October 1 the men received a hat,
the women two handkerchiefs, and each man and woman a suit
of clothes. The regulations were not published on St. John until
1821 (*LA* 159: October 13, 1832; *STG* 1: February 9, 1831).

In 1830, a law was passed permitting evidence to be given in
the courts by slaves who were baptized and understood the meaning of the holy oath so long as they did not witness against their
owner (Lawaetz 1940: 147). While this law appears to have been
rather progressive, it was in fact largely intended to encourage
slaves to witness against each other and against poorer whites
suspected of criminal behavior. It was noted on St. John, for ex-

ample, that the inadmissibility of slave testimony as the basis of conviction had previously prevented slaves from being prosecuted for poisoning masters (*LA* 6: August 29, 1825; 72: November 30, 1804) and conspiring to organize an uprising (*LA* 6: August 29, 1825); and it had made it impossible to charge whites suspected of having collaborated in abducting slaves and taking them to Puerto Rico (*LA* 72: April 19, 1806).

An even more elaborate slave code followed in 1834. This law appears to have been the response of the Danish West Indian government to the proclamation of emancipation on the British West Indian islands in 1834. While Denmark had banned the slave trade before Great Britain, it was not prepared to emancipate its slaves also, perhaps because the country could not afford to pay compensation for their loss of property to the planters. As some of the British islands were within sight of the Danish West Indies (the British Virgin Islands, for example, were a few hundred yards from St. John), it was not unlikely that the Danish West Indian slaves would be incited by the British emancipation. The Danish governor-general, Peter v. Scholten, suggested that the 1834 code be formulated to placate the slaves by improving their living conditions and to allow the colonial government greater control over the planter-slave relationship. The new code granted the slaves legal right to own all property they managed to acquire and to purchase their own freedom with whatever funds they accumulated. If mistreated, the slaves were to be removed from their owner; punishment by owners was limited to flogging, no more than twelve lashes for men, six for women. More severe punishment was to be meted out by the *landfoged* (Lawaetz 1940: 149–50).

The 1834 code was followed by a number of decrees that further specified the rights of the slaves. In 1838, Peter v. Scholten issued a placard that reiterated the food allowances in the 1817 decree. In 1840 a further interpretation of this decree, specifically with regard to conditions on St. John, stipulated that each slave receive a Christmas allowance of four Danish pounds of pork, five quarts of white flour, and one quart of sugar. The slaves' houses had to be of "wall- or masterwork, with an inside dimension of 18 Danish feet by 12, partitioned with boards into a room and a chamber for one family, calculated to consist of man, wife and 2 or 3 children." Slaves with no families were to have a room each in similar housing. The law also suggested a distance of 30 Danish feet between the houses wherever possible. Further-more, sick houses were to be erected on plantations where there were none, doctors were to be employed to look after the slaves, blankets were to be given to slaves at least once every three years. Planters were not to prevent slaves from attending church on Sundays and holidays (*LA* 28: May 1, 1840).

In 1838, another placard prohibited the sale of slaves at auc-tions and the sale of children under ten years old without the consent of the parents (*LA* 76: December 24, 1840). An 1839 law required that slave children attend schools built by colonial trea-sury funds and run by the Moravian missionaries (see N. Hall 1979). In 1843, Peter v. Scholten made a special agreement with the planters on St. John to make Saturday a free day (similar agreements on St. Croix and St. Thomas were only partially suc-cessful). If the plantations had to use the slaves on Saturdays, payment or other privileges had to be granted for this work (*LA* 160: September 13, 1843). The daily work hours on the planta-tions were reduced so that work began at 7:00 A.M. and ceased at sunset (around 6:00 P.M.). Slaves received a two-hour break at noon but were still required to find grass for the estate's animals during the noon break (*LA* 59: February 1, 1835; 35: July 15, 1848). Pregnant women had to be excused from the hardest physical work in the fields, could not be subjected to hard physi-cal punishment, and were not to work at all for five to six weeks after giving birth (*LA* 34: January 25, 1847; March 26, 1845). In order to give them sufficient time to nurse their babies, they were allowed to begin the noon break at 11:00 A.M. and to stop the day's work at 5:00 P.M. up to a year after the birth of their child (*LA* 35: April 28, 1847; July 15, 1848). Apparently Peter v. Scholten instituted several of these regulations on his own, with-out the authorization of the Danish government (Lawaetz 1940: 150–51).

The slaves assert themselves

Compared to eighteenth-century codes, these may seem to repre-sent a great improvement in the position of the slaves. Governor-General v. Scholten even stated that he wished to prepare the slaves for freedom gradually through reforms (ibid.: 149). Not only were the slaves granted the right to be provided with the means of existence, but they were also protected by restrictions on the work to be extracted from them and the punishments to be suffered by them. The decrees even seem to reflect a greater recognition of the slaves as human beings with emotional needs and intellectual abilities.

In reality, however, the codes and decrees were not just the result of progressive thinking by the colonial government; they are evidence of the increasing difficulty with which the government was controlling the slaves. After the ban on the slave trade, the slaves realized that the planters were completely dependent upon them for the continued operation of the plantations. The slaves therefore pressed for better conditions, knowing that it was difficult for the *landfoged* to refuse their requests because they were essential to the reproduction of the slave labor force. The planters, on the other hand, owning only marginally profitable plantations, sought to circumvent the laws that called for improved standards of living among the slaves. The result was a long series of conflicts between slaves and planters/overseers, many of which were brought before the *landfoged* by the slaves to be settled according to law. While eighteenth-century records contain very few references to complaints brought to the *landfoged* by the slaves, nineteenth-century records abound with such complaints. More and more of them were settled in the favor of the slaves. The slaves knew the laws, which were promulgated on the plantations or at the missionary stations, and they continuously used them to push for better conditions.

A common complaint of the slaves was that they did not receive an adequate allowance of food from the plantations. The slaves on Enighed Estate complained in 1814 that they had not received any food allowances for several years and no clothing for a very long time (*LA* 73: June 7, 1814). The following year fourteen female slaves on Bordeaux complained that they got very little food and that this was the reason at least seventeen slaves had left the plantation for five to six weeks (*LA* 73: July 4, 1815). When the Bordeaux planter continued to ignore the food requirements of the slaves, the plantation was placed under the administration of the colonial government for a number of years (*STG* 1). Complaints became a regular occurrence after the 1821 decree on food allowances. In 1840 slaves on Annaberg and Mahobay refused to accept the food allowances handed out to them because they thought the measures used were too small (*LA* 5:

July 18, 1840). In most cases the *landfoged* had to give in to them and reprimand the planters.

Slaves also protested that the planters made it difficult for them to bear and rear children and lead a secure family life. Three slaves on Cinnamonbay Plantation complained that they were beaten because they did not work enough, despite the fact that they were pregnant (*LA* 34: March 26, 1845). Another Cinnamonbay slave reported that his wife, who belonged to Rustenberg Plantation, had been arrested with their three-month-old infant (*LA* 33: February 9, 1841) and that the Rustenberg overseer refused to let him visit his wife on Rustenberg (ibid.: February 13, 1841). Another Rustenberg slave complained that the owner had demanded that the slave's daughter be sent to St. Thomas, even though she was only seven years old and had no family on that island to protect her (*LA* 35: May 25, 1847). Again and again, the *landfoged* had to order planters and overseers to respect the slaves' family relations and be more considerate in the treatment of pregnant women and infants. In 1844, after a visit to the island, the governor-general issued a warning to the planters on St. John about their treatment of the slaves with regard to allowances of food and clothing, housing, prison facilities, and schools (*LA* 7: November 26, 1844).

The records of the *landfoged* reveal, however, that the slaves were not confining their protests to official complaints at the office of the *landfoged*. They sought in various ways to escape from their toil and from conflicts with the overseers—for example, by pretending to be ill. When forty slaves checked into the sick house on Abrams Fancy at one time, the overseer believed that they were pretending to be ill and forced several of them to work. This action led to the death of a slave woman, prompting a police investigation and, apparently, the dismissal of the overseer. When the new overseer tried to be more accommodating, the slaves took advantage of his forebearance; it proved almost impossible for him to get any of them to work until the *landfoged* stepped in and helped him (*LA* 40: February 18, 1831). Similar cases were reported for the British West Indies, and "Slave-owners were driven to desperation trying to outsmart the plans of slave-malingerers" (Mathurin 1975: 11).

Marooning continued to be a problem. *Landfoged* cases include those of Backeroo, who feared punishment when the cows he was supposed to tend got away (*LA* 33: September 19, 1843);

Curtis, who was not being provided with any food on Bordeaux Plantation (*STG* 1); and Cornelius, who was not allowed to be treated in the sick house for wounds on his legs (*LA* 32: May 6, 1839). Some of the maroons desperately tried to remain free; one "took to the sea, but had to give up, when follow^{d} by boat" (*LA* 83: November 1, 1819); another tried to fool her owner by placing her clothes at the seashore, hoping that she would be presumed drowned (*LA* 88: July 10, 1834). When caught, some preferred suicide to returning to slavery (*LA* 88: January 2, 1844). Others decided to commit suicide rather than try to escape (*LA* 32: June 14, 1837; 88: April 10, 1844), or they mutilated themselves in order to escape the hardest labor (*LA* 32: December 24, 1839).

The records also contain examples of more organized protests against the slave system. In 1818 at Leinsterbay on St. John, forty-seven slaves left the plantation fields for the bush because a slave died a few days after having been subjected to excessive punishment by the overseer. When colonial officials attempted to force the slaves to return to the plantation, the slaves threw stones at them. The governor sent a contingent of thirty soldiers to quarantine this minor rebellion. Even though the *landfoged* was not convinced that the slave had died as a result of his punishment, only one of the rebels was found guilty. He was originally from Trinidad and had allegedly been a conspirator in a similar rebellion on that island and thus deported to the Danish West Indies. Though the rebel denied both his Trinidad involvement and his leading role in the rebellion on St. John, he alone was regarded as responsible for the unrest and was deported from the Danish West Indies (*LA* 15: September 21, 1818; 39: September 23, 1818; 73: October 23, 1818; 81: September 15, 1818). This tactic of punishing only the one or two slaves suspected of being the ringleaders was common whenever slave protests involved groups. Obviously it was difficult and potentially dangerous to administer punishment to the entire slave population on an estate at one time; singling out one or two for punishment was an attempt to break up the feeling of solidarity that naturally existed among the slaves as a result of their common exploitation and deprivation.

This same method of using a few slaves to control the entire slave population was also employed in reverse. It was common practice in the West Indies to favor a small number of slaves with a special status in order to gain their loyalty and confidence and thus separate them from the rest of the slaves (James 1980 [1938]: 36–45). The largest proportion of slaves were field workers; of the 1,760 slaves counted in the 1846 census on St. John, 1,359 were active in the work force, 1,149 as field slaves. These slaves were scattered on the island's different estates and were supervised by a head driver, or *bomba*, who had been appointed from their ranks. The head driver was responsible for the daily work in the fields and was allowed to use a whip. The drivers received special privileges—for example, a double allowance (*LA* 33: July 26, 1841). The Carolina Plantation journal indicated that the total work force on the plantation sometimes was placed at the driver's disposal; one Saturday entry shows that the driver got "all the slaves to clean his corn piece" (*SAA* 62: September 5, 1767). A driver on Hermanfarm Estate got a bottle of rum on Sundays; although he did not drink the rum himself, he was able to make other slaves work for him in exchange for some (*LA* 31: April 24, 1835).

On each plantation a few slaves were used as artisans and house servants and did not have to work in the field. The 1846 census lists 208 such slaves on St. John. They were regarded as especially privileged because their work was less strenuous and monotonous than that of the field slaves. The artisan slaves were trained in a craft and had the opportunity to earn some money in their free time by working as artisans outside the plantations. The domestic slaves were envied too, because their chores were light compared with those of other slaves. They also lived and worked in close contact with the families they served, which often made it possible to get extra favors. In some instances the special position of these slaves caused others to suspect their loyalty to the slave group. A driver on Leinsterbay was hated by the field slaves, who took the first opportunity to plot against him and have him brought to the *landfoged*, who dismissed him from his post (*LA* 33: September 21, 1844). Nanny, a house slave on Annaberg, was slandered in a field slaves' work song because she was believed to be a gossip.[1] Though many of the work songs mocked or even threatened the planters and overseers, they were not prohibited, probably because they constituted useful "institutional releases" that served to help "maintain the slave system" (G. Hall 1971: 35).

Although the drivers, house slaves, and artisans were often resented, they were also envied, and the slaves competed with each other to attain the desired positions. Some of them even resorted to *obeah* in their efforts to become drivers or to be sent to St. Croix to learn a craft (*LA* 33: July 26, 1841; September 27, 1842; January 26, 1844). Thus the planters, using this system of favoring a few slaves, succeeded in pitting some slaves against one another and were able to better control the slave population.

Disintegration of slave owner control: emancipation

During the eighteenth century, the planters had sought to control the slaves by dehumanizing them. In the late eighteenth and early nineteenth centuries, this strategy became increasingly unworkable, partly because the slaves' living conditions needed to be improved in order to encourage their biological reproduction, partly because the slaves were beginning to resist debasement by their owners. The slaves' subsistence activities involved extensive cultivation of foodstuffs, the surplus of which could be marketed. Colonial authorities tried to regulate this cultivation, but they had to tolerate it since the plantations depended on the slaves' labor. The marketing of goods gradually increased, permitting a large number of slaves to accumulate cash, then to purchase their own freedom.

Another problem for the plantation owner class was the increasing number of colored children, the offspring of black-white unions. When a white woman was involved, the colonial authorities reacted angrily. In the reverse situation, the children of slaves by law belonged to the mother's owner; but a free white mother placed her family in the embarrassing situation of having to accept a colored child. The authorities attempted to discourage public displays of affectionate relationships between white men and black women, but it proved impossible to prevent white planters and overseers from having sexual intercourse with slave women on their plantations. The colored offspring were often freed by the fathers, and in some cases the mother as well.

By the late 1820s the population of free colored had grown to close to 9,000 on the three Danish islands, most of them on St. Thomas, where they could make a living in the harbor city. Some free colored men were quite well-to-do and ran large businesses, having arranged for whites to be the nominal owners. Many free colored women lived in unofficial unions with planters or colonial officials; the most prominent was Anna Heegaard, who lived with Governor-General Peter v. Scholten (see N. Hall 1976). But the colonial government initially sought to subjugate the free colored by limiting their rights. For employment, they were technically restricted to fishing, small farming, and being artisans. Thus restricted, some were barely able to eke out a living, and they represented a potential problem to the social and economic well-being of the colony.

In an effort to normalize and improve the situation of this group, a law was passed in 1834 granting equality on par with the white population to all free colored who had acquired their freedom by April 1830. The remainder could attain this status after a trial period of three years. The free colored also were organized into their own military regiments, headed by a white captain. Governor-General v. Scholten placed himself in the forefront of the struggle to raise the social status of the free colored by inviting the most prominent among them to dinner in Government House together with colonial officials and planter families; apparently he succeeded to the extent that, after a time, even the white ladies attended the parties and did not snub the free colored (Lawaetz 1940: 142–46). Significantly, these efforts by the colonial government to improve the lot of the free colored came at the time of emancipation on the British islands.

On St. John, the free colored constituted a small and impoverished population. In the late 1820s there were about 100 free colored on the island, comprising less than 5 percent of the population. Throughout the slavery period they remained quite poor because their economic opportunities were limited by law; their main occupations were fishing, cultivating provisions, and burning lime. The *landfoged* recorded many cases of free coloreds requesting funds from the public treasury to pay for funerals. In one case of a woman who asked for help to bury her son, the *landfoged* noted that the public treasury had already paid for the burial of three of her other children (*LA* 33: February 13, 1841).

The improved legal position granted to freed persons by the colonial government and the economic aid given to the most destitute caused many of them to view the *landfoged* as their protector and benefactor (*DK*: Breve 2041–2300). They even participated in hunting maroons and helped catch runaway slaves that they encountered on their own. They were paid for this kind of cooperation (*LA* 34: September 3, 1846). Thus the granting of equal rights to freed persons created a cleavage between the slaves and the free colored and, to a certain extent, weakened the solidarity among people of African descent. A slave named Lucia expressed the frustration felt by many of the slaves when she said in the course of an argument with Johnny, who had recently been freed: "since the Basses [Moravian Church] gave you free you become damn'd mannish" (*LA* 34: June 22, 1846).

The colonial authorities appealed to the Moravian missionaries on the island for help in controlling the slaves. Planters were instructed to ensure that all slaves received religious instruction and that children were baptized. When it was discovered that Godfry, who had been brought to court for burglary, was not baptized, he was asked why. He replied that he had no desire for religious education. This argument was dismissed by the government, and it was impressed upon Godfry's owner that it was his duty to have Godfry baptized (*LA* 17: October 21, 1843). The missionaries were also asked to help the slaves who seemed to have difficulty adjusting to slavery. Kilmannock, who belonged to Caneel Bay Estate, was sent to the missionaries after he had been a maroon several times and had attempted suicide (*LA* 32: April 24, 1839). One of the missionaries was asked to try to persuade slaves from Leinsterbay Plantation who had fled to the British Virgin Islands to return to St. John; he did not succeed (*LA* 32: May 25, 1840). Like the planters, the missionaries imposed a hierarchical structure on the slaves, which accorded them different statuses within the church and singled out a few leaders. The members were divided into three classes: apprentices for baptism, the baptized not yet ready to receive communion, and communicants. Among the communicants, a few helpers were chosen who were perceived as displaying highly moral conduct. These helpers had the confidence of both the missionaries and the planters, and they held positions of great respect in the church (Lawaetz 1902: 202–3; *LA* 35: November 1, 1847). The *landfoged* realized the importance of the missionaries as far as public order was concerned. In 1840 he noted in one of his reports: "the peace and the state of things, the usual good order here on St. John rest primarily, if not singularly, on moral grounds, i.e. on the influence of the missionaries on the slaves, and on the slaves' conviction that, through the former's peaceful intervention, or, at least, through the *landfoged*'s aid, their complaints will be investigated in an impartial way and set right" (*LA* 5: May 27, 1840; cf. Goveia 1969: 305; G. Hall 1971: 45).

In the long run, neither peaceful intervention by the missionaries nor the *landfoged*'s aid succeeded in salvaging the

plantation system on St. John. Many planters were not financially able to maintain the slaves as the law prescribed, and they
resented the colonial authorities' interference in the operation of
the plantations. The attitude of the plantocracy is expressed in a
letter written by one of the most important owners of St. John
plantations, Judge H. H. Berg, who owned Annaberg and Leinsterbay. Reflecting upon the last years of slavery, he wrote:

> Whatever the Master formerly did from kindness to his people
> was made a legal obligation although no law was needed to
> that effect. Thus nobody thought of taking away his slaves'
> property, nobody thought of refusing their slaves, who had con-
> ducted themselves well, their usual Christmas presents, flour
> and pork. Hardly any refused to sell a slave who deserved it for
> his freedom [i.e., refused to let him buy his freedom], and many
> masters of their own accord gratified their slaves with a free
> Saturday even unasked for, when they had worked well during
> the week. All these favors were done away with—law made it
> the Masters' bound-in duty, and instead of gratitude you heard
> the Negroes say: 'de debil thank Massa for de, de no be di Gen-
> eral do ha order di'. Public authority both plunged and crept in
> betwixt master and slave, the bonds of affection, of respect,
> of subordination were severed and—we now have the effect,
> ruin staring us in the face. (*STG* 2 1848–52; English in the
> original)

Certainly not all planters were as kind as Berg seemed to
think. Many (including Berg, who lived on St. Thomas) were
often absent from St. John, where they were represented by overseers. In the *landfoged*'s words, these men were "raw and uncultivated people" who knew little about operating a large sugar
plantation (*LA* 5: May 12, 1833). In the latter days of slavery, the
knowledge that the *landfoged* would help them and the realiza-
tion that many overseers were ignorant newcomers emboldened
the slaves; some openly showed their spite for the overseers. In
an encounter with the assistant manager on Carolina Plantation, a slave exclaimed: "Mass' John, why are you picking at me
in this way, and what can you do me? You may lick me and luck
me up, that's all—but you can't kill me or shoot me" (*LA* 32: May
11, 1839; English in the original). In another instance a slave
displayed his contempt for the low position of overseers in the
white planter class, shouting to the overseer on the neighboring

estate: "Do you know whom I belong to? I belong to Judge Berg, you are a come-and-go, my master is head-judge. You, pshaw! You a shitting ass blanco!" (*LA* 35: April 24, 1847; English in the original).

The slaves, becoming more and more confident in their protests, expected emancipation to be proclaimed on the Danish islands in 1838, when slavery ceased on the British West Indian islands (after an apprentice period that began in 1834). When instead the governor-general merely issued a placard reiterating the food allowances specified already in the 1817 code, they were disappointed and believed that the placard should have contained further rights that had not been published. The *landfoged* had to go to all the plantations himself in order to assure the slaves that the placard had been read in full (*LA* 5: May 27, 1840).

Although the colonial government realized that the British islands would provide a safe harbor for any slave who managed to escape from the Danish islands, it was believed that this would not occur. The St. John *stadshauptmand* (a planter who was in charge of the white militia and the corps of free colored) explained why: "Negroes have strong local attachment and the comfortable houses and a piece of good land for cultivation which our people all enjoy and which the[y] are tought [*sic*] to consider as their own, together with the stock which they all more or less raise, will I think form ties, which they will not easily be endured to sever" (*LA* 159: May 23, 1838; English in the original). The *landfoged* agreed. The slaves have a "particular preference for living and being buried on their place of birth: 'the place where my navel string lies', as they express it" (*DK* Breve 2041–2300: November 6, 1841). Essentially, the planters and colonial authorities were hoping that the slaves would be tied down by their own system of food production. They did not consider that this very system gave the slaves the choice of settling on the British islands because they already were largely self-sufficient economically and knew how to provide for themselves.

The first major escape to the British islands from St. John occurred in May 1840, when eleven slaves fled from Leinsterbay and Annaberg to Tortola, and a few days later four slaves belonging to Adrian, Brownsbay, and Hermitage followed (*LA* 32: May 25, 1840; *SP* 33: June 10, 1840). The colonial government responded by issuing a series of regulations restricting the usage and storage of boats (*LA* 32: May 30, 1840; 17: January 1, 1842;

33: March 31, 1842; 29: July 6, 1844). But the slaves who wanted "to look for freedom" (*LA* 34: October 26, 1846) could not be stopped. They made arrangements with the freed on Tortola to pick them up at night on one of the many cays on St. John, or they made their own boats or rafts out of wood from the bush or doors stolen from estate buildings (*LA* 33: October 29, 1842; 29: December 2, 1844; 34: August 4, 1845). The government stationed a naval ship on the north shore overlooking the British island to prevent further escapes (Lawaetz 1940: 156), but without success. During the 1840s, well over a hundred slaves fled from St. John (*LA* 30: May 8, 1846; *RD* Box 1904). The many slaves who chose not to flee to the British islands but to wait for freedom on St. John became increasingly impatient.

In 1847, a royal resolution issued freedom to all slaves, effective after a twelve-year transitional period, as well as immediate freedom to all children born after the date of the law. When the resolution was published in the Moravian churches on St. John, the slaves loudly protested, "That is too long," and the slaves at Caneel Bay Plantation even refused to attend the church to hear it (*LA* 35: October 12, 1847). On the other islands also, especially on St. Croix, the resolution was received with great dissatisfaction.

From St. Thomas and St. John, slaves had relatively easy access to the British islands. Because St. Croix was much more isolated, even the most dissatisfied Crucian slaves had little chance of escape. Furthermore, while the slaves on St. Thomas and St. John had found a certain measure of independence in their system of food production, the Crucian slaves had been worked much harder as field slaves and had not learned to provide for themselves as well as had the slaves on the other islands. By the 1840s, most of the Crucian slave population was not a proto-peasantry, as was the case on St. John, but rather an emerging rural proletariat (cf. Rodney 1981: 647–48). In July 1848, they staged a strikelike action, demanding freedom before they went to work; this soon developed into a threat of rebellion, as the participants began to drink and displayed their anger more violently. Rather than undertake a major battle with the slaves, Governor-General v. Scholten decided to issue general emancipation on the Danish islands. The slaves were freed July 3, 1848 (Lawaetz 1940: 176–91; N. Hall 1976).

3

The Emergence of an
Afro-Caribbean Culture

As far as the planters were concerned, the reproduction of slave labor was merely a matter of sufficient food production and, after 1808, procreation to maintain the proper number of slaves. Labor reproduction was regarded by planters as a necessary evil that should interfere as little as possible with the plantation enterprise. As far as the slaves were concerned, labor reproduction presented the opportunity to engage in activities that were not controlled by the planter class but were initiated by slaves to maintain the well-being of the slave group. Though their labor reproduction emerged as an integral part of plantation society, it nevertheless constituted a socioeconomic subsystem that formed the basis of an Afro-Caribbean community.

Production

It was common in the West Indies to allow slaves, in their limited free time, to cultivate their own provision crops, thus saving the expense of importing foodstuffs from Europe and North America. On St. John, the slaves engaged in a variety of subsistence activities. C. G. A. Oldendorp had been sent to the Danish West Indies in 1767–68 by the Moravian church to report on the progress of their missionary efforts among the slaves (Ramløv 1968: 149). He was particularly interested in the culture and economy of the slaves, including their subsistence activities:

> Every single household receives a small piece of land from the master, which is used for their subsistence. Usually it is so large that, through industrious work, it can provide not just

the necessities of life but also something extra. . . . This custom
frees the master from all further care for the slaves' support;
and for them it is much more convenient and advantageous
than if their necessary support should be given them in natura,
which occurs on some English plantations on St. Croix. The
Negro enjoys on his own plantation a form of freedom: He
works it as he pleases; and as he owns everything that he ac-
quires from it, this is quite encouraging and leads to greater
industriousness. The Negro becomes, in this way, much more
tied to the master's plantation, as it is almost as if he has his
own property and owns a little plot on it. . . . On his piece of
land the Negro plants primarily cassava, potatoes and yams.
The first mentioned constitute his daily bread and, lacking
this, he makes do with the two others. Maize and "Welsh grain"
are also comprised in the Negro's most necessary crops. Apart
from what he can derive from his ground, the wild forest also
presents him with a plentitude of fruits which cost him nothing
but the time to collect them. With little trouble he can also provide for himself from the sea with fish, crabs and mussels. The
fish are so plentiful from July to October, that one can accumulate as large a supply as one believes one needs. These small
fish can be preserved well after they have been dried. Apart
from this, industrious housekeepers also raise fowl and good
pigs, which they use for money and acquire in this way other
food stuffs and necessities. If some of the Negroes eat dogs and
cats this is not out of need, but out of an abnormal craving.
Usually the Negroes have most difficulty acquiring their food
from September to the end of November, but this is the case for
the whites also. (1786: 348–49)

From this account the slaves appear to have exploited all subsistence possibilities available to them, ranging from agriculture
to fishing and gathering. Oldendorp seems hesitant to recognize
the difficulties the slaves experienced acquiring sufficient food,
perhaps because he was eager to see the activities as the cradle of
moral virtues such as industriousness and pride in property and
of greater attachment to the master's plantation. Though the ethnographic detail contained in Oldendorp's book has been praised
by Melville Herskovits, among others (Ramløv 1968: 150), Oldendorp's description of the slaves' system of production is rather
general and does not seem to reflect an intimate knowledge of

their methods and techniques or the organizational structure of the subsistence system.

Like Oldendorp's report, the records of the St. John *landfoged* from the eighteenth and early nineteenth centuries reflect almost complete indifference to these matters. For example, a slave was brought to the *landfoged* because he had refused to work for his master on Sundays, and the *landfoged* asked whether the slave really knew the religious meaning of the day. When the slave replied that he did not, the *landfoged* asked, "Why, since he knew that he was Burke's purchased property, did he not then obey his orders?" The slave answered that he obeyed during the six days, but the seventh, he believed, was for him to work on his own provision ground (*LA* 70: April 3, 1788). Sunday, despite the missionary efforts of the Moravians, had become not the day of the Lord but the day of the provision ground. Similarly, the *landfoged* had little idea of the economic system that had evolved in connection with subsistence activities. He was quite surprised, for example, when a slave woman explained to him that she wanted to go to St. Thomas in order to collect some money that was due her. "What kind of debt," asked the bewildered *landfoged*, "could be due to her as a slave?" She explained that it arose from some trading that she had been involved in (*LA* 72: October 5, 1804). In another case, the *landfoged* expressed astonishment when he learned that the house of the old "royal slave" Matheus, which was located on a bay, served as a storage place for products such as yams, tannier, and beans that the slaves wished to send to St. Thomas (*LA* 58: May 20, 1796).

One reason for this lack of knowledge may have been that the planters and colonial officials, in relegating the slaves to a subhuman position, chose not to acknowledge socioeconomic independence among the slaves as long as it did not interfere with the operation of the plantations. Another reason may have been that most of the slaves' activities took place outside the main plantation area that was used by and well-known to the planters. The slaves' provision grounds were usually located on the periphery of the estate (Carstens 1981 [1740s]: 88) and were accessible only by foot and donkey path. A case in the *landfoged*'s records indicates that the white population might not even have known the location of the slaves' provision grounds. A party of whites hunting for maroons had to ask a slave on the estate to show them the way to the provision grounds (*LA* 89: November 18, 1787). This ignorance is not really surprising; most of the estates on St. John included large tracts of mountainous land covered with tropical forest cut only by small, inconspicuous paths. In 1805 the average area left uncultivated on every sugar plantation, at the peak of sugarcane cultivation, exceeded 175 acres. Carolina Plantation had more than 1,500 acres in bush. To the whites, St. John was comprised of the cultivated areas of sugarcane and other crops situated in valleys with their main estate grounds. The surrounding mountainsides were regarded as more or less impenetrable bush, which served largely to isolate the estates from each other. To the slaves, the bush lands were not foreign territory but their own land, where they could make their gardens in small clearings and create an existence for themselves outside the direct control of the planters.

Because the colonial authorities and the planters lacked interest in and knowledge of the slaves' social and economic system, it is almost impossible to reconstruct the details of this eighteenth-century system. References to it in the archival materials before the nineteenth century are few, and even here much of it must be inferred from slaves' testimony about other matters, which incidentally contains a wealth of brief descriptions of the slaves' "free time" activities and social customs (cf. N. Hall 1980). By piecing together scraps of information contained in the records of the *landfoged* and cross-examining them against the background of the plantation society within which the slaves existed, it is possible to assemble a picture of the system of production experienced by the slaves. I have included many quotations from the records, "witnesses in spite of themselves" that give a less biased, livelier impression of slave life than accounts abstracted primarily from the somewhat dubious statistical data and descriptive reports of the time.

The provision ground

Provision farming is pictured in detail in a lithographic illustration and its accompanying explanatory text in an 1855 atlas of Denmark and its colonies (see Figure 2). The provision ground, shown as it looked about the time of emancipation in 1848, is located in a mountainside clearing, far above the sugarcane fields in the valleys. The text, probably written by the Danish botanist A. S. Ørsted, who visited the Danish West Indies in 1843–44, explains that

This picture places us in the interior of St. John in the vicinity of Bordeaux, which is toward the east end [of the island]. . . . In the picture's foreground we see several plants which show that this is a so-called provision ground, or a small plot which has been left for the Negroes to cultivate. The little tree on the right resembles, in several ways, the palms. . . . This is the *papaya* or the melon tree (Carica Papaya), which bears great fruits like melons that sit in great numbers (30–50) by the base of the leaves' stems. Behind this, one sees the big light green leaves of the *plantain* (Musa paradisiaca) and the *banana* (Musa sapientum), the nourishing fruits of which are used in all tropical countries to a great extent instead of bread. Next to these we easily recognize the coconut palm and the sugarcanes. The plant which sends its vines along the earth with great heart shaped leaves, is a kind of pumpkin (Curcubita Pepo), whose fruits are boiled and constitute a favored meal among the Creoles. (*Danmark* 1855: "Parti af det Indre")

This is followed by a further description of the forest vegetation.[1]

While the text is mostly in rather dry botanical language, the scene itself, by the Danish painter Frits Melby, has a highly romantic gloss and shows a picturesquely dressed couple resting by a fire, where they are probably cooking some of their produce. One can get an impression of a field with intercropping blending into the forest.

The mountaintop site of the provision ground in the picture was quite typical. Because the slaves cleared their provision grounds by cutting and burning the bush, they were located as far from the plantation fields as possible. Fires were otherwise a threat to the highly flammable sugarcane fields if the weather was dry (*LA* 35: March 16, 26, 1847). The records of the *landfoged* indicate that the provision grounds often were situated along the borders of the plantations and that slaves from neighboring plantations worked in the same general area. For example, when a fire broke out near the border between the estates of Annaberg and Varinisberg, slaves from both plantations arrived quickly to help because they were in the immediate vicinity working on their provision grounds. The provision grounds, in fact, may have constituted small, hamlet-type settlements that were on the outermost fringe of the plantation society. Despite laws explicitly prohibiting slaves who belonged to different plantations from congregating (*LA* 40: June 16, 1828), the provi-

Figure 2. A provision ground, about 1848. Lithograph by Frits Melby, in *Parti af det Indre, Danmark* 1855.

sion grounds must have provided ample opportunity for slaves to get together without the planters' knowing it.

Slaves had permission to use the marginal land around their provision grounds for other economic activities in addition to farming. While slaves kept poultry at their houses in the slave village on the estate, they often chose to raise livestock such as pigs and goats near the provision grounds, where there was more room. They also used materials gathered in the bush to make tools. Certain kinds of wood were used to weave mats, fishing equipment, and possibly baskets. The house depicted in Melby's scene was constructed out of wood and grass from the bush (*LA* 33: April 6, 1841; 40: August 19, 1828, October 19, 1826; Morton 1975 [1843–44]: 169).

Sidney Mintz, who has made extensive analyses of slave agricultural practices, notes that he found no evidence that "land was ever afforded other than to male slaves—though their families (and it does bear noting that their families are referred to with surprising matter-of-factness in the literature) commonly helped them on the provision grounds" (1974: 216–17). However, archival data from St. John indicate that women as well as men had the right to use land on the plantation to which they belonged. Provision farming was not a secondary subsistence activity but provided the basic daily sustenance for the vast majority of slaves. The slave decrees of the nineteenth century specified the amount of food allowances to be granted to individual adult slaves, and cutbacks in food rations were permitted if slaves were given extra free time in which to cultivate provisions. The use of a plot of land was not regarded as a privilege but as a right of all slaves, regardless of sex or marital status, who did not receive full allowance (*LA* 17: September 30, 1843). The *stadshauptmand* did not distinguish between the sexes when he wrote in a letter to the governor on St. Thomas that the "people" have "the choice of land for the cultivation of provisions" (*LA* 159: October 6, 1840).[2] The fact that women were independently engaged in provision farming is also clearly shown in the *landfoged*'s records. The slaves on Bordeaux, for example, complained that women nursing infants were finding it difficult to subsist on their own provision grounds (*LA* 59: March 30, 1830). Women actually seem to have had something of a monopoly on the raising of pigs (compare Oldendorp's description above). The court records contain no references to males raising pigs, and they indicate that women regarded the pigs of the household as their own, even when they lived with a man. When, for example, a man once sold a pig without giving his wife any of the money, she became so angry that he felt he had to move out, despite the fact that they had been married in the church (*LA* 88: September 20, 1835). In another case, a man had placed a pig with his common-law wife's mother to be raised by her. When he came to collect the pig after having broken up with the daughter, she refused to turn it over to him unless he paid her for her work (*LA* 34: June 22, 1846).

Fishing

The sea was an important resource for the slaves. Carstens noted that the slaves on St. John hollowed out big trees to use as fishing canoes (1981 [1740s]: 38), and Oldendorp emphasized the importance of seafood in the slaves' diet (1786: 349). Eighteenth-century archival sources describe fishing by hook and line, with the slaves making their own hooks (*LA* 64: July 14, 1756); nineteenth-century records describe this and a number of other fishing methods. The slaves fished with hook and line from steep cliffs that bordered the sea at some places on the island (*LA* 35: November 22, 1845). They knew how to catch fry with nets in order to use them for bait (*LA* 81: February 29, 1816). They wove fish pots out of thin strips of wood and tended them using an estate rowboat placed at their disposal. During the last years of slavery, this was done under strict supervision, because the boat offered too ready a means of escape to the British islands (*LA* 35: November 1, 1847; 42: November 7, 1843; 40: October 19, 1840). At night, the slaves fished with torches for crabs and lobsters, even though this was prohibited (*LA* 33: August 31, 1843) to prevent slaves from fleeing under the cover of darkness. They also collected whelks along the seashore and gathered shells to burn for lime (*LA* 88: July 10, 1834; 159: October 6, 1840). References to fishing indicate that women fished and collected shellfish along the shore but did not fish from boats. Since the fish pots often were tended by one or two slaves under the supervision of a free fisherman, women may have owned fish pots.

In a discussion of the historical background of Caribbean fishing in slavery, Price emphasizes that fishing was rarely used by the planters as a means of acquiring "cheap food for their field hands" but rather was seen as a way to obtain fresh fish for the planter family (1966: 1370). In the St. Johnian data, however, there are many references to fishing as a means of feeding the slaves. For example, during the harvest season, when the slaves were given less time to provide for themselves, the planter on Lamesure purchased a sprat-net, which all the slaves were allowed to use; he often let one of the slaves catch fish for the whole work gang (*LA* 5: July 2, 1841). Another planter apparently decided to give the slaves extra free time to cultivate their provision grounds and to fish instead of providing them with the allowances that the 1817 law called for (*LA* 5: July 2, 1841). On St. John, where all slaves had easy access to the sea, fishing was an integral element in the slaves' system of food production and therefore figured in the minds of the planters as yet another way in which to cut the costs of maintaining the slaves.

Trading

On many of the West Indian islands, the slaves' system of food production provided the basis for an internal market system. Mintz and Hall, in their study of the development of the markets on Jamaica, show that by the eighteenth century an extensive internal market system had emerged, which was largely run by the slaves. Through this system the slaves managed to control as much as 20 percent of the money in circulation on Jamaica (Mintz and Hall 1960). A similar market system evolved on the Danish islands, where, as already noted, the eighteenth-century slave codes reflect attempts to check these economic activities.

On St. John, where there was no real town, a major weekly market never became established. A minor market was held in Coral Bay—the location of Carolina Plantation, the Moravian mission station at Emmaus Estate, and a number of free colored settlements (*LA* 6: September 7, 1832). In the early 1840s, planter Alexander Fraser characterized the Sunday market on St. John as "a mere nominal thing altogether," which "does not deserve the name" (*LA* 120: n.d). Instead of a regular public market, trade on St. John involved informal arrangements and was often based on bartering. A number of women (many of them free colored) regularly visited the different estates to sell goods brought to the island from St. Thomas, especially clothing. In 1840 the *landfoged* noted that since there was little money on the island, these women instead received "fruit, fowls and small livestock—

which leads the Negroes to steal from each other and their masters, when the time comes to pay for the dearly bought wares"
(*LA* 5: April 29, 1840). He sought to prevent this by enforcing a
governmental regulation that a permit must be acquired to carry
on trade, and during the 1840s as many as twenty-five permits
were issued yearly to traders, virtually all of them women. Some
of them were slaves, but they appear to have traded on behalf of
women who made their living from trade. White women who
were the spouses of planters also received permits to sell store
goods on the estates (*LA* 149, 150).

The slaves often bartered with free colored, who were eager to
acquire cornmeal and salt fish from the slaves rather than pay
cash for these imported goods. For example, a slave from Hope
Estate traded cornmeal for rum with a free colored woman, and
slaves on Carolina Plantation hired free colored women to sew
clothes for them in exchange for cornmeal (*LA* 42: August 5,
1846; 40: June 27, 1828). On the large sugar plantations, the
slaves would seem to have been more financially secure than the
poorest free colored, if they received regular allowances and had
free access to unused land. There is a case on record of a free man
who was visited on the night before he died by a number of slave
men and women from Hermanfarm who wanted to get the money
he owed them, before he expired (*LA* 107: September 29, 1837).

A certain amount of bartering went on between slaves belonging to different estates. There was a great difference between the
resources available to slaves on the large sugar plantations and
those belonging to small estates. Whereas slaves on the large
plantations were able to use large tracts of marginal land and
were provided with allowances whenever this was required by
law (with the help of the *landfoged* if needed), the slaves on the
small estates had little land at their disposal and often received
no allowances at all. During one of the governor-general's visits
to St. John, a slave belonging to a smallholder complained to him
about receiving no allowances from his owner. The governor referred the case to the *landfoged*, who was told by the smallholder
that his slaves' working conditions were as follows: They "were
off on Saturdays and received other days when they demanded it.
They go to work in the morning at the time they determine and
cease work in the evening in the same fashion. Lunch and noon
breaks are determined by the Negroes themselves, as no signal is
given." When the *landfoged* heard this, he turned to the slave

and asked whether he would like to be sold to a sugar plantation, to which the slave quickly replied no. He was given thirty whiplashes for having complained without a cause (*LA* 41: April 5, 1836; 31: February 28, 1836). Thus, to compensate for the lack of allowances on the small estates, the slaves received extra free time to work for themselves. They were able to offer certain services in exchange for cornmeal and fish from the slaves on sugar plantations, who had less free time but received allowances; the records show several references to such services, which included clothes washing and gathering firewood and whelks (*LA* 88: July 10, 1834, October 1, 1834; 41: August 5, 1839).

Though there was no regular market on St. John, the slaves were able to sell their produce at the public market on St. Thomas, where they sold almost all of their wood and lime. Most plantations allowed the slaves either to go to St. Thomas on the estate boat to sell their goods or, more commonly, to send their goods on the boat to be sold at the market (*LA* 159: October 6, 1840; 77: July 11, 1844; 35: August 23, 1845). The slaves often made private arrangements with boat captains to transport their wares to St. Thomas and then to purchase certain items for them with the proceeds. Some planters opposed these activities and sought to curb them; during the last years of slavery, when slaves began to escape to the British islands, the trafficking of boats to estates was strictly controlled (*LA* 31: January 23, 1832; 40: August 19, 1828; 41: February 1, 1832; 34: November 23, 1845). The slaves were dependent on the honesty of the boat captains if they could not go to St. Thomas themselves. The slaves on Enighed Plantation, for example, complained that the captain who ran the boat on that estate did not always give them the money that was due to them. He excused himself by saying that often he had to leave their goods on St. Thomas to be sold there and could not collect the money until he returned at a later date (*LA* 77: July 11, 1844).

The system of food production that had emerged among the slaves on St. John by the end of the slavery period enabled them to provide for themselves if the planters granted them extra time off from plantation work. Although this practice was against the law after the proclamation of the 1817 regulation, it seems to have been common on many of the estates and it was accepted by the slaves as long as the weather conditions and the work hours on the plantations made it possible for them to cultivate sufficient crops for their subsistence. When slave women with infants on Bordeaux Estate in 1830 complained about having difficulty cultivating their own provision grounds, their main grievance was that they received no breaks during the day and, because of caring for their babies, had even less time than the other slaves to work on their provision grounds (*LA* 40: March 30, 1830). When the *landfoged* asked the slaves whether they preferred "half allowance and half Saturday or remain as they are, getting the whole day without allowance ... they replied they preferred the latter" (*STG* 1). When a royal code of May 1, 1840, emphasized that slaves on St. John were to receive full allowance and work six days a week, the slaves complained about it, asking the planters to continue their old, informal arrangements whereby they worked only five days against receiving half allowance (*LA* 28: October 3, 1842). When Saturday was given free with half allowance in 1843, the colonial government was requested to permit the slaves to be off on Wednesday or Friday afternoon against their receiving no allowance. This was allowed, if both parties agreed (*LA* 33: October 6, 1843). The slaves could not be forced to relinquish their allowance, however, if they could demonstrate that the provision grounds had failed to bear because of poor growing conditions (*LA* 33: October 2, 1842). The old and disabled, who did not have the physical strength to cultivate their own provision grounds, had to be provided with full allowances throughout the year; in 1844 the *landfoged* registered fifty slaves who qualified for such allowances (*LA* 33: October 6, 1843; June 13, July 5, 1844).

Eventually, all adult slaves who were able to cultivate their own foodstuffs were required to do so and were not entitled to full provisions when the provision grounds were bearing (*LA* 33: November 5, 1844). By the end of slavery almost all slaves were actively involved in a system of food production that entailed cultivating crops, raising animals, and fishing. The Saturday-free regulation specified that all slaves were entitled to work a piece of land, to keep fowl, and to other privileges that had to be worked out with the planters (*LA* 33: October 6, 1843); these included keeping livestock, cutting wood, burning lime, sending goods to St. Thomas on estate boats, and using estate rowboats to tend fish pots. All slaves thus had access to the means of production by virtue of their belonging to a plantation, and there apparently was little differentiation in the treatment of men and women. As noted by Mathurin, "Slavery, in many essentials, made men and women roughly equal in the eyes of the master. Legally they had identical status as chattels, as objects which could be owned. They were seen, not so much as men and women, but as units of labor" (1975: 5). The plantation society therefore appears to have induced only a limited differentiation of labor by sex.

Procreation

As the bearers of children, women had the heavier responsibility for the infants' care; this placed them at a disadvantage in provision farming. Sometimes new mothers received neither allowances nor enough free time to care for their babies and provide for themselves; nursing women had the most difficulty cultivating their provision grounds. Ordinarily, however, the extra work involved in caring for infants was acknowledged by the plantation managers, who permitted a shorter workday for women with children below one year of age.

After the ban on the slave trade in 1808, when the planters began to depend on procreation among the slaves for the maintenance of the slave population, it was expected that slaves would settle as married couples and establish nuclear families with children. The scene in Figure 2, with its couple having a common provision ground and sharing a meal together, reflects this conception of the slave family. But the reality of the slaves' system of marriage and kinship was quite different.

There are few explicit data on the slaves' conjugal arrangements, and the few descriptions that exist are biased by ethnocentric notions of what constitutes a family. During recent years, historians have turned to church records and census materials. In the case of St. John, there is a certain amount of such statistical material, but here, as elsewhere, it is difficult to ascertain the exact meaning of the different categories that can be elucidated on the basis of such information. Furthermore, some of the church and census data were collected in such an ambiguous and unprofessional manner that their value is questionable. In this discussion I have therefore combined a quantitative analysis with qualitative information from the court records—information that refers to the slaves' family arrangements, whether they involve affinal or kin ties. This qualitative information has been used to determine the social, economic, and cultural context within which the slaves lived and thus to find a framework within which to interpret the statistical data of the census and church records.

Kinship ties

An understanding of the genesis of kinship ties among the slaves can shed light on the important issue of the Afro-American family. Virtually all African slaves arrived on St. John spouseless and virtually without relatives. The records indicate that during the eighteenth century, when the slaves on an estate were mostly unrelated, they tended to form sexual unions within the estate. As children were born, kin groups began to emerge on the estate, and during the nineteenth century slaves were surrounded by large networks of relatives if they lived on the estate where they were born. Thus the slave population of an estate was turning into one large kindred, and eventually some of the slaves began to look for spouses outside their own estate. This was especially the case on estates with a relatively small stock of slaves. The children who resulted from these extra-estate relationships always belonged to the mothers' owners. By the end of slavery, the slaves therefore had most of their matrilateral relatives on the estate, whereas the affinal and patrilateral ties in many cases extended to other estates. This general development can be seen in the records available for St. John.

Statistics on the slave population after 1806, according to estates, indicate that there were 817 men and 699 women twenty years old and above on the island (see Table 2). The excess of men was accounted for, in the main, by four large sugar plantations, which had a total of 226 male and 148 female slaves. Apart from these plantations, the sexual composition was fairly equal on the large estates, thus enabling the slaves to find spouses within the estate if they wished. A total of 148 slaves twenty years old and above lived on small estates having up to 50 slaves. On these estates, the adult population was quite small, ranging from 1 slave to 28 slaves, with an average of 10. The opportunity to find a spouse within the estate was limited, especially as the sexual composition and the age range varied a great deal. Many of the slaves on the small estates therefore were forced to look for their spouses outside the estate where they lived.

Figures on the "slaves who are known to have engaged in marriage with Negroes on other estates" confirm that the smaller the slave population, the greater the number of slaves who had relationships outside the estate; though the statistics refer to "marriages," it is likely that common-law marriages are included insofar as they were known to the planters. On the estates with up to 50 slaves over twenty years old, more than 25 percent of the slaves married outside the estate, whereas on the largest estates, with more than 100 slaves over twenty years old, only 10 percent were known to do so (see Table 3). In the case of the largest estates it is important to consider that the figures include only marriages that were known to the planters; the planters on the large estates probably were much less informed about the slaves' conjugal relationships than were those on small estates. Also, six of the nineteen estates with more than 50 slaves actually consisted of more than one property owned and operated by one owner; while the slaves belonged to the same master, they may have been dispersed on different estates and thus involved in extra-estate marriages, at least in the territorial sense. Nevertheless, most seem to have limited at least their more established, known relationships to slaves living on the same estate. This is confirmed by statistics on married and unmarried slave couples included in the same survey, as seen in Table 2.

The statistics refer to the slave couples on the various estates. A total of 69 married couples and 199 common-law couples are listed. These figures should refer only to those unions where both slaves belonged to a single estate, since otherwise extra-estate unions would be reported twice. If the 268 couples are regarded as involving only those slaves who belonged to the same plantation, 536 slaves found their partner within the same estate compared to 259 who were known to have relationships outside the estate. This means that of the unions known to the planters, 68 percent were confined to the estate and 32 percent were not. The figures on couples are not entirely consistent internally, and it must be expected that some of the extra-estate couples may have been counted twice and also listed both in the category for couples and in the category for extra-estate marriages. Table 2 also shows, however, that there was a great deal of variation from estate to estate in the relative numbers of slaves seeking mates on other estates. Other important factors influencing the choice of a mate included the proportion of African to Creole slaves (and thus the slaves' potential kin ties within the estate) and the relative ease

Table 2. Slave Population of St. John, 1806[a]

Name of estate	No. of slaves	Males	Females	Creoles	Africans	20 years old and above		Couples		Known to be married to slaves on other plantations	
						Males	Females	Married	Unmarried	Males	Females
East End											
Hermitage	25	9	16	23	2	2	10	—	1	—	3
Hallover	12	4	8	1	11	4	5	—	1	—	1
Mount Pleasant	27	10	17	27	—	4	7	—	2	2	4
Cruz Bay											
Pastory	3	2	1	1	2	2	1	—	—	1	—
Bethany	16	9	7	12	4	4	3	—	—	2	1
Enighed	65	40	25	53	12	29	21	1	2	1	3
L'Esperance	81	41	40	39	42	21	17	3	9	12	12
Adrian & Trunkbay	125	63	62	76	49	47	42	3	17	1	3
K. Caneel Bay, etc.	118	63	55	69	49	34	32	—	17	1	6
Susannaberg	143	71	72	109	34	35	45	4	9	9	17
Cathrinaberg	117	56	61	77	40	39	40	1	16	2	—
Beverhoudtsberg	58	30	28	31	27	19	24	2	1	4	7
Reef Bay											
Sieben & Mollendal	124	60	64	93	31	34	36	3	9	17	14
The Gift	2	1	1	2	—	1	1	—	—	—	—
Parforce & Little Reefbay	70	36	34	45	25	26	20	1	9	7	4
Hope & Misgunst	61	33	28	55	6	20	18	2	14	2	3
Bakkero	50	31	19	20	30	15	13	—	6	1	1
Bordeaux & Lamesure	165	84	81	86	79	62	33	1	52[b]	2	—

Maho Bay											
Varini & Winthberg	128	76	52	75	53	48	30	3	10	8	4
Great Caneelbay (Cinnamonbay)	116	67	49	77	39	47	30	9	4	9	4
Rustenberg	84	42	42	62	22	24	28	7	6	3	3
Brownsbay	70	42	28	64	6	27	21	—	14	5	2
Munsberry	131	67	64	54	77	47	44	10	7	3	7
Annaberg	147	83	64	67	80	66	47	1	10	1	11
Leinsterbay	182	115	67	99	83	69	38	11	10	11	3
Coral Bay											
Zootenval	26	14	12	26	—	4	8	—	1	1	5
De Kooningh	14	7	7	7	7	5	4	—	3	1	3
Kambrechs	30	14	16	24	6	9	12	—	2	6	5
Lohmann	8	4	4	2	6	2	2	—	—	1	—
Mollendahl	6	2	4	4	2	2	3	—	1	1	1
Carolina	169	88	81	109	60	57	51	7	17	4	7
Emmaus	28	12	16	25	3	4	7	—	1	2	1
Fortsberg	1	—	1	1	—	1	1	—	—	—	—
Reynolds	9	5	4	3	6	4	3	—	—	1	1
Fries *alias* Johns Folly	6	4	2	3	3	4	2	—	—	2	—
Total	2,417	1,285	1,132	1,521	896	817	699	69	251	123	136

a. The information in this table was gathered by a commission investigating the state of the transatlantic slave trade with a view to its possible abolition. The commission was particularly interested in ascertaining whether the slaves' marital and sexual relationships were of such a nature that they could be expected to provide the base for the maintenance of the slave work force by procreation as an alternative to importation of slaves from Africa.

b. Excluded in statistics; as the figure for unmarried couples is inconsistent with figures for other estates, a zero value is quite unlikely given the number of slaves 20 years old and above on the plantation.

Source: *G1*: 1806.

Table 3. Slave Marriages outside the Estate
(according to Size of Slave Population)

Size of slave population 20 years old and above per estate	Total number of slaves 20 years old and above	Slaves known to be engaged in marriages outside estates	
		Number	Percent
50 or fewer slaves	441	109	25
51–100 slaves	885	127	14
101–150 slaves[a]	221	23	10

a. Excludes figures given for Bordeaux and Lamesure (see Table 2).

Source: *G*1: 1806.

of access to other estates. Despite this uncertainty, the percentages provide a rough indication of the nature of the slaves' sexual unions.

The Moravian records on the parentage of children baptized in the Emmaus church during the last years of slavery, covering the eastern half of the island, furnish more exact information on the relationships that resulted in the birth of children. Table 4 shows that during the last five years of slavery, of the 215 slave children (born to slave women) who were baptized, 42 percent were born of slave parents belonging to the same estate, 41 percent to slave parents belonging to different estates, and 16 percent to slave mothers and free men who probably did not live on the same estate. Therefore, perhaps close to 60 percent of these sexual unions were oriented toward spouses outside the estate. The smaller the estate, the greater the number of slaves who formed sexual unions outside the estate. On Carolina Plantation, which had approximately 150 slaves during the last fifteen years of slavery, 70 percent of the children were born to parents who both belonged to the plantation. At Lamesure, which had approximately 45 slaves, only 45 percent of the children born were to parents who both belonged to the plantation. Tables 5 and 6 show that while some of the intra-estate unions were monogamous and of long duration, others were rather short-lived or were not mutually exclusive. The Carolina Plantation unions, for example, included monogamous, permanent unions such as those between Jacob and Maria Elizabeth, Peter and Ana Luise, and Emmanuel and Anna Christina. The union between Johan Moses and Maria Magdalene, however, was rather brief, and three years later she

Table 4. Slave Children of St. Johnian Mating Relationships,
Baptized 1843–47

	1843	1844	1845	1846	1847
Female slave and:					
Male slave, same estate	22	12	19	16	21
Male slave, other estate	19	14	19	14	22
Male slave, unclassifiable estate	0	1	0	0	0
Free man, same estate	0	0	0	1	0
Free man, other estate	0	0	0	3	1
Free man, unclassifiable estate	1	7	11	4	8
Free woman and:					
Male slave, same estate	0	0	0	0	0
Male slave, other estate	0	0	0	0	0
Male slave, unclassifiable estate	1	2	0	1	3
Free man, same estate	1	2	0	1	3
Free man, other estate	0	0	0	3	1
Free man, unclassifiable estate	3	10	12	1	7
Unclassifiable relations	7	1	3	2	0

Source: *M: J.* 1.

had a child with Stephanus. Eva Maria, though she remained with George for at least seven years, from 1835 to 1842, had a brief prior union with John William (1833). After George she had brief unions with Wilhelmus (1844) and Christian (1846). Several of the men also had more than one woman at a time, as in the cases of Benjamin, Stephanus, Samuel, Gottlieb, Christophal, Ernst, and Johan Marcus.

The records of the *landfoged* contain many references to the great variety of unions and shifts of partner among the slaves. The most elaborate is one from 1845, describing the life history of Petronella, 37, who was born on St. Croix but as a child was brought to Beverhoudtsberg on St. John:

In her youth she was a house slave on Beverhoudtsberg and had a relationship with her master's son, William Beverhoudt, but she had no children with him; thereafter she got together

Table 5. Mating Relationships on Carolina Plantation, 1833–47 (according to Male Partner)

Father	Mother	Child	Year
Benjamin	Abigail	Johan Petrus	1835
	same	Mathilde	1840
	same	Maria Cecilia	1843
	same	William James	1846
	Rudi	Sophia	1841
Nathanael	Sophia	Paulus	1838
	same	Ane Catharine	1841
Johan Moses	Maria Magdalene	Rosina	1835
Stephanus	Maria Magdalene	Jan	1838
	Margreth (free?)	Mary Johana	1842
	Franziska	Ana Elisa	1843
	same	Mary Jane	1845
	same	Sophia Marg.	1847
	Ana Elizabeth v. Usher[a]	Joseph Alwera	1845
	same	James Mortimer	1847
Martin	Anna Susanne	Johann	1835
(possibly	same	Philippa	1838
2 persons)	same	Timoth	1841
	Apolonia	Magdalene	1837
	same	Gabriel	1839
	Priscille	Ane Louise	1841
Samuel	Anna Susanne	James	1842
(possibly	Agnes	Christian	1844
2 persons)	same	Adam	1847
	Maria Susanna	Johannes	1833
	same	Carl	1836
	same	Abraham	1839
	same	Wm. Thomas	1844
	same	Christian Friedrick	1847
	Anne Margrethe	Daniel	1839
	Anne Maria	Jan	1839
Jacob	Maria Elizabeth	Petrus	1836
	same	Albertus	1838
	same	Charlotte Louise	1842
	same	Veronia	1845
Gottlieb	Anna Luise	William	1836
	Agnes	Adam	1834
	Ana Rahel	Carolina	1833
	same	Paulus	1836
	same	Christian	1837
Peter	Ana Luise	Frederieka	1837

Continued

Table 5 continued

Father	Mother	Child	Year
	same	Anne	1840
	same	Rosaline	1841
	same	Alberta Earthenia	1843
	same	Rosalinde	1847
Johan Petrus (possibly same as Peter)	Apolonia	Marian Dekoning	1845
	same	Susane Catharine	1847
Johannes (possibly 2 persons)	Agnes	William	1839
	Lucia v. Usher	Christian	1844
Matheus (possibly same as Johannes)	Catharina	William Henry	1835
Johan Godfried	Anna Christine	Jan Joseph	1834
Jeremias	Catharina	Friedrick	1835
John William	Eva Maria	Luise Charlotte	1833
George	Eva Maria	Daniel	1835
	same	Sarah	1836
	same	Josua	1839
	same	Maria	1842
Wilhelmus	Eva Maria	Nathanael	1844
Johan David	Ana Rahel	Johanne	1839
Christophal	Ana Rahel	Alexander	1843
	same	Mary Julia	1845
	J. Elizabeth	James Joseph	1844
Christian	Eva Maria	Susane Pauline	1846
Immanuel	Anna Christina	Cornelis	1834
	same	Susanna	1836
	same	Stephanus	1839
	same	Emilie	1840
	same	Johannes	1842
Philippus	Lea	John Petrus	1841
	Philippa	John Charles	1842
Johan Josua	Dorothea	Carl	1836
	same	Charles	1838
Ernst	Ana Rosine	Margretha	1838
	Kitty v. Sally Haragin	Edward	1835
	same	Caroline	1838
	same	Sally Margaretha	1841
	same	Juliana Celestina	1844
	same	Henry Walter	1847
Johan Marcus	Ana Rosine	William Henrick	1843

Continued

Table 5 continued

Father	Mother	Child	Year
	same	Jinnet	1846
	same	Maria Louise	1847
	Helena v. Dr. Raphael	Rosina Olivia	1847
William	Ann Maria	Marie Aletta	1842
	same	David	1845
Carl	Philippa	Maichel	1845
Christian Ludvig	Philippina	Mariane	1847
Alexander	Johanne Gertrud	Joseph	1839
	same	Clara Adeline	1842
	Rebecca v. Abigail	Anna Elise	1833
Tony	Rudy	Kitty	1844
Henrich	Priscille	William	1843
Michael	Juliane	Maria Magdalene	1841
Johan Jacob	Juliane	Ernestina	1844
	same	Petrina	1846
Thomas	J. Elisabeth	Mary Johane	1847
Andreas	Catharina Elisabeth	Ana Maria	1845
	same	Simon	1847

a. "v." refers to the German *von* and indicates ownership. I have listed this only when the mother does not belong to the same plantation as the father.

Source: *M:* J.1.

with Ben, but at that time had no children with him. Ben left her and started a relationship with Anna Johanna with whom he had children. . . . When Ben thus had left her and overseer Sprat came to Beverhoudtsberg he took up with her, and had a mulatto boy with her, i.e. Sprat (George) who now is with her and is 14 years old; then she got together with unfree Christian belonging to Hope and she had a son with him, that is Christian, 11 years old. Since then Ben again began a relationship with her, and she has had three children with him, the eldest of whom is 7 years old. At the very time that Ben started seeing her, she remembers that he no longer had anything to do with Anna Johanna, and he took her [Petronella] into his house, where she still lives. She learned later, however, that Ben also lives with Anna Johanna, with whom he has had 2 girls, one born in 1841 and the other in 1843. (*LA* 34: June 18, 1845)

Though Petronella was annoyed that Ben still was seeing Anna Johanna, she showed her anger only toward Ben and apparently did not quarrel with Anna Johanna, who was living on the same estate as she. Petronella's history indicates that a person might go through a variety of unions, with free and unfree; with persons on the same estate and on other estates; of a residential and extra-residential character.

Slaves who lived on the same estate had the most opportunity to get to know each other and to form sexual unions. They worked together throughout the day and at night stayed in the slave houses, which usually were located close to each other in the slave quarters of the estate. Slaves from neighboring estates, however, also had opportunities to meet. Much of their free time was spent in the provision grounds, located on the estate borders. Slaves on neighboring estates knew a great deal about each

Table 6. Mating Relationships on Lamesure, 1833–47
(according to Male Partner)

Father	Mother	Child	Year
Luis	Christine	Lucia	1835
	Maria Elisabeth	Mathias	1837
Pier	Lydia v. Cath. Michel	Christian	1837
	same	William	1839
	same	Elisabeth	1842
	same	Ane Marie	1842
	same	Nekelaus	1845
Kitt	Margretha	Thomas	1837
	same	Luisa	1839
	same	Cathrine Elisabeth	1842
Christoffel	Jinny	Maria	1837
Johannes	Mar. Elisabeth	Anthony	1841
Samuel	M. Theresa	Johannes	1844
	same	William Charles	1846
	Sebera v. Mr. Enon	Charlotte Amalia	1844
John Abr.	Dorothea Emilie	Amalie Elisabeth	1847
Friedrich	Salome v. Hope	Amalie	1847
Jacob	Susane v. Hope	Antoni Petrus	1844

Source: *M:* J.1.

others' comings and goings in the provision grounds, and they saw and talked with each other regularly. After the slaves were entitled by law to attend church, most of them went to one of the two Moravian churches on the island. This involved as much as an hour's walk passing several estates and thus the possibility of talking to and meeting with many slaves on the way. Those who attended the same church had further opportunities to get acquainted.

The rise in the number of slaves with extra-estate partners might also have been caused by the fact that the slave population on the home estate was becoming more and more interrelated. Michael Craton, in his study of a Jamaican plantation, observes: "Looking back, it seems that many a slave plantation after four or five generations must have been virtually one huge extended family" (1978c: 166). Since by law all children belonged to the mother's owner, groups of matrilaterally related kin emerged on each estate. At the same time, because the slaves also formed unions within the estates, succeeding generations became increasingly related to other slaves on the same estate. After the slave trade ceased and further importation of new slaves stopped, the estate population must have become completely interconnected to form one network of affinal and kin relations (cf. Craton 1978c: 166). This trend is illustrated in the case of the slave woman Susanna (see Figure 3), whose descendants were written down to determine the security for a loan.

Susanna had been purchased by the owner of L'Esperance Estate sometime in the eighteenth century. In 1820, when the plantation was appraised, she had founded a large, matrilaterally related kin group that included two sons, three daughters, and a host of grand- and great-grandchildren. (Her oldest son had died, and the second son had been sold to another plantation.) The oldest daughter, Beata, had borne nine children, eight of whom were still alive. The eldest of Beata's daughters also had had a daughter. Susanna's other two daughters, Dorothea and Rachel, each had had one child by 1820. Thus, out of the sixty-six slaves who belonged to L'Esperance Estate in 1820, fourteen were descendants of one African slave woman (*LA* 109: March 10, 1820). The records do not list the fathers of Susanna's descendants. If any of them belonged to similar family groupings on the estate, the result would have been that most of the slaves on the estate were tied together into a large network of relatives.

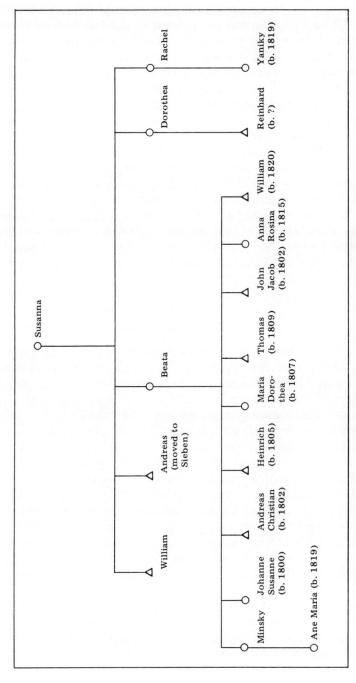

Figure 3. Susanna's descendants through the female line, March 10, 1820. Source: *LA* 109.

The slave group on L'Esperance Estate cannot be followed after 1830, when sugar production stopped and the slaves were removed. This led twelve of the slaves to complain to the *land-foged* that they did not want to be moved from the island since many of them had spouses and family on other estates that they did not wish to leave behind (*LA* 31: July 6, 1830). That so many at this time had spouses on other estates may, of course, be indirect proof that the slave population of one estate had become one large kin group and its members had sought spouses on other estates. This contention is strengthened by evidence from other plantations, which indicates that large family networks were created. When John William in 1845 was asked about his family, he explained that his father belonged to Mr. Richardson, but that he, his mother, and his eight brothers belonged to Brownsbay Plantation. He added that "he was related to almost all the slaves on the plantation" (*LA* 42: June 25, 1845). A slave population of 96 (*VRR* 1: 1845) therefore appeared as a single network of relatives.

The household

Historians' discussions of the slave family have centered to a great extent on whether the nuclear family was important among slaves and have used household censuses as the main indicators of family units. The many references to slaves' living arrangements in the *landfoged* records allow certain generalizations. A fairly large proportion of the slaves did live in households with a nuclear-family structure inasmuch as partners on the same estate having fairly permanent common-law unions often lived together. This is illustrated in the above-mentioned case of Ben and Petronella, in which Ben took Petronella into his house, when they resumed their relationship; however, Ben's second spouse, Anna Johanna, lived with her children in her own house, and Ben visited her there frequently. Judging from the many women who were either "second wives" or were engaged in relationships with men on other estates, the woman-headed household, consisting of a mother and her children, was another numerically important household type on St. John. The *landfoged* records, in fact, often refer to such households that were visited regularly by a man living elsewhere. Also mentioned are households inhabited by single men; some young single men appar-

Table 7. Household Types, St. John, 1855

Type of household	Number
Couple plus eventual children and/or other relatives	117
Kin group	
Male head	7
Female head	167
Single men	67
Single women	29

Source: *F* 1855.

ently did not live permanently in any household, but moved around and stayed with different persons. Daughters tended to stay at home until they began to have children of their own, at which point most of them seem to have acquired their own house. As all slaves were entitled to housing from the planter, obtaining a house presented little difficulty. The number of persons per house on the plantations seems to have been quite small; appraisals from five plantations display slave-per-house averages ranging from 1.9 on the small estates to 3.0 on the large estates, where co-resident unions were most likely to develop (*LA* 85).

The population census from 1855, which for the first time groups the entire population into households, confirms the general housing pattern already described on the basis of the qualitative records (see Table 7). Though this census was taken seven years after the emancipation of the slaves, the living arrangements had not changed much except that couples living on different estates had been able to move in together on one of them if they married. The statistics from 1855 thus can be expected to show a higher percentage of co-residential couples than was the case during slavery.

The kin group as a network of cooperation and reciprocal support

The *landfoged* records indicate that actual residence patterns reflected little more than where the slaves slept and stored some of their belongings. Residential units were not important socioeconomically, and they cannot be characterized even as households in that many of the domestic functions were taken care of by kinsmen and affines. During the nineteenth century most of the slaves, as noted earlier, were surrounded by an extended family of mainly matrilateral relatives on their estate and a more extensive network of patrilateral and affinal relations on others. These relationships were the avenues for mutual aid and cooperation that reached almost all the slaves. This web of socioeconomic exchange provided the lasting context for the often impermanent unions between spouses and among the households, unions that were formed and dissolved at the wish of the partners. The matrilateral relatives were most important as the source of reciprocal help in everyday life on the estates.

One of the most important tasks normally associated with households is the preparing of food. In the St. John slave households food was cooked on a small fire a few steps outside the house itself. Often the residents of a particular house did not cook but relied on relatives living outside the household to cook for them. Thomas, a carpenter on Carolina Plantation, explained that, on the day he held watch, he went "to his own house to cook a pot of food, which he had to do himself, because his grandmother, who otherwise usually did this, was ill" (*LA* 41: August 5, 1839). Christopher, belonging to Hermanfarm Plantation, received a visit from his wife, who belonged to Cinnamonbay. After they had eaten together in his house, she went home to fetch clean clothing. When he became hungry again, he asked his mother, Johanna, to cook some food for him, which she did (*LA* 42: January 2, 1844). Gotlief, a cooper belonging to Munsberry, lived by himself but chose to cook his food on the fireplace outside his mother's door (*LA* 33: July 28, 1840). Cooked food was shared with people outside the household. For example, Rebecca, a cook for the manager at Parforce, sent a lunch of salt fish, johnnycake, and coffee to her husband, a driver who worked in the field. He gave some of this food to Magdalene, one of the slave women working in the field, because she had no lunch. Rebecca also brought food to her mother, who lived by herself and was seventy years old and incapable of working (*LA* 39: May 22, 1824).

Uncooked foodstuffs were also given to relatives; for example, it was customary to give meat to relatives when animals were slaughtered. When Johem, belonging to Rustenberg, stole a pig and butchered it, he was questioned about who had been given the meat. He had only given meat to his roommate, Polydor, and two other friends; he had not given any to his wife on Hope Estate or his mother and two sisters on Rustenberg, he explained, because he had been quarreling with all of them (*LA* 41: October 26, 1837). In another case, Juliana, belonging to Reefbay, slaughtered a pig and gave her nephew Petrus, who also belonged to the estate, a big piece of the meat (*LA* 35: April 19, 1847).

Meat and other produce were given to relatives and spouses in return for various kinds of assistance, like the cooking discussed above. Juliana gave her nephew a good portion of the meat because he had cut wood for her at her request. Juliana did not expect help from her spouse, Kitt, because he lived on another estate, Lamesure (ibid.). Besides, Kitt was quite busy helping his relatives on Lamesure—for example, making a box for his sister Charlotte's clothes (*LA* 34: November 25, 1845).

Child care, like provisions, cooked food, and favors, was passed freely among relatives living in different households. Penny and Christian, for example, had two small children. Penny belonged to Rustenberg, Christian to Cinnamonbay. The children were often brought to stay in the house of Christian's mother, Rebecca, on Cinnamonbay, where Christian's sister Esther also lived. Penny's mother, who lived by herself on Rustenberg, was not suitable as a minder of the children because she had leprosy (*LA* 42: November 7, 1843). It seems to have been quite common for children to be taken from the plantations to which they belonged. The overseer on Cinnamonbay notified the *landfoged* that he was missing a three-year-old girl. He had learned that the mother had brought the child to stay with its godmother, who belonged to Mrs. Johnson. He did not know what she intended with this move and asked the *landfoged* for advice on what to do, because he often had unpleasant encounters with the slaves concerning their children and did not know what might happen to them when they were removed from the estate (*LA* 29: February 1, 1845).

Just as parents relied on others, such as godparents and grandparents, to help care for their young children, the old depended on their grown children to provide for them when they became unable to work. Johannes Mike was devastated when his son Mingo escaped to the British islands, because he "for the greatest part depended upon Mingo for his upkeep" (*LA* 42: March 18, 1845). Marotte, seventy years old and born in Africa, was most unhappy over "being left by her child in her old age" (*LA* 41: May 25, 1840). Curtes herded animals on Bordeaux Estate, probably because he was too old to do ordinary work in the field. He complained because he was given no free time to cultivate his provision ground, stating that, as he received no allowances, it would have been impossible for him to live if he had not received help from his two children on the estate (*LA* 31: September 13, 1831).

The importance of close relatives who were always nearby on the estate is revealed in the following *landfoged*'s report:

> Towards five o'clock Sunday evening on the second of this month, the slave woman Christiane and the slave Marius, both belonging to the plantation Adrian, came down to Cruz Bay to complain about the overseer Cameron's treatment of them. The overseer had ordered both the plaintiffs arrested because Christiane had sent her bundle of grass, which every working slave on the plantations must fetch in the evening, to the [plantation] yard with Marius to be given by him for her, as she was baking or preparing her . . . cassava bread. During the roll call, Marius answered for Christiane, after which overseer Cameron asked where Christiane was, and why she did not come to the yard herself instead of sending Marius. When the latter gave the reason for her absence, he ordered him arrested until Christiane showed up. She was therefore called for and brought with her a trough of manioc or cassava flour to the yard and explained that as all the Negroes' cassava on the plantation had been pulled up during the last hurricane, they all had been occupied with preparing and baking throughout the day of Sunday the second of this month, for which reason the iron plates that are used for this had been used throughout the day, so that she, Christiane, was not able to have her cassava flour baked. She therefore felt compelled to make hers in the evening in order to prevent the flour from becoming bad or sour—this circumstance alone was the reason why she had not appeared in the yard with her cut grass, although she also had to care for her five small children. Even though Christiane asked that her misdemeanor be forgiven this time, the overseer held to his order that she Christiane as well as Marius were to be arrested. These two slaves believed that they were treated in an unjust manner.

The *landfoged* apparently agreed, for he added: "As I was going to Adrian plantation the following day, that is Monday the third, on other business, I let the slaves Christiane and Marius stay in

Cruz Bay, the first to make her cassava bread, which otherwise would have become bad, and Marius to help her, as he is her brother" (*LA* 5: September 5, 1827). Even though Christiane had five small children and must have had at least one spouse somewhere, this spouse does not figure in the story, probably because the brother was the person closest at hand to help her.

The Christiane story shows how relatives tried to help and protect each other against harsh treatment. The records contain many references to such help among relatives. In one instance, Caritta, belonging to Leinsterbay, did not follow the driver's orders, and he hit her with the cart whip. She fought back and soon her brother Johannes came to her aid. When the overseer intervened in the fight, he was knocked down by Johannes (*LA* 32: June 20, 1838). Similarly, the overseer at Cinnamonbay complained to the *landfoged* that after he had flogged a slave his sister "kept cursing me all the time. I locked her up till noon and had her flogged by the Driver, which so enraged the Brother that he came to the Yard Gate and called out to me that if the Judge— the Commandant and the whole of them was here, they (meaning himself and sister) would curse me . . ." (*LA* 58: October 17, 1826; English in the original). Another case involved Adam, who was punished because he had mistreated a sheep. When he had been flogged twenty times by the overseer, his relatives asked to have the flogging stopped (*LA* 73: July 7, 1815). If disagreements erupted between slaves on the same plantation, close relatives rallied to each other's defense. During the festivities celebrating the end of the sugarcane harvest, a little girl accidentally stepped on Johannes's ailing foot. When he expressed his anger about this, her uncle became furious and attacked Johannes (*LA* 35: August 2, 1847).

Whereas the largely matrilateral kin ties on the estates were important in daily life, affinal and patrilateral ties outside the estates were most important on special occasions. For example, the father was expected to provide support for the mother during her confinement and for the newborn child; when Henrik escaped to Tortola at the time that Magdalene was having his child, she complained to the *landfoged* that he had not left the slightest support for her and the infant (*LA* 28: February 22, 1842). Spouses frequently brought complaints to the *landfoged* on behalf of their mates. While it could be risky for a relative living on the same estate to complain against the manager or plantation owner, a spouse living on another plantation could freely do so, and the records of the *landfoged* contain many examples of such complaints. Henry of Hermanfarm, for example, complained that his spouse, Nancy, with whom he had three children, had been whipped and arrested on Susannaberg, where she was a slave. Christian of Cinnamonbay complained that his wife Penny, belonging to Rustenberg, had been arrested with their three-month-old infant; the overseer, annoyed at this complaint, later attempted to prevent Christian from seeing his wife on Rustenberg, and Christian complained again (*LA* 33: February 9, 1841). Maroons also sought help from their spouses on other estates. January, belonging to Parforce, was a maroon for eight months and spent half that time with his wife, Catherine, at Little Reefbay, working on her provision ground (*LA* 40: October 19, 1826). The colonial authorities discovered this practice early on; a reference from 1788 notes that maroon hunters searched Friderica's house to find her husband, Mingo, who had been a maroon for almost two years. The slaves on Friderica's estate became so irate over this that they threw stones after the maroon hunters, forcing them to leave the estate (*LA* 70: February 29, April 14, 1788).

Spouses also provided a possibility for using resources on other estates—for example, in cultivating a provision ground together. Phoebe belonged to the relatively small plantation Little Reefbay, located in an area with rather poor soil suitable for limited plantation cultivation. This left Phoebe with free time, which she usually spent working on her spouse's provision ground, located on the much larger and more fertile Hope Estate (*LA* 88: February 25, 1845). The female slaves especially were often engaged in relationships with free persons, who helped them improve their economic situation. Juliana, belonging to Enighed Estate, had lived with a boat captain, Viggo Toy, for seven years; she stated that he had given her a couple of barrels of flour and had brought her things from St. Thomas. Though the relationship was over at the time that Juliana was asked about him, she emphasized that he had been good to her and that she had nothing to complain about as far as his treatment of her or his moral character were concerned (*LA* 77: July 11, 1844). Helene, also belonging to Enighed Estate, relied on her free spouse, Friederich Christian, who worked on the estate as a mason, for her food and clothing. When the overseer forbade him to visit her, she asked the *landfoged* that she be sold from the plantation (*LA* 31: August 29,

1836; 41: August 29, 1836). A free mate sometimes made it possible to be freed by purchase, as was Eliza of Bordeaux. After she
had lived in "natural marriage" with Powler for about three
years and had had a child with him, he offered to purchase their
freedom (*LA* 41: March 30, 1832). The possibility of freedom
probably was a major reason that slave women engaged in sexual
relationships and had children with overseers and planters.

Just as spouses had important functions when they lived on
other estates, relatives (particularly patrilateral ones) belonging
to other plantations helped out when normal socioeconomic relations broke down on an estate. When the owner of Hope Estate
left for England without giving the overseer any money to purchase food, the slaves told the *landfoged* that they naturally had
all helped each other with what little they had, but on Sundays
when they had no work, they had had to go to relatives on other
estates and ask them for food (*LA* 40: August 19, 1828; March 30,
1830).

Family life among the St. Johnian slaves thus does not seem to
have centered on the household or a nuclear-type residential
family, but rather on networks of relationships involving various
relatives and spouses. The matrilateral kin groups, whose members lived on the same estate, constituted an essential source of
socioeconomic aid and support in everyday life. Through spouses
on other plantations, slaves extended their relationships outside
their own estate, obtaining access to resources that would not
otherwise have been available to them and sources of assistance
when ordinary mechanisms of plantation life broke down. The
primarily patrilateral relatives on other estates had the same
function, though perhaps to a lesser degree. The importance of
these relationships was demonstrated in the rituals surrounding
the main rites of passage in the slaves' lives.

Childbirth was the occasion for a major festivity called the
wake. It was held on the night between the eighth and ninth day
following the birth of the child, probably the time when the
mother and child came out of confinement (*LA* 39: March 1,
1825).[3] By attending the wake, the slaves on the mother and
child's estate recognized the admittance of a new member to their
community. The father of the child was expected to help organize
and pay for the wake, even if he did not live on the estate. Slaves
from different estates usually attended (especially if the father
belonged to another estate), and because such congregating was

considered dangerous, wakes were illegal; the *landfoged's* records include several references to wakes that were stopped by the authorities. In one case, it was learned that a large party was being planned on Brownsbay Plantation, occasioned by "a child's birth or something like it." Slaves had been invited from several plantations to "supper and ball," but they had to pay a small amount of money to help cover the expenses. Two pigs and one young goat had been prepared, and the driver Christian was to have been master of ceremonies. The *landfoged* forbade the celebration, noting that similar parties previously had been held on the estate (*LA* 31: March 27, 1829).

One of the most important functions of the wake was probably to establish publicly the child's paternity. The Moravian missionaries attempted to convince the more established couples to marry, but fewer than 15 percent of the slaves were married in 1846 (*Statistiske Meddelelser* 1852: 178–79). Those who were married sometimes separated for seemingly minor reasons—for example, George and Kitty's marriage broke up when George sold a pig without giving any money to Kitty. Sometimes slaves who escaped to the British islands left their spouses behind. In one case, the overseer on Cinnamonbay Estate had permitted a slave to use the estate's fishing boat; the slave was married and a helper in the church—thus, in the eyes of the overseer, a trustworthy man. However, he escaped when the opportunity presented itself, leaving his wife (*LA* 35: November 1, 1847). Spouses seem to have led fairly independent lives; they depended mainly on their kindred for the socioeconomic functions otherwise associated with conjugal unions. Since most of the spouses did not depend upon each other in their daily living, they were not prone to maintain relationships for practical reasons but based their unions on love and passion. The lack of economic ties meant that the unions were easily dissolved by either spouse, often because of infidelity. When Elsy heard that her spouse, Jacob, was seeing a woman on Munsberry, she decided to move out of his house on Annaberg Plantation, to which they both belonged. She told the overseer that he had beaten her now and then when he was drunk, and that she saw no reason to tolerate this now that he was seeing another woman (*LA* 88: June 18, 1834). Similarly, Jørgen decided to leave his wife, Helena, when he found another man with her (*LA* 34: June 22, 1846).

This does not mean that the slaves approved of indiscriminate mating relationships. The relatives of a couple attempted to make sure that sexual unions were publicly recognized, and they disapproved of relations on the side. When Daniel found his wife in Joe's house on Brownsbay Plantation, he immediately started a fight with Joe. He was soon arrested by the driver, who was the wife's brother; the driver demanded however, that his sister be punished, as she had been wrong in seeing another man (*LA* 33: April 14, 1844). In another case, John had left his wife Beata to live with another woman, the cook Maria. Subsequently he rarely went to the slave houses on the estate hill, "because he was not highly regarded by the slaves living there," including his mother, two sisters, and one brother (*LA* 34: November 20, 1845). Sexual unions were socially sanctioned, probably to ensure that the resulting offspring could be accorded a father as well as a mother. Anney, belonging to Brownsbay Plantation, claimed that Jacob William, who was married in the Moravian church to another woman, was the father of her newborn child; Anney's family was placed in an embarrassing situation when Jacob William denied paternity. The incident led the kindred of the two to take sides, resulting in a "major row" on the estate (*LA* 33: July 21, 1843). With sexual unions in relative flux, it was especially important that the father acknowledge paternity of a child and agree to help organize the festivities in connection with the child's birth.

Consanguineal and affinal relations also gathered at the death or serious illness of a relative. When Johanna on Brownsbay was believed to be dying, slaves stayed with her through the night and sent for her spouse, a free man, to attend the wake. Later, when Johanna was ill after an abortion, her father and sister stayed with her to see her through the night (*LA* 85: September 28, 1840).

African and Creole family patterns

In a study of household structure among slaves on two Jamaican sugar estates, Higman has found that African slaves, to a greater extent than Creole slaves, when they lived in a household containing more than one person, tended to form nuclear family–type households consisting of man, woman, and possibly children. Higman concludes that this "might suggest that the Africans attempted to maintain nuclear families, while the Creoles, dislocated by the experience of slavery, were unable to do so; or it may simply signify that the ramifications of Creole kinship were that much greater" (1973: 536). The recorded experiences of the slave community on St. John suggest that the Creoles did form residential, nuclear families; but they also formed an increasing number of relationships with partners on other estates that did not unite them in a single household. On St. John, the networks of Creole affinal and kin relationships provided many of the socioeconomic functions elsewhere associated with the residential, nuclear family. The case of the African slaves was quite different. Dislocated by the slave trade, they could form enduring bonds only by establishing conjugal families and having children. Their lack of kin networks on St. John upon their arrival made the nuclear family much more important to them. The *landfoged*'s records attest these different systems of kinship and marriage among the African and Creole slaves.

As I have noted, most slaves depended on their kindred, especially those who resided with them on the estate, as a source of help in everyday living. Whereas there are no recorded complaints from slaves not being able to subsist because they had no spouse (apart from the cases of Helene, who relied on her free spouse, and Magdalene, who was abandoned at the time of childbirth), there are several complaints from Creole slaves who could not manage because they had no kin on their estate. Kilmannock, who had been moved from St. Croix to St. John, eventually attempted suicide because he was hungry and lonely (*LA* 32: October 31, 1837). Later he ran away; when caught, he refused to work on the estate, asking to be returned to St. Croix (*LA* 33: February 11, 1843). Petrus, who belonged to Hallover Estate, was very upset at having been removed from his estate to Brownsbay; he asked to be returned to Hallover because his family lived there and he did not get along well with the slaves on Brownsbay (*LA* 41: April 11, 1832.)

On the other hand, the Africans depended to a much greater extent on their affinal ties for mutual help and support, having no kinsmen on the island, and they therefore tended to maintain their conjugal ties. When Lydia was moved to Caneel Bay from St. Thomas, she protested because she had lived on St. Thomas since she had been sold as an African slave, and her husband was there (*LA* 31: July 6, 1832). To make up for their lack of relatives, Africans created kinlike relationships based on their ethnic origin and past companionship on the slave ship. Frederick answered no when asked whether he was related to anybody on St. John, but added that he was a countryman with John Usher and that "both of them had arrived together from Africa, when they were small" (*LA* 34: January 25, 1847). Such relationships were used, much as the Creole slaves used their kindred, as a source of help; Swame, for example, went to one of Mr. Wellem Barry's slaves who was a countryman of his to get some salt (*LA* 65: May 20, 1760). Polly, an African who was an "ignorant wretch," moved in with "another Guinea family" after she had a quarrel with her husband and was thrown out of the house (*LA* 33: December 28, 1843). Descendants of African slaves honored these relationships and treated such Africans as kinsmen. When Susanne died on Hope Estate, Martha asked to be allowed to hold the wake because Susanne had "come from Africa together with her parents" (*LA* 33: November 7, 1840).

In general, the lot of African slaves was regarded as unenviable because they lacked a network of social and economic relationships as extensive as the Creoles'. Thus Murphy of Rustenberg, when she was ordered to move to Josygut to become a house slave for an estate manager there, complained that she "had her whole family, her small animals and her other things on Rustenberg, and . . . she therefore could not move to Josygut, where she would be just like a Busal Negro [slave just arrived from Africa]" (*LA* 33: April 6, 1841). The attachment to kin and the fact that the estate had become the birthplace of part of the family deterred many slaves from fleeing to the British islands after emancipation there. Christian, who was suspected of having conspired with others to escape to Tortola, thus explained that "it had never occurred to him to leave the plantation where he was born, has his mother and sister, and quite recently has built himself a new house" (*LA* 41: January 15, 1840). Christine of Munsberry refused to escape to Tortola with a man who offered to marry her because her father and mother were buried on St. John. She knew nobody on Tortola and wished "that her child should rest by her parents" (*LA* 41: November 19, 1841). On the other hand, slaves who had close kin outside St. John were quite tempted to leave the island. Lettice, who was born on Tortola and had five sisters on that island as well as many other relatives, attempted to escape to Tortola taking her two children, who had been born on St. John (*LA* 33: November 17, 1841). When Doris considered fleeing to Tortola with her brother Boy and common-law husband Gutlief, she backed out when she learned that Gutlief was planning to steal a boat belonging to Doris's cousin Blyden. Doris told Gutlief off, saying that "she had stronger feelings for Blyden, who is her cousin and whose boat she herself has great advantage of together with the whole family, than she had for Gutlief" (*LA* 33: January 10, 1842).

The conflict is clearly illustrated in the case of John and Thony. They were fishing together in a rowboat when John, who had family on a nearby British island, suggested that they flee there. Thony, whose mother and sister were back on St. John, refused (*LA* 31: October 10, 1831). The fact that only 120 slaves fled to the British islands during the last years of slavery can be attributed largely to the hesitancy that many felt about leaving their family and place of birth forever.

Conclusion

Historians interested in the slave family have largely been concerned with determining whether slaves had a nuclear family structure or whether other family forms predominated. They have relied primarily upon census data or birth records as the basis for their research and have concentrated on the plantations for which such material is available (see chapter 1). This case study of St. John has adopted a somewhat different approach to the family, taking its point of departure in the development of an Afro-Caribbean system of labor reproduction within a particular plantation society as a whole. The family has been seen as a constellation of consanguineal and affinal relationships that were employed and valued by slaves in their daily struggle to support their existence. In this context, the issue of the nuclear family form loses significance. Though the nuclear family did exist during slavery as a household group, the data suggest that it was not the slaves' primary socioeconomic structure for biological reproduction or child rearing. Rather, kin networks were the foundation upon which the Creole slaves of St. John depended for the sharing of tasks and goods that spouses, children, and parents commonly share in the nuclear family. Even historians who have devoted so much attention to ascertaining whether the slaves had nuclear families have noted the importance of such networks.[4]

The emergence of an Afro-Caribbean community

The kinship system on St. John was part of the larger system of labor reproduction which included a wide array of activities as well as the bearing and rearing of children. As this system evolved, it no longer pertained mainly to the biological replacement of the slave group but to the survival of the Afro-Caribbean slave community. Though this community existed within the plantation society, it transcended individual estates and formed the basis of a group identity among all slaves.

The community manifested itself in many ways that were hardly recognized by the planter class. Cultivation of the provision grounds resulted in the establishment of more or less hidden village-type aggregations along the borders of the estates and led to numerous private economic transactions that crossed estate boundaries and extended as far as St. Thomas. The slaves regarded the bush lands surrounding the estates as their home territory and traveled freely through them, avoiding the public roads and evading the planters' control of their movements (*LA* 5: December 7, 1843). Procreation had created consanguineal ties, and the recognition of biological parenthood created "affinal" relations. These bound the slaves together in large networks that included almost all the slaves on the island and provided them with reciprocal social and economic assistance. The slaves' rituals connected with birth and death brought slaves from several estates to festivities organized on a large scale.

The slaves were essentially leading a double life as plantation laborers and as small farmers and fishermen; as chattels of the planters and as members of large family networks; as cultureless, ignorant savages being civilized through legislative reforms and missionizing efforts and as Afro-Caribbeans proud of the culture they had created and that they regarded as the true basis of their existence (cf. Craton 1978c: 383).[5] The slaves became increasingly impatient with this schizophrenic way of life and were eager to establish their own communities outside the estates. By the time of emancipation it was clear, even to the planters, that the slaves were ready to do just that.

4

The Peasant Society

THE PEASANT society that emerged after emancipation must
be understood in terms of the form that slavery had taken on
St. John. Since the slaves had become largely self-sufficient
through subsistence activities, it was quite obvious that when
they were free they would seek to establish their own Afro-
Caribbean society of independent, self-sufficient small farmers
outside the estates. The estates would thus lose their laborers, an
outcome that representatives of the planters tried to prevent.
Emancipation on St. John caused an even more intense struggle
than slavery had, with the freed trying to break away from the
plantations and the owners attempting to retain them as a dependent labor force. This conflict was never quite resolved. To a
great extent, it barred the freed St. Johnians from attaining an
adequate economic base for establishing a community of free
farmers. It also weakened the plantations and eventually led to
their downfall.

The relatively peaceful appearance of St. John, where there
had been no recent slave uprising as there had been on St. Croix,
was deceptive. The plantation society there was actually under
much greater threat than on more volatile St. Croix, for beneath
the calm surface, the freed were busy expanding the independent
socioeconomic relationships they had developed during slavery.
On St. Croix, where the slaves did not have such an extensive
system of social reproduction, partly because they had been
maintained by the planters to a greater extent, their general dissatisfaction with the planters and slavery had led to a violent con-
frontation. Thirty years after emancipation, when the St. Johnians had succeeded in establishing the beginnings of a peasant

society, Crucian laborers were confronted with such great problems that they staged another uprising against the plantation system. While an economically independent society of farmers did not become a reality on St. John, the Afro-Caribbean system of social reproduction nevertheless was strong enough to become an important factor in destroying intensive plantation agriculture. This system of social reproduction, which had been born under the difficult conditions of slavery, proved to be a viable basis for the development of a strong Afro-Caribbean community and culture.

Before emancipation was proclaimed on St. John, the planters and colonial officials had observed emancipation on the British islands, where the freed had left the estates en masse, leading to a decline in production and the collapse of the plantation system on Tortola and other islands. The *landfoged* noted that it was "a warning to us that the English government, after an intermediate period of a few years of so-called apprenticeship, has placed the emancipated in her West Indian colonies on an equal footing with the other English subjects, and that the result has been the almost total ruin of the colonies" (*LA* 7: November 11, 1848). The newly freed persons had experienced work only under force, explained the *landfoged*, and they regarded labor as equivalent to slavery, preferring even hunger to work. It was necessary, he argued, to force the freed persons to work (ibid.).

On July 6, 1848, he reported having completed the announcement of emancipation on the island's plantations: "The emancipated were so surprised and happy that they hardly knew which leg to stand on. In general they declared immediately that they would like to work; but a few added the exception that they would not 'dig caneholes'; others stated that they first wanted to go to St. Thomas to have a good time for a couple of weeks, before they would think of work; one has said to the overseer 'now I am just as good as you'" (*LA* 6: July 6, 1848). The *landfoged* already had taken precautionary measures to prevent the freed from leaving the island by promulgating on July 5 a police placard prohibiting all "owners and captains of boats and other vessels in St. John . . . under *severe penalty*, to bring persons belonging to the laboring classes away from this island, unless such persons have obtained a special permit for the passage from this office" (*LA* 6: July 5, 1848, emphasis in original). On July 10 he promulgated another placard, which compelled the freed to sign contracts with their former owners for terms of three to six months. The planters were ordered not to pay the ex-slaves more than a fixed sum. The working conditions were to be the same as during slavery, except for the fact that the laborers now received pay instead of allowance. They continued to live on the plantations and kept the usual privileges (housing, provision cultivation, etc.) that they had held as slaves. Those who formerly had worked in the big gang now were called first-class workers and received six dollars for three months' work. Second- and third-class workers were paid less, and children were paid only with food and clothing (*LA* 35: July 8, 15, 1848). The wage structure was explained in a circular from July 26, which stated: "Being free, the people must support themselves by labor. The wages in money which they receive for their labor should accordingly supply them with nearly the same quantity of food and laboring-clothes which they formerly received as allowance." Rather than establishing stores on the plantations, the *landfoged* suggested, the planters should give allowances directly to the laborers (*LA* 35: July 26, 1848).

To prevent the laborers from moving onto surplus land, a placard was published early in August prohibiting "proprietors or possessors of land" to sell or lease it to the estate laborers unless they could provide security to ensure that the laborers would not become "a burden to the public" (*St. Thomæ Tidende*, August 2, 1848). The following year, the *landfoged* negotiated an agreement among the planters not to hire any laborers from each others' estates. In this way, he hoped to avoid competition among planters for laborers and thus the possibility of some planters offering better working conditions and higher pay (*LA* 42: October 23, 1849). To help control the laboring population, the *landfoged* appointed as constables some of the most "trustworthy and most respectable among the laborers on the various plantations and elsewhere on the island." He placed at least one constable on each estate to keep an eye on what happened and report unusual events to the *landfoged*. The constables were instructed to seize "any vagrants, idlers, unknown persons without passports, or others who violated the law" and in general were to obey all instructions from their superiors, whether overseers of the estates or the colonial officials. Most constables appointed were either drivers or artisans on the estates (*LA* 77: July 21, 1848). Firm treatment of the laborers was regarded as necessary because of their "low" level of civilization: "According to the level of culture on which most of the emancipated are situated, a given agreement with them is nothing but a given agreement with a minor; they need, just as much as the minor, that their well-being is cared for and protected by law and administration. . . . Physical punishment will yet for a long time remain indispensable" (*LA* 7: December 21, 1848).

The *landfoged* saw many of the problems of the plantation society as caused by the laborers' "level of culture." The fact that common-law marriages were more frequent than legal marriages he saw as a manifestation of poor moral character among the slaves (*LA* 7: December 31, 1848). The lack of "proper" marriages he saw as an important reason for the instability of the labor force; contrarily, he regarded the "marital relationship" as "a further guarantee for good behavior and steadiness in service" (*LA* 7: June 13, 1850). A lack of civilization was also viewed as one of the main causes for the high rate of infant mortality—about 50 percent—that plagued the island in the 1850s. The *landfoged* hoped that the "mothers' well-known great carelessness and indifference toward their children" would be remedied as the working class "became more civilized" (*LA* 1: October 8, 1858). When St. John was ravaged by cholera epidemics in 1854 (218 died) and 1856 (132 died), the health authorities blamed their severity on the victims (*SS* 1854, 1856). The medical report for 1856 described the plantation laborers as "being among the most uncivilized inhabitants of the West Indies" and

> only little above the animals. They have huts themselves woven of branches, plastered with clay, and covered with sugarcane tops. The huts are low, have one door and one shutter, which never is opened. They know of no beds, and they lie on the humid floor on a mat of straw. They live on the cornmeal, which is common in the colonies and is eaten either as a gruel or hard as a firm pudding or as half-baked cakes. Supplementing this, salt, ill-smelling fish, half-ripe fruits. When to this is added the fact that they have a unique mistrust of all that is white, as they have the belief that self-interest is the basis of the whites' goodness towards them, and an incomparable laziness and indifference, which extends so far, that the one spouse hardly will get up to assist the other, I probably don't have to mention the result of the epidemic. (*SS* 1856)

To raise the laborers' cultural level, the *landfoged* endeavored to introduce marriage and the stable nuclear family among them. He allowed the couples who worked (and thus lived) on different estates to move in together on one if they married (*LA*35: September 25, 1848). While the slave fathers had been denied any official right and obligation vis-à-vis their children, they were now made legally responsible for supporting them. If they failed, they were brought to court and forced to make a legal contract with the mothers for child support (*LA* 43: December 4, 1852). The Moravian missionaries joined the *landfoged* in promoting legal marriage among the laborers by refusing, after 1859, to baptize children born out of wedlock. They explained that the church only wished to have members who led a strictly virtuous life, and that they would rather have a small, chosen congregation than a large one (*LA* 1: July 30, 1859); in the end a small congregation was what they got.

The results of these efforts to create a docile laboring class living in orderly nuclear families were not encouraging. While the newly emancipated slaves, stunned by the rapid changes in their status, had agreed to make contracts with their former owners, they reacted quickly when they realized that they had been effectively re-enslaved. A few weeks after emancipation, they began to boycott their work in the sugarcane fields. On July 24, the laborers on Carolina Plantation were reported to be slow at work or shirking it entirely. The *landfoged* reprimanded them severely, threatening to withdraw their wages and give them jail sentences if the behavior continued; they resumed work. On July 25, the laborers did not report for work on Enighed Estate. When the *landfoged* reprimanded them, they said that they had misunderstood orders; they escaped punishment only because the planter interceded on their behalf. Labor problems were reported on the same day on Caneel Bay Plantation, where a laborer who had resisted orders from the planter received a severe whipping. On July 27, the laborers refused to work on Brownsbay, a few days later on Reef Bay, Leinsterbay, and so on. Wherever the laborers boycotted their work or gave the planters trouble, the *landfoged* was called for and he threatened them with "judgework" (i.e., punishment by working without pay for a period of time), jail, or flogging. Though the *landfoged* prevented an island-wide uprising, the laborers continued to cause problems on the estates. In October 1849, Carolina Plantation experienced problems with the laborers for the third time. They had re-fused to work, claiming that it was the queen's birthday and therefore a holiday! The constable had refused to help the over-seer make them work (*LA* 42: October 17, 1849).

When the first three-month contracts expired, no less than 150 slaves applied to discontinue their contracts. According to the *landfoged*, the following reasons were given for leaving: (1) Some wanted to move out to settle as squatters outside the estates. This was refused entirely. (2) Some wanted to move to St. Thomas to look for work or live with their family there. They were told that permission could not be granted for the time being: St. Thomas had more than enough vagrants. (3) About ten wished to visit kin on Tortola and then return. They were informed that they had to wait for the colonial government to decide on this matter (*LA* 6: September 9, 1848). In short, all 150 were denied permission to leave the estates.[1]

The laborers then sought to avoid the labor contracts by other means. Many already had decided to send their children to school rather than have them work on the estates, knowing that the missionaries would not refuse them. In August 1848, the plan-ters complained to the *landfoged* that many children who were old enough to be of use on the estates had been removed from the work gangs to attend school. Despite the *landfoged*'s professed desire to "civilize" the freed, he suggested that an ordinance be introduced to regulate school attendance of the laborers' chil-dren, and in 1849 a law was passed, allowing only children from five to eight years old to attend school every work day from 8:00 to 11:00 A.M. Older children (ages nine to twelve) were limited to going to school on Saturdays (*LA* 35: November 5, 1849). In 1853, the law was changed so that children six to ten years of age could attend school daily from 8:00 A.M. to noon; children eleven to thirteen had to go to school on Saturdays. The publication of the school ordinance included a reminder that children as well as adults had to have a permit from the *landfoged* to travel to St. Thomas, noting that "during the latter years, a considerable number of children have been removed clandestinely from the es-tates to St. Thomas" (*LA* 35: November 25, 1854). The population censuses after emancipation show an increase in St. Johnian children on St. Thomas. Whereas there were 7 St. Johnian slave children and 38 free children fifteen years old and younger on St. Thomas in 1846, the 1857 census lists 52 St. Johnian children and the 1860 census 65. Only about 25 percent of them lived with parents, indicating that most had probably been sent clandestinely to St. Thomas by parents on St. John eager for them to avoid becoming plantation laborers (*F* 1846, 1857, 1860).

Some laborers began fleeing from the island again when they realized that there was no other way to escape the plantation system. In 1850, 25 laborers fled from Brownsbay to Tortola (*LA* 35: December 13, 1850). In 1853 a total of 44 laborers fled from various plantations. In October 1854, 17 escaped; and in June 1855, 10 fled from Carolina Plantation alone (*LA* 6: July 14, 1853, November 1, December 12, 1854; 44: June 14, 1855). Many of the escapees did not stay on Tortola but went on to St. Thomas, where the labor regulations did not apply in Charlotte Amalie. It was relatively easy to find work with good pay, and it was impossible for the authorities to track down the St. Johnians in the large city. One of the few workers who was caught and sent back to St. John claimed that he had worked at the harbor for as much as $1.25 a day, though there had not been work every day. This was quite a change from the two dollars a month that could be earned on St. John (*LA* 44: June 1, 1855). The St. Thomas censuses show an increasing number of St. Johnians living on that island; many others may not have reported their correct place of birth for fear of being returned to St. John. The recorded St. Johnian population of 193 on St. Thomas in 1846 had grown to 263 in 1857 and 315 in 1860 (*F* 1846, 1857, 1860).

While the *landfoged* seems to have had little luck changing the slaves to a stable, dependable, and willing labor force, he and the Moravian missionaries apparently had some success in changing the marital relationships among the freed. In 1846 the slaves twenty years old and above had a marriage rate of 13 percent. In 1855 this had rather drastically increased to 50 percent for the men and 42 percent for the women, and in 1860 to 60 percent for the men, 48 percent for the women. Not all laborers, however, complied with the wishes of the Moravian missionaries that they marry before having children. Many children were baptized in the Lutheran Church after July 1859, when the Moravians stopped baptizing children born out of wedlock.[2] The Lutherans had been a minor influence up to that time, baptizing only 17 children from emancipation in 1848 to July 1859; but they baptized no less than 196 from 1859 to the end of 1869. The census returns also show that a rather large number of children still were being born to unmarried parents or grew up in single-parent households. Of the children who resided in households headed by persons thirty-five years old and under in 1860, 31 percent lived in a woman-headed household that included no spouse; in 1870, the figure was 36 percent (*F* 1860, 1870; *STP* 2; *M* J.1).

The question thus arises: were the laborers who married changing their family system to that of the monogamous, father-headed nuclear family advocated by the missionaries and the *landfoged*, or were they marrying to ensure that the child could be baptized in the Moravian church and that they would have the privilege of living together on the same plantation? References in the *landfoged*'s records indicate that networks of cognatic and affinal relationships remained the basis of the Afro-Caribbean community, and that the legal marital tie was seen as only one of several types of relationships the laborers employed to advance their socioeconomic position. Kin ties still appear to have been more important than affinal ties. Sambo, for example, who wanted to move to St. Thomas, explained that his wife would not come with him because "she would not leave her mother and other kin here on the island" (*LA* 43: August 19, 1853). Kin also had a great influence on the relationship between the spouses. Anny's brother forced her to leave her spouse because he had quarreled with Anny and their mother (*LA* 42: January 11, 1851). When Mathias suspected his wife of infidelity, he appealed to her brother, Wilhelm, to talk to her. Wilhelm promised to do so, but in the meantime Mathias and his wife had a fight in which Mathias hurt her. Wilhelm, upon hearing this, immediately went to his sister to dress her wound and "spoke seriously" with Mathias about the incident (*LA* 45: November 1862). The laborers do not seem to have developed the stable, father-headed, nuclear families based on marriage that the *landfoged* was looking for.

Despite the heavy-handed way in which the *landfoged* was enforcing the labor code and attempting to "civilize" the laborers, the estates were rapidly losing their labor force. The St. Johnian population of 2,450 in 1846 had declined to 1,574 in 1860. Apart from the 350 who had died in the cholera epidemics, the population had decreased by 526 (*Statistiske Meddelelser* 1865: 142). The plantations suffered from the declining number of laborers,

Table 8. Acreage in Sugarcane Cultivation,
St. John, 1845–1902

Year	Acres
1846	839
1850	774
1855	686
1860	547
1865	559
1870	126
1880	8
1902	7

Source: *VRR* 1846–1902.

sugar production fell (see Table 8), and the planters began to break the labor code themselves.

The St. Thomas planters had found it impossible to enforce the labor regulations because the city of Charlotte Amalie attracted large numbers of laborers. They attempted several times to recruit laborers on St. John illegally (*LA* 43: August 19, 1853; 47: October 1, 1867). The Caneel Bay planter accused the Susannaberg planter of having tried to convince a laborer to apply to change employment to Susannaberg (*LA* 45: March 27, 1865). The Cinnamonbay planter was brought to court for using piecework and offering higher pay to induce the laborers to work harder (*LA* 46: November 29, 1865).

In 1867 a hurricane hit the island, followed by an earthquake. The estates and their crops were seriously damaged, and sugarcane cultivation was abandoned on most of the estates. By 1870, only three plantations still cultivated sugarcane. Only Adrian and Hermanfarm continued to produce sugar systematically, and these two estates were owned by the colonial treasury. Sugarcane cultivation was restored by a few plantations again in 1880, but it was short-lived.

To the old planter families it had long been apparent that the days of sugarcane cultivation were over on St. John, and they attempted to make the best of it by selling out before sugar production ceased entirely. Seven of the fifteen estates that grew sugarcane at the time of emancipation had changed owners by 1860. In the 1861–70 period, ten of the plantations changed hands, and

during the 1871–80 period, seven. With the departure of the
sugarcane planters the most prominent and economically powerful estate owners severed their ties with St. John, among them
the Danish noble family Schimmelmann, which owned Carolina
Plantation, and H. H. Berg, the Norwegian owner of Annaberg
and Leinsterbay, who had been a vice-governor of the Danish
West Indies. Most of the new families who took over the faltering
sugar plantations were colored people who moved to St. John
from other West Indian islands and became the core of a new upper class on the island. This new owner class had neither the
financial capacity nor the desire to reintroduce sugarcane cultivation on the former scale, but rather wished to develop stock
raising, using casual laborers.

Stock raising, unlike sugar production, did not require a large,
steady labor force. The major tasks on a cattle estate involved the
clearing of new pastures and the removal of weeds and bush from
existing fields, the watering of animals, and, in the case of sheep
and goats, regular tethering and restaking of the animals. The
cattle estates could make do with a few full-time laborers for the
daily work and an occasional larger work force to clear and clean
the pastures periodically. They were not interested in bonding a
great number of workers, who had to be paid continuously, but in
having an intermittent work force. This goal would be attained if
the laborers were allowed to squat on surplus estate land.

The *landfoged* strongly disapproved of these developments.
The slaves' system of labor reproduction had been tolerated, even
encouraged, as a way of maintaining the labor force and tying
the slaves to the plantations and to slavery. After emancipation
and the cessation of sugar production, the *landfoged* saw this
system of social reproduction as a serious threat to the plantation
system. It provided an alternative to intensive plantation cultivation and portended the takeover of the island by the former
slaves and the eventual collapse of the plantocracy. It also meant
a weakening of the tax base necessary to maintain the colonial
structure. Therefore the *landfoged* reacted quickly when he saw
any signs of the laborers moving away from the estates to settle
on their own. When Mr. Weinmar (the owner of Enighed Plantation, which had stopped producing sugar in 1855), employed Ludvig to cut wood for him, the *landfoged* invalidated the contract
because he suspected that Ludvig worked mostly on his own in

exchange for giving shares to the estate or doing occasional work for Mr. Weinmar (*LA* 1: September 10, 1860). A few years later, Weinmar made a contract with Ben and Christina to work on Enighed, but let them move to a small estate, Freemansground, to work for themselves. As soon as the *landfoged* learned about this, he forced the couple to move back to one of the major estates and fined Weinmar for circumventing the law (*LA* 45: November 13, 20, 1862). Alexander Fraser, the owner of a small estate, Fries, made a contract with Johannes Henry but only gave him irregular work. Fraser was forced to discontinue the contract and Johannes Henry was jailed for three days for vagrancy (*LA* 45: July 26, October 26, 1864).

It was becoming increasingly difficult to find employment on the estates, since they needed fewer permanent laborers than formerly and the new estate owners were not able to pay even the minimal wages that the contracts called for. Anne Helena Hendrick, who was bonded to Annaberg, complained that her son did not receive the allowance from the planter that he was entitled to. The planter replied that "the workers could take their children and do with them what they wanted to, as he could not afford to support them." The *landfoged* intervened and arranged an agreement between the planter and the workers. Two months later, however, the planter gave up and moved to Tortola, abandoning the estate (*LA* 47: August 5, October 17, December 27, 1867). He left about 200 laborers behind on Annaberg and Leinsterbay with nothing to do. They asked to stay on the estates and work on their own, but the *landfoged* refused, ordering them to leave the island if they could not find employment on an estate (*LA* 1: September 16, 1868; 2: July 2, 1869; 47: December 27, 1867; 48: August 31, 1868).

The *landfoged*'s strict enforcement of the labor code was intended to maintain a strong plantation economy, but in fact it had the opposite effect, depriving the island of most of its laboring population. During the late 1860s and early 1870s, the new estate owners complained to the Colonial Council for St. Thomas–St. John, which had been established on St. Thomas after emancipation, about the administration of the labor code and asked that it be repealed. The members of the council, most of whom were merchants and planters, agreed that this was desirable because the law ought to serve the current needs and conditions. In 1872 the law was repealed (*Proceedings of the Colonial Council* for St. Thomas and St. John, June 24, 1869; April 11, 1872; May 8, 1872). At that time the population of St. John had already been reduced by more than half, falling from 2,450 in 1846 to 1,054 in 1870 (Statistiske Meddelelser 1865: 142; 1883: 162).

While the new estate owners were eager to have the cumbersome labor code repealed, they did not advocate the development of an independent community of Afro-Caribbean peasants. They wanted the laborers to be able to purchase small lots or squat on estate land, but to remain dependent on the estates for the cash income needed to pay taxes and purchase staples; this dependence would guarantee the estates a stable labor force. During the last decades of the nineteenth century, a few smaller estates were parceled out and sold at approximately four dollars an acre. Some former sugar plantations also sold or even gave some of their marginal land to a number of former workers (VK 8: 132). The total acreage owned by persons owning less than 50 acres increased as the peasants acquired land (see Table 9). The number of owners also increased; however, 88 percent of those owning 50 acres or fewer had only 10 acres or fewer (see Table 10). The total acreage owned by the 137 smallholders in 1902 was 512.58, averaging less than 4 acres per person (VRR 1902).

After the repeal of the labor code, stable conditions returned to St. John. The drastic population decline leveled off at the number attained in the early 1870s (see Table 11). It appeared that the repeal of the code had had the effect desired by the estate owners.

When St. Croix experienced labor problems in the late 1870s, the colonial government attempted to establish a cottar class like the one on St. John. St. Croix had been the most developed plantation society during slavery, and after emancipation a labor code had been introduced on that island to maintain a plantation la-

Table 9. Acreage Owned by St. Johnians
(up to 50 Acres)

Year	Average
1846	223.50
1870	232.50
1880	546.00
1902	1,128.83

Source: VRR 1846–1902.

Table 10. Number of St. Johnian Landowners, 1846–1902

Year (1)	Owning 50 acres or fewer (2)	Owning 10 acres or fewer (3)	Column 3 as percent of Column 2 (4)	Owning more than 50 acres (5)
1846	23	19	83	41
1870	77	68	88	39
1880	85	72	85	35
1902	156	137	88	36

Source: *VRR* 1846–1902.

Table 11. Population of St. John, 1846–1911

Year	Number
1846	2,450
1855	1,715
1860	1,574
1870	1,054
1880	994
1890	984
1901	925
1911	941
1917	959

Source: *Census of the Virgin Islands of the United States* 1918: 37.

bor force. The Crucian plantations, having a sounder economic basis for sugar production than the St. Johnian plantations, succeeded in maintaining sugarcane cultivation. However, it was reduced by almost 50 percent as sugar production decreased in profitability and the laborers left the plantations for the cities on St. Croix and St. Thomas (Sveistrup 1942: 87, 143; *Statistiske Meddelelser* 1883: 162). Dissatisfaction with the labor code and the generally poor socioeconomic conditions on the plantations led the laborers to stage a major uprising in 1878, which forced the colonial government to repeal the code. In the 1880s the government decided to parcel out a plantation to the laborers, hoping that they might form "a class of smallholders, who will feel tied to their little plot, where they can work almost without capital and come to regard work as a blessing. This group of cottars will form an excellent counterweight against the large group of propertyless Negroes ... for whom the normal development of conditions is rather indifferent. They have nothing to lose because they own nothing, and therefore they are always a dangerous ferment among the rest of the population" (Lassen 1895–96: 85). This attempt to create a cottar class on St. Croix as a stabilizing factor was a failure. The Crucian laborers, unlike the St. Johnians, had not developed a strong system of production based on small farming and fishing during slavery, and they had little desire to become peasants. They gradually turned into a rural proletariat that organized industrial action (Nørregaard 1966).

Even though the smallholders on St. John were held up as an example of a stable class of small-property owners, who were presenting no problems to the colonial government, they did not turn out to be the labor force that the estate holders wanted. The St. Johnians generally wished to live and work on their own plots rather than on the estates, where the pay was minimal. Alternatively they chose to leave the island to find employment and send their wages home. The cattle estates never became a powerful economic force, and visitors to the island reported a general collapse of plantation society. The journalist Henrik Cavling described one of the largest plantations on the island as consisting of "several miserable huts, which, under the circumstances, struck one as a good sized village" (1894: 137–40). The painter A. Riis Carstensen depicted a society of peasants who, much to his regret, were not preoccupied with laboring: "When I passed blacks who were busy with their daily occupation: resting, or, exceptionally, working on a little piece of cultivated land, they stared after me in a way which indicated how seldom it was to see a stranger. Several ran a long ways after the horse and asked for dollars, possibly thinking that a riding white at least was a millionaire" (1897: 110).

Despite the "general collapse of civilization," the *landfoged* made a heroic effort to keep up the pretension that St. John was still an important plantation society and had not become an insignificant peasant backwater. Cavling describes how the *landfoged* greeted him "as would a sovereign monarch greet an emissary from a foreign power. ... By just changing place he was transformed to Mr. District Court Judge, Mr. Police Chief,

Mr. Veterinarian and Mr. Coroner, not to mention that now and then, outside the normal daily routine, he could be called Mr. County Medical Officer or Mr. Pastor. [He] . . . gave his verdict following the letter of the law, and down below he executed the punishment—for he was also keeper of the local jail!" (1894: 134–35).

Even this modest administration on St. John was regarded by the colonial government, which earned practically no revenues from the island, as expensive. St. Croix, declining in sugar production, also presented the government with a deficit. Only St. Thomas, which was not dependent on plantation production, remained profitable because of its fine natural harbor. However, the profits were not substantial and did not provide a sufficient economic base for maintaining the Danish West Indian colonial structure. It was suggested as early as 1842 in Denmark that the colonies ought to be disposed of "to any Christian power" (Vibæk 1966: 281). The idea of selling the islands cropped up again and again, and in 1864 and 1902 the Danish government negotiated with the United States. This preoccupation in Denmark with selling the islands had the effect of restraining any initiative to invest in them or to press for major reforms, which might have improved the socioeconomic conditions (Lawaetz 1916: 35; Nørregaard 1966: 144).

While the Danish government continued its benign neglect of St. John and made few economic initiatives on St. Thomas and St. Croix, a group of "patriotic" Danish citizens decided to form a company to promote Danish economic interests on the West Indian islands and create a greater awareness of the islands among Danes. The company, called the Plantation Company Danish West India, purchased several plantations, among them 237-acre Cinnamon Bay on St. John, and in 1903 began cultivating fruits and bay leaves for export. The company made little money on the fruits because they spoiled before reaching continental markets. The extraction of bay oil from the bay leaves, which was then mixed with rum and sold as bay rum lotion, was a greater success, and inspired other plantations to cultivate bay trees (Jørgensen 1953: 56, 65, 70–72).

The Plantation Company never made a major impact on the economy of St. John and was unable to reverse the general economic decline that had long characterized the plantation society. In 1917 an agreement finally was made between Denmark and the United States; the islands were sold for $25 million and became the American Virgin Islands. The transfer of the islands to American rule did little to reverse the downward economic trend. The United States had purchased the islands to be used as a naval station during World War I because of their strategic position at the entrance to the Caribbean Sea. When the war ended in 1918, the islands lost their immediate military significance; though they were placed under naval administration, they never became an important naval base. The three islands passed rather unnoticed from the backwater of the Danish "empire" to that of the American. Though the transfer was marked by elaborate ceremonies on St. Thomas and St. Croix, no immediate change occurred when the Danish colonial government was replaced by an American navy administration. On St. John, least important of the American Virgin Islands, the transfer was marked only by the *landfoged*'s proclamation of the change in nationality, the lowering of the Dannebrog and the raising of the Stars and Stripes, and the replacement of the Danish administrator by an American who soon fell into the traditional "monarchical" role.[3] The American government had purchased St. John as an appendage to St. Thomas and had no military, political, or economic interest in the island. No major investments were made, and the cattle estates continued to be the major economic enterprises.

The tax records at the turn of the century listed a total of 192 landowners (see Table 12). Twelve owned 73.5 percent of the acreage on the island; 137 owned less than 4 percent; and 67 owners, with up to 2 acres each, owned .6 percent of the island's acreage (*VRR* 1902). Despite the small amount of property owned by the peasants, about 80 percent of the population lived on its own land or squatted on peasant holdings (*F* 1901). Even though the island had been abandoned by the powerful plantation interests, it was still controlled to a great extent by a few estate owners. However, these owners were relatively poor and used only a fraction of their land, primarily for cattle raising, which provided only a few poorly paid jobs. In 1902, out of 12,251.25 acres held by estate owners (those owning more than 50 acres of land), only 539 acres, or 4 percent, were used. In 1902 the small farmers (those who owned up to 50 acres) held a total of 1,128.83 acres and cultivated 244.75 acres, or 22 percent, despite the fact that much of it was of poor quality and a relatively large portion had to be used for housing (*VRR* 1902). The peasants were free to

Table 12. Landholdings by Ownership, St. John, 1902

Acres of land owned by individuals	Number of owners	Percent of total number	Total acres	Percent of total acres
0–1	47	24.5	42.06	0.3
1+ –2	20	10.4	37.80	0.3
2+ –3	6	3.1	18.00	0.1
3+ –4	14	7.3	56.00	0.4
4+ –5	8	4.2	38.00	0.3
5+ –6	18	9.4	107.50	0.8
6+ –7	2	1.0	14.00	0.1
7+ –8	7	3.6	57.00	0.4
8+ –9	6	3.1	53.00	0.4
9+ –10	9	4.7	89.22	0.7
10+ –11	1	0.5	11.00	0.1
11+ –15	2	1.0	27.00	0.2
16–20	1	0.5	19.00	0.1
21–30	2	1.0	45.00	0.3
31–40	6	3.1	214.25	1.6
41–50	7	3.6	300.00	2.2
51–60	4	2.1	212.25	1.6
61–70	0	0.0	0.00	0.0
71–80	8	4.2	597.50	4.5
81–90	0	0.0	0.00	0.0
91–100	3	1.6	289.00	2.2
101–150	6	3.1	790.75	5.9
151–200	2	1.0	308.75	2.3
201–250	1	0.5	224.00	1.7
251–300	1	0.5	285.00	2.1
301–400	2	1.0	703.00	5.3
401–500	4	2.1	1739.75	13.0
501–1000	2	1.0	1454.00	10.9
1001–1500	1	0.5	1429.00	10.7
1501–2000	1	0.5	1687.00	12.6
2001–2500	0	0.0	0.00	0.0
2501–3000	1	0.5	2531.25	18.9
Total	192	99.6	.08	0.0

Note: One lot on 19 acres, owned by "different persons," is not included.

Source: *VRR* 1902.

leave the estates, but they did not have the opportunity to acquire sufficient land to establish a solid economic basis for the
development of an independent community of small farmers. An
ever-increasing number of St. Johnians preferred to leave the island to find wage employment. Many children of the original
settlers on the peasant land departed to work outside the island.
Many went to St. Thomas, where the 1901 population included
395 St. Johnians, about half of them thirty-five years old and
under (*F* 1901).

In 1902 the major landowners on St. John presented a petition
to a Danish West Indian Commission investigating island conditions. They suggested that all who did not own more than five
acres of land be forced to take work if they had no steady employment, and that a suitable plantation be parceled out to cottars.
The petitioners wanted to expand the landed peasantry (so that a
greater labor force would be available), and they also wanted to
compel this landed peasantry to work for them. The petition was
ignored by the commission (*VK* 8:91)

The economic situation on St. John improved slightly during
the 1930s. The United States was experiencing a major depression
and had instituted the New Deal programs to alleviate its socioeconomic problems. The relief and make-work programs were applied to the U.S. Virgin Islands, including St. John, after the islands were transferred from military to civil administration in
1931. The New Deal on St. John largely took the form of relief
work employment by a Civilian Conservation Corps project; the
encouragement of home industry, notably basket weaving, and
the formation of cooperatives to help distribute and market the
products; and, finally, improved health services. The work camps
employed young men full time in "planting coconut groves and
stands of mahogany, building and repairing roads, digging drain-
age facilities, uncovering new water sources, combatting soil erosion, and helping eradicate animal ticks" (Grede 1962: 108).

The New Deal programs were introduced on the islands following the preparation of a report on the political, social, and
economic conditions on the islands, which drew a pessimistic picture of St. John and concluded in rather exaggerated fashion that
"*The plain fact is that many of the people are gradually starving
to death*" (H. Brown 1930: 280, emphasis in original). Clearly
there was widespread poverty on the island, and the New Deal
did not change this markedly. Its employment and assistance

programs did not induce any economic growth nor did they help
the St. Johnians to become self-sufficient, which was their stated
goal. They failed to generate growth because they did little to
alter the basic structure of the island's economy. At this time,
80 percent of the land was owned by twelve families (Grede 1962:
49), who were not willing to parcel out land to the St. Johnians
nor able to develop much agriculture on the property themselves.
A 1935 survey showed that there were only five major cattle estates on the island, owning an average of 156 cattle each, and
four smaller estates owning an average of 35 cattle each (*EMB* 1:
1935). The St. Johnian peasants lived on their small lots of land
in houses characterized as "uninhabitable, being merely two
room shacks holding as many as four people in numerous cases"
with "all sewage disposal ... confined to the bush" (*EMB* 1:
1935). Though the American administration was embarrassed
that such conditions existed on one of its possessions, a major
land reform would have been required to improve on them.

The failure of the New Deal programs was blamed, to a great
extent, on the local population. Grede reports that "the instability
of the Virgin Islands family presented the New Deal with some of
its most difficult problems" (1962: 38). Improving the wages was
regarded as having done little good, because for the peasants the
symbol of success was the white plantation owner sitting on the
porch and enjoying himself (ibid.: 41). With more pay, the workers would just do less work! By 1937, when the economic situation had improved in the United States, the federal support of the
programs began to decline. At this time, St. John was not substantially better off than before. Some estates had been forced to
curb operations, as wages had increased. Many St. Johnians who
had experienced the higher pay of the CCC programs were reluctant to return to small farming and fishing and instead looked
for better-paid jobs elsewhere. Though there was no work to be
found on St. John immediately after the withdrawal of the federal programs, St. Thomas was offering jobs related to war preparations that included improving naval facilities in the harbor.
Many St. Johnians were moving there as well as to the United
States. The increasing emigration is reflected in the population
statistics of the early American period. In 1917, when the islands
were transferred from Danish to American rule, there were 959
persons on St. John; by 1930, this number had decreased to 756,

and in 1940 and 1950 it was below 750 (*Census of the Virgin Islands of the United States* 1950).

In 1945 a land sales program was introduced on St. John, based on the parceling out of estate land near the village of Cruz Bay in the westernmost area of St. John. By the end of 1946, the homesteaders had deposited about 20 percent of the "aggregate selling price" (Boyer 1949: 116–17). Though the land was of poor quality, St. Johnians were eager to acquire it in order to have house lots near Cruz Bay, the main point of communication with St. Thomas. As people moved to Cruz Bay, they left their old peasant settlements, a movement that correlated with the reduction in the relative importance of agriculture. When the anthropologist Robert Manners spent a few months on St. John in the mid-fifties, he found that the small island community could subsist only because it received substantial remittances from relatives who had left the island for wage employment: "No more than 10–15 families of some 175 resident on the island had even modest kitchen gardens. Bay leaves as a cash crop had, to all intents and purposes, disappeared. Fishing provided partial support for about a dozen families on the eastern end of the island. But *all* St. Johnians were dependent upon cash for their survival, and almost all cash . . . derived from the wages of family members working in St. Thomas or the United States" (1965: 186). Even though agriculture had ceased to be of major economic significance at the time of Manners's stay on the island, traditional agriculture never disappeared entirely and continued to play an important social role.

The socioeconomic development of St. John typifies, in many respects, changes that occurred on many other West Indian islands after emancipation. In areas where the conditions for sugarcane cultivation were poor and where there had emerged relatively independent systems of production among the slaves, the freed managed to establish themselves as peasants wherever land was available for purchase or squatting. In the case of St. John, only limited land areas were available, and the peasants had to move either to the larger sugar islands for temporary work as laborers or to urban areas for wage employment. Such migration for employment was characteristic on many West Indian islands by the nineteenth century (D. Hall 1971; Thomas-Hope 1978), and during the twentieth century it has developed into large-scale emigration—which has deprived many island societies of their most able work force and has led to the collapse of their local economies (Manners 1965; Frucht 1968; Philpott 1973). The peasant society of St. John, like any peasant society, was not self-sufficient but existed on the periphery of economic centers that were essential to its continued existence.

It might appear as if the St. Johnians never managed to establish their own independent society. Insofar as the economic base of the society is concerned, this is probably correct. Nevertheless, the St. Johnians did establish a socioeconomic system rooted in native history supporting a distinctive peasant society. This system was a further development of the Afro-Caribbean community that had emerged during slavery from the slaves' system of labor reproduction.

5

The Households

PRESENT-DAY African peasantries have been defined as being "primarily the result of the interaction between an international capitalistic economic system and traditional socio-economic systems" (Saul and Woods 1975 [1971]: 106). The Caribbean peasantries do not fit this description. As Mintz has pointed out, there never were any "traditional socio-economic systems" in the Afro-Caribbean, because the West Indians are "peoples whose ways of life were disrupted by migration, enslavement, labor contracts and the like. Rather than 'primitives' whose homelands were conquered from afar, or 'peasants' within archaic imperial states invaded or crushed by European newcomers, Caribbean peoples were always migrants, or the recent descendants of migrants, compelled to design new patterns of life in an alien environment, and usually under rigidly coercive conditions" (1973: 100). It would be wrong, however, to assume that such coercion destroyed all sense of social continuity or "tradition" among West Indians. The St. John peasantry did not originate as a means of survival after the collapse of plantation society; its social forms had long been the basis of the Afro-Caribbean community. The peasantry was, rather than a new phenomenon, a "reconstituted" peasantry, which provided the means of subsistence and was part of a distinct cultural system (Mintz 1974: 151–52). Whereas contemporary African peasantries can be seen as characterized by an interplay between tribal socioeconomic forms and Western society, the peasantry on St. John emerged from a tradition that had grown up within, and in certain respects in opposition to, Western society. It was not based on large, permanent socioeconomic units rooted in ancient traditions of relatively undisturbed existence in the same area. Rather, it was based on households and flexible networks of exchange providing a means of living with, yet resisting, oppression by the colonial order. I shall here focus on the reproduction activities that centered on the households.

Production

St. Johnians clearly recognized the roots of their peasant society in the slaves' system of reproduction. When describing the establishment of one of the first peasant settlements on the island, a St. Johnian emphasized how his great-aunt had been able to build a very nice house because of her economic activities as a slave: "After slavery my great aunt built the first house in Pastory on her land. Pastory was in wilderness at the time, there was no plantation there. She was quite prosperous and a very active lady. As a slave she had to work certain hours, but in her spare time, which for most others seemed not adequate to do anything, *she* would raise hogs and cultivate the ground. . . . She sold her products to others on the island, who weren't as industrious as she was. . . . So the result was that she had the money to build a house, when she acquired her property. She used to say that she paid two carpenters each one stocking of money to build the house. Most houses at that time were made of thatch and the tops of sugarcane and wattle. But her house was built of wood and shingles in the form of a hip roof."[1]

Most St. Johnians were able to acquire only very limited land-holdings; however, these modest tracts of land had a significance much greater than their economic value. Based on them, the Afro-Caribbeans, who possessed a subsistence system developed during slavery, formed a community that enabled them to generate a living from the scarce resources of St. John. The importance of the land as the seedbed of freedom and self-worth is explained by an older St. Johnian, born in the 1880s: "I like to think of people having land wherever they are born. To me, they are more stable and much more secure when they have a foundation of their own. If not, you will keep paying, and even if you own a million dollars, you don't own anything. If not, there will be people begging. I believe that there were slaves, because the people had no home to go to. It is terrible to live so. Here you can work all right, but when you are finished, you can just pick up your tools and go home. But if you have to live on somebody else's place, when the month comes up, you must pay, otherwise you go into the street. And after all, a person can't live on the street. You can always manage when you have a place of your own, and that is why I will not sell any of my property, so that anybody in the family who wants to live on it can do so."

The official St. John records do not reflect the social significance of the peasant landholdings. When a census was conducted by the American government after purchasing the Danish West Indies, the small farms on St. John were not even recorded. The census reflected the modern American business approach to farming, defining a farm as "the land under the personal management of a single individual or firm, though consisting of different tracts, used for raising or producing animals, poultry, and agricultural products, and operated or farmed by his labor, the labor of the members of his household, or by hired employees working under his personal direction" (*Census of the Virgin Islands 1917*, 1918: 114). The many small holdings owned by the peasants were not seen as fitting this description and therefore were not reported as farms.

Most St. Johnian peasants were by no means full-time farmers. They engaged in a number of economic activities such as provision farming, animal husbandry, charcoal burning, fishing, basket weaving, lime burning, bay leaf picking, sailing, carpentry, wage labor on estates, and migratory wage labor off the island. Many of these occupations supplemented one another, offering a variety of resources which St. Johnians could utilize to design their individual constellation of activities. I shall discuss them each separately, showing how they were interrelated in one coherent peasant economy. Data for the analysis come from historical documents (e.g., records from the Danish *landfoged/* American administrator, population census returns, land records, and various publications) and from field data gathered among St. Johnians through oral history interviews, life history narratives, and genealogies.

Farming

Though the small farmers owned little land, they were responsible for much of the farming on the island. The tax records from 1902 show that the small farms (up to 50 acres) cultivated a total of 244.75 acres, whereas the estate owners cultivated a total of

Table 13. Acres in Cultivation on Small Farms and Estates, St. John, 1902

Acres under cultivation	Number of		Total acres under cultivation on		Percentage of cultivated land on	
	Small farms	estates	Small farms	estates	Small farms	estates
0	51	24	0	0	0	0
0.01–1	71	4	67.5	4	27.5	0.7
1.01–2	22	0	44	4	18.0	0.7
2.01–3	12	2	36	3	14.7	0.6
3.01–4	6	1	24	8	9.8	1.5
4.01–5	4	3	20	10	8.2	1.9
5.01–10	6	6	53.25	43	21.8	8
10.01–20	0	6	0	98	0	18.2
20.01–30	0	1	0	25	0	4.6
30.01–40	0	0	0	0	0	0
40.01–50	0	4	0	192	0	35.6
50.01–100	0	2	0	152	0	28.2
Total	172	53	244.75	539	100.0	100.0

Source: *VRR* 1902.

539.00 acres (see Table 13). In other words, almost a third of the cultivated land was located on the peasant plots.

The peasants' cultivation of land was not limited to their own small plots; they commonly received permission from neighboring estates to stake out plots on marginal, unused land to cultivate provisions. In fact, some peasants, whose plots were quite small and had poor soil, did their farming primarily on estate land. Of the plots owned by small farmers, 30 percent had no acreage in cultivation. One St. Johnian explained that in his village, they did not farm much of their own land: "Even though we owned some land, this was not important for farming. The land was used mostly for house sites and places where we could keep a few things. The main farming was done on the surrounding plantations, that were waste land. On these plantations we could get permission to burn charcoal, keep some animals or have a little garden. We did not have to pay for this, but it was customary to give some of the produce, for example a few bags of charcoal." The records do not indicate how much land was cultivated in this way, and it likely that no taxes were paid on cultivated land that was located in the bush on the estates. Descriptions of St. John by Danish and American visitors give the impression that the island was almost completely uncultivated. One wrote: "At first glance the place looks uninhabited and quite untouched by human life and activity. Then the gaze falls upon a single house and some palms—a Moravian minister's modest dwelling, which in a curious way melted together with the surroundings" (Christmas 1923: 142). Another wrote: "Since the land has been virtually entirely uncultivated since the emancipation of the negroes in 1848, one meets everywhere complete wilderness" (Børgesen and Uldall 1900: 16).

St. Johnians often cultivated plots in several places, working out different arrangements with the landowners. One St. Johnian explained, "My father had three grounds when he died. One was at our own place. ... Another ground was on land that he hired from the [Moravian] mission, and it was when he worked at that place that he was wounded so that he died. He was cleaning the ticks out of his horse's ears, and was kicked in his head, so that he fell to the ground. ... The third ground he had was on a cattle estate. This land he didn't actually rent, because he used to go fish there and then it was arranged that he could have a ground over there." This small farmer thus owned some of the land he cultivated, rented some, and used some by an informal agreement with the estate owner, which probably involved exchanging fish and produce for the use of the land. By using land in several locations, the farmer had access to different geographical environments and could more easily mix farming with fishing or charcoal burning.

On estate lands the peasants practiced extensive cultivation. They cut the bush with machetes and burned it to clear the land. A large root net in the soil formed by bushes and small trees had to be broken up with a hoe or ax. Large trees were spared to hold the soil during sudden rainfalls and to provide shade. Fields on mountainsides had to be terraced by piling up stone walls that could retain banks of earth. Before planting could begin, fields had to be surrounded by a stone wall or a prickly brush fence to protect them from animals. Planting was done throughout the year whenever there was sufficient rainfall. Although there is no true "rainy season" on St. John, November is generally the wettest month, February and March the driest months (Shaw 1934; *H*: n.d.). The annual rainfall varies greatly, from less than thirty inches to more than sixty inches, and periodically droughts threaten to destroy the crops.

To use the fields most productively, St. Johnian peasants practiced intercropping much as it had been practiced during slavery. This method permitted the faster-growing plants, such as sweet potato vines, to cover the soil and keep it moist and thus to retard soil erosion during heavy downpours. The produce grown was similar to that grown during slavery, the important staples being sweet potato, tannier, cassava, and pigeon peas. After being cultivated for two to four years, depending on the soil's fertility, a field was abandoned to lie fallow until it was again covered with bush. This would take two to three years, depending on the rainfall. Since plenty of land was at the farmers' disposal, a new area for cultivation was not difficult to find and farmers were not forced to return to sites that had already been used. If great effort and energy had been expended on terracing and fencing, the field would likely be cultivated again within a few years when soil fertility had been restored. Only on the estates did the St. Johnians practice such shifting, bush fallow cultivation. Provision farming on the peasants' own grounds adjacent to their houses, where little land was available, took the form of kitchen gardening on permanent plots; in such locations, one section might be in fallow for a season. Provision farming was done primarily to supply vegetables for the household.

St. Johnians did not regard provision farming as a separate occupation but saw it as part of other farming activities. When the fields were cleared, a great deal of wood was cut, which could be used for charcoal burning: "Charcoal burning was really part of the general farming—an important link in the farm work. When this land was first settled there was bush all over, and this had to be cleared in order to use the land. When the fields were cleared the wood would be lying right where the fields were to be as an embarrassment. So before the wood rotted, it would be burned for charcoal. Everybody, almost, would burn their own charcoal to get the money for it." Charcoal was sold for cash on St. Thomas, where it was used for cooking. It was not used on St. John, where wood was readily available. Charcoal burning involved cutting a large quantity of wood, which was then chopped into smaller pieces, tightly packed, covered with bush and dirt to reduce oxygen, and burned at a very low heat. The coals were bagged and shipped to St. Thomas on sailboats owned by estates or individuals who specialized in carriage by boat. Because selling charcoal was one of the few means of procuring cash, St. Johnians often cut wood just to make charcoal without using the land cleared in the process. The cattle estates took advantage of such clearings; when an estate needed a new pasture, charcoal burners were often allowed to cut as much wood in the area as they wished before the final clearing was done by hired labor.

Shifting cultivation was also compatible with animal husbandry. It was common for a field to be changed into pasture before it was left entirely to go fallow. In this way, the land was used in three successive economic activities: "I have cut wood all the way from the bay down from my house to up the hill by the estate. But to make a living from it I had to cut wood in the hills where the land would serve me better. I could then cut wood, burn it, and then plant the ground, which I had cleared. . . . I had to let a place grow up again and get covered by bush, when I had cultivated it for two years. If there was good rainfall, and the bush came up again, I could clear it after two, three years and start cultivating the banks again. . . . And then, when I decided to move to another spot, I could let the pieces grow up completely, or I could turn them into animal feed, grazing for the animals. I would grow grass there, and open a new place for cultivation." St. Johnians kept several kinds of farm animals, the most important being goats, cattle, chickens, and pigs. Pigs and chickens usually were kept near the house, while goats and cattle were staked out in the bush on peasant-owned or estate land. Cattle were grazed wherever pastures were available. A census of animals owned by individual households on St. John in 1935 indicates that 163 out of 189 households inhabited by small farmers had some animals; most owned just one or two pigs, goats, and/or cows and a few fowl (see Tables 14 and 15).

Goats, sheep, and swine were primarily kept for meat, cows for milk, fowl for eggs. The primary meat animals, including bull calves, were usually slaughtered only on special occasions to provide many people with meat; or they were sent live to St. Thomas to be sold for slaughter. Meat could also be sold on St. John, but the sale had to be arranged in advance so that the meat would not spoil: "I had several cows and I milked two of them to have milk for the family. We then also made butter out of it. ... We reared the pigs until they came to perfection, and then we killed them and sold the meat. We would tell people that we were going to kill a pig one Saturday, and then we had engagements for selling the pig. People would come for five, six pounds or whatever they could afford to buy." It was common to sell animals at times of drought, when provision farming failed and there was no feed

Table 14. Number of Farm Animals Owned by
St. Johnian Farmers, 1935

	Total	Small farms (up to 50 acres)	On plantations (over 50 acres)
Mules	13	0	13
Donkeys	183	117	66
Horses	125	32	93
Cows	1,172	165	1,007
Swine	122	66	56
Goats	536	340	196
Fowls	737	638	99
Pigeons	19	19	0
Ducks	11	11	0
Dogs	120	104	16
Cats	10	9	1
Sheep	49	10	39

Source: *EMB* 1.

Table 15. Number of Small Farms with Animals,
St. John, 1935

	Number of animals											
	1	2	3	4	5	6	7	8	9	10	11–15	16+
Donkeys	48	20	4	3	1	—	—	—	—	—	—	—
Horses	9	6	1	2	—	—	—	—	—	—	—	—
Cows	17	11	7	5	3	4	2	1	—	1	2	—
Swine	26	6	3	—	—	—	1	—	—	—	1	—
Goats	20	15	10	5	3	1	1	4	1	4	4	2
Fowls	3	12	13	12	8	14	5	6	3	10	8	4
Pigeons	—	—	—	—	—	—	—	—	—	—	—	1
Ducks	—	1	—	—	—	—	—	—	1	—	—	—
Dogs	56	21	2	—	—	—	—	—	—	—	—	—
Cats	9	—	—	—	—	—	—	—	—	—	—	—
Sheep	—	1	—	—	—	—	—	1	—	—	—	—

Source: *EMB* 1.

for the animals, or when major purchases requiring relatively large sums of cash had to be made. The animals owned by the small farmers thus constituted a form of savings.

Fishing

St. Johnians depended on fish rather than meat for protein in their daily diet. The records of boat taxes show that the number of rowboats that were taxed from 1912 to 1919 ranged from thirty-eight boats in 1916, immediately after a hurricane, to fifty-six in 1918 (*EMB* 2: 1912–19). These rowboats were used mainly for fishing. The fish pot was a favorite fishing tool. During slavery it was made of wood cut in the bush on estate land, later on from imported chicken wire or telegraph wire. Since fish pots could usually be tended only from a rowboat, rowboat owners often helped tend other people's fish pots; thus the number of rowboats does not reflect the total number of St. Johnians actively engaged in fishing with pots. It was also common to fish by hook and line from the cliffs. More specialized fishing techniques included seining, which was organized by boat owners and involved a number of people. Seining occurred when certain fish were running, and usually the catch was sold on St. Thomas, the crew receiving part of the proceeds. A few St. Johnians caught turtles and sold their valuable shells for export.

A few other activities produced wares for export to St. Thomas. Lime was made from coral and shells collected on the shore and burned in a kiln. Baskets were woven out of materials found in the bush on the marginal estate land. A number of people picked bay leaves, which grew in only a few areas, and sold them to the few estates that distilled bay oil. Leaves picked on the peasant's own land brought a higher price than leaves picked on estate property. A few St. Johnians had special skills by which they earned a significant portion of their livelihood. Carpenters built wooden houses for persons who could afford them; the boat carpenters living in East End who made rowboats and sailboats on special order from people on or off the island made a substantial living. Even the boat carpenters, however, engaged in farming on the side. A few seamstresses worked for hire, but their pay was low and sewing was largely seen as an aspect of general housework. In certain areas of St. John, topographical conditions favored some specialization. On Bordeaux Mountain, for example, the soil was excellent for farming and the rainfall was good, so this area was cultivated intensively. The southeastern shore of the island had poor soil but excellent access to fishing. These regional specializations led to some exchange or even outright sale of produce. It was possible to sell some goods to the few persons who lived primarily by their crafts, but because most of them farmed on the side, they purchased little. To sell produce in any quantity, it was necessary to ship it to St. Thomas.

Trading

In the late Danish and early American period there were between twenty and thirty sailboats on the island that were owned either by the estates or the more prosperous small farmers (*EMB* 2: 1912–19). Every week they hauled animals, charcoal, and fish to market. The St. Johnians had developed an intricate system whereby different types of cargo were shipped for different rates according to their value and how hard it was for the captain to dispose of them on St. Thomas. Livestock was sent to St. Thomas, strapped to the mast of the small sailboats; the slaughterhouse usually had been notified in advance and was ready to receive the animals. The captain therefore received only a 10 percent commission. Charcoal was usually sold by the captain himself, though he had to leave it with a tradesman if the market was poor and he could not sell it during his short stay. Early in the century, charcoal sold for as little as twenty-five to thirty cents a bag; of this, the captain took five to ten cents per bag for transporting it and gave five to ten cents to the seller, if he engaged one, leaving only ten to fifteen cents for the farmer. The captain's and the seller's rates were the same, regardless of the selling price of coal, because "they had the same trouble with it." Charcoal burning therefore was rather risky business, and the St. Johnians used to say that if they fetched forty cents for a bag, they had won the grand prize (see *VK* 8: Journalsager 91).

Fish were usually not sold by the captain. When the sailboat arrived on St. Thomas, it was met by the *bom boat*, a little rowboat that distributed cargo within the harbor. If there was fish on the sailboat, it would be thrown into the *bom boat* and delivered to the market women. The fish had been put on strings, which were tied together and identified with a special label, such as a piece of coral or shell. At the fish market, the market women examined the labels in order to see whether they belonged to fishermen for whom they customarily sold fish. Exporting fish to St. Thomas was a very uncertain business. If the boat took a long time getting to St. Thomas, the fish might spoil, or if too much fish had already been brought to market, much of it spoiled before it could be sold. Because the selling of fish was so uncertain and was done only when extraordinarily large catches had been made on St. John, the captain did not charge the fisherman any money but had the right to take one out of every four strings he transported. The *bom boat* charged ten cents per string for distributing the fish, the market women kept half the selling price of the fish, and the captain gave the remainder (not even half of the selling price) to the fisherman on St. John.[2]

The captain usually was responsible not just for collecting the money, but also for spending the proceeds on purchases that he had been instructed to make in Charlotte Amalie. If St. Johnians needed shoes, cloth, or hats, women might go along in the boat to pick out what they liked. They were not charged for the trip because they caused the captain no extra work and they might even help him purchase the many items that he wanted to buy for his other customers. If the St. Thomas market was good, the boat stayed until everything had been sold and the money collected. Such a trip took two days. But if the market was poor, the money had to be collected on later trips: "It was the boatman's responsibility to remember where he placed the products, to whom, and how much, and to get back the money from them. He never kept long accounts of it, but remembered it all in his head. We did it so often that it wasn't anything to remember it." With many boats plying the waters, many young St. Johnian men took part-time jobs on sailboats to supplement their small farming.

Wage labor

Despite the fact that the St. Johnians attempted to be self-sufficient through their small farming and fishing, the proceeds were not great. One captain once stated that it was almost more important to remember to bring back the coal bags than the money, the bags having the greater value. The St. Johnians had to supplement their income with wage labor, and the cattle estates offered virtually the only wage labor on St. John. Estate work had not changed much since the days after emancipation, when the rules were laid out by the *landfoged*. Work began at seven in the morning and stopped at five in the afternoon with a noon break. The pay had risen from the ten cents a day stipulated in the first labor code to twenty cents a day in the late nineteenth century, and twenty-five to forty cents in the early twentieth century. With the New Deal the wages increased to sixty-five cents a day. St. Johnians were reluctant to work and live on an estate full-time, feeling that this was only for those who "couldn't do any better." When they took estate work, they remained in their homes and walked the often long distance to the estate every day. Although the peasants had an amiable relationship with the estate owners about using the estates' resources, they were generally skeptical about becoming estate laborers, suspecting that they would be exploited as much as possible. Many resorted to estate work only when it was absolutely necessary. An elderly St. Johnian recalled with bitterness the estate work he had done at the turn of the century: "My father was sick and couldn't work, so I told him about an estate where there was work, and he said that it was all right for me to work there. We had to get up at four

o'clock in the morning to be there at seven. We used to walk to
the point and then row across the bay where we left the boat to
climb over the hill to the estate. If we were just a little late, the
estate owner took money out of our wages. We had to work until
five in the afternoon, but when he said that it was five, it must
have been nearly seven o'clock. We had no watches so we had to
accept anything he said. He told me that I couldn't work for more
than twelve cents a day. It must have been because I was so
young. The men were getting twenty cents a day." Years later he
was still angry enough about this to say to a descendant of this
estate owner: "Your grandfather thiefed me, and he is dead and
has gone to hell!"

Rather than work on an estate, many St. Johnians chose to
leave the island to find higher paying wage labor. During the
Danish and the early American periods, they commonly worked
on sugar estates in the Dominican Republic or Cuba. Sailboats
would pick up workers in November and December, in time for
the sugarcane harvest, and returned them to St. John in July and
August, when the harvest was finished. A few St. Johnians went
to Central America to work on fruit plantations. During the
American period an increasing number went to the United States;
and throughout the Danish and American periods, St. Thomas
remained a popular destination for St. Johnians seeking work.
Some St. Johnians who left never returned, or they came back
only for brief visits. Those who did return, however, had often
been able to save enough money to improve their economic position substantially. At a time when local estate work paid only
twenty cents a day, it was possible to make what seemed like a
small fortune outside: "I worked for thirty-five dollars a month
in Guatemala. They took fifteen dollars out for food, which left
twenty dollars. I sent seven-fifty to a woman I had children with
on St. Thomas. . . . I then had thirteen-fifty left and I saved all of
that. So I was quite rich when I came back, and I bought land
right away." Most St. Johnians who left had an obligation to support their family on St. John. Those who worked on St. Thomas,
particularly, were expected to send regular supplies to parents on
St. John on the sailboats that ran between the islands. With 395
St. Johnians on St. Thomas in 1901 and a resident population
on St. John of 941, this income was probably an important feature of the peasant society's economy.

A number of St. Johnian children went to live and work with more well-to-do people on St. Thomas. In 1901 thirty-five St. Johnian children fifteen years old and under lived on St. Thomas without their parents. Fifteen were living with relatives or godparents, twenty (as servants) with strangers. The children were sent to St. Thomas because their parents were having a hard time supporting them and because St. Thomas offered an opportunity to learn trades that were difficult to acquire on St. John, where there were so few artisans: "As a boy I was brought to St. Thomas, and I was fourteen years when I came back, so all my schooling was there. I lived with a Smith family, and they were no relatives to me. My aunt was living on St. Thomas, and she sent for me to live with these people. Things were quite hard on St. John, and the St. Thomians were better off than we were. Besides, my parents liked to send their children to St. Thomas, so that they could learn different trades there. On St. John you only learned how to cut bush and burn charcoal, but there were more opportunities on St. Thomas. Mr. Smith was a carpenter, and so I used to learn some of this trade from him."

St. Johnians tried to make the best of the connections they developed on St. Thomas through their children or other relatives. One man sent his daughter to live with a woman who was a baker and therefore needed to buy fuel regularly. He sold the woman most of the wood he cut; she also gave him a place to stay when he had occasion to be on St. Thomas overnight, which he repaid by giving her provisions from St. John. The woman, who was childless herself, received a child who helped her with her business as well as a steady supply of fuel and fresh provisions from the country.

The nature of economic activities on St. John changed somewhat during the approximately seventy-five-year period in which the peasant society predominated. Estate work decreased during the twentieth century, and small farming declined after the New Deal period. Wage labor off the island increased so much in importance that it provided a substantial part of the income base of the island society. The St. Johnians seem to have engaged in what Comitas has termed "occupational multiplicity," in which "the modal adult is systematically engaged in a number of gainful activities, which for him form an integrated economic complex" (Comitas 1973 [1963]: 157). This economic pattern is common throughout the Caribbean, and it seems to be ruled by a philosophy of taking advantage of the opportunities that are available without becoming too dependent upon one of them in case it might fail.

Division of labor

There was a general but not a clear-cut sexual division of labor on St. John, and few tasks were strictly partitioned. Sailing and carpentry were confined to men, sewing to women. Men were generally most active outside the house, clearing the land of bush, building terraces, fencing fields, planting and tending the crops, producing charcoal, and fishing; wage labor on the estates was also done mostly by men. Women were most active in work around the household, which could be combined with child care. They tended to be in charge of the household, the care of the animals kept near the house, and the tending of the kitchen garden. When a household included both an adult man and an adult woman, they tended to abide by this division of labor, though it was generally accepted that they could help each other: "The husband will attend to the outside work, the wife to the inside work, from the house to the kitchen. They could help each other, if they were quite busy. I have known men who helped their wives with the wash tub on a busy day, both of them scrubbing. . . . The wife could also help outside then. If you were making a garden, she would come many times to help pull the grass, to help you plant. I have know women to help their men in the charcoal business." A few St. Johnian men expressed the opinion, however, that a couple living in a household as man and wife should not interfere in each other's work: "My wife worked in the home, you can't allow your wife to work [outside] . . . and I wouldn't help her in the house. Since the house was built, I haven't put a broom in it yet. When a man is by himself he must do his own housework, but not when a man is married. This would make the wife lazy. Not only that but then you take away her job and get mixed up with regard to what she is supposed to do and he is supposed to do. . . . I didn't want her in my [provision] ground even though I knew that she knew all about grounds."

Housework was arduous and could easily take up an adult's full attention. All cooking was done over an open fire using wood that had to be collected in the bush; some vegetables required extensive preparations before they could be eaten. Cassava bread involved hours of work grating the cassava, wringing out the juices, and drying and sifting the starch before it could be used as flour. Laundry had to be carried to a spring in one of the "guts" (ravines) and boiled in a kerosene tin over an open fire; if the Sunday clothes were to be ironed, starch had to be boiled and the iron heated. In many cases there were several children to be looked after.

The woman could give all her attention to household activities only when the household also included an adult man who was able to do all the outside work on his own or had the economic means to hire workers, if extra help was needed. These preconditions were rarely present, and both men and women were capable of performing the tasks associated with small farming. The St. Johnian quoted above, who insisted on a strict division of labor, added that he realized that his wife was perfectly capable of managing a provision ground by herself, and that the division of labor was only for couples who were married or living together. Rather than emphasizing a general sexual division of labor, St. Johnians placed great value on the ability of persons of either sex to perform a wide range of tasks and thus be self-sufficient. Many women told with great pride how they had worked to make a living on their own: "I planted pigeon peas, potatoes, tannier—I planted all kinds of things. . . . I used to go to the tip of the cliffs where there was a boulder with a hole where I fished with a rod. I put on a bait and caught fish there, I got a basket full of fish. I fished all over the whole place. . . . I burned charcoal. I was never brought up to burn charcoal, but I did it. I would cut up the wood, pack it up, bush it, light it. . . . I worked very hard all my life, and they all said that they never saw a woman work so. I never asked anybody for anything, but I got it myself. I never begged a neighbor for nothing." The importance of women in economic activities outside the household is clearly shown by the fact that women as well as men emigrated to work. The population on St. John in 1901, for example, was just slightly in favor of women, with 52 percent. In fact, there were more St. Johnian women than men on St. Thomas, where there was a good job market for women in domestic work, trading, and loading coal onto the many ships that used St. Thomas as a refueling station.

Women were able to play such an active role in the extra-domestic activities partly because children were used as labor-power as soon as they were old enough. Children were sent to the spring to get water when they could carry a pail on their head, and to find firewood in the bush. They also had to sweep the yard and help with food preparations. They were usually responsible for watering and restaking daily the animals that were kept in the bush. They helped cultivate the provision ground and burn the coal, and often had to "hold water" (i.e., keep the boats in position) when the fish pots were hauled. As mentioned above, children were sometimes sent to St. Thomas to work for their own upkeep when they were quite small. Their most important job, however, was minding younger siblings; it was not uncommon for the oldest child to be kept home from school to look after the small ones, so that the adults could work away from the house. During the Danish period the school commission fined many parents because of their children's absence from school (*STP* 3).

If a woman had nobody to run the house while she worked outside, she often had a little bush house of wattle and grass built beside her field or charcoal pit in the bush. In this way she was able to care for small children and prepare food while working away from the main house. The general flexibility in the division of labor and the heavy usage of child labor made it possible for households to function even if adults of both sexes were not included in the household.

Procreation

The structure of the household, which was the basis for the day-to-day economic activities of the peasants, was determined largely by procreation and the system of kinship and marriage. As already noted, in the years following emancipation the colonial authorities, aided by the Moravian missionaries, had attempted to promote among the freed a family structure that resembled the European nuclear family. As a result the marriage rate among St. Johnians quadrupled during the first decades after emancipation. It is questionable whether this increase in the marriage rate reflected a radical alteration in the pattern of procreation and the system of kinship and marriage. Baptismal records indicate that the Lutheran Church grew rapidly because it accepted illegitimate children, whereas the Moravian Church declined. Census returns show that in 1860, about a third of the children who lived in households headed by persons thirty-five years old and under were living in woman-headed households where no spouse was present. This indicates that even though a rather large percentage of St. Johnians were marrying, a significant number of St. Johnian children were born out of wedlock and the resulting households were often woman-headed. The statistical materials from the period after 1870, when the plantation system lost its dominant position on the island, show that, as the peasantry began to assert itself, the nuclear family based on marriage, which had been advocated by the colonial authorities, began to lose its popularity among the St. Johnians. The marriage rate, as revealed by the population censuses, peaked in the 1860–80 period, after which it declined to the level attained immediately after emancipation (see Table 16).

The marriage statistics are paralleled by statistics on the frequency of marital and common-law relationships as shown in the household censuses (see Table 17). The frequency of marriage increased until 1860, but in 1870 it had already begun to decline. While the marriage rate increased, the number of households headed by women declined. After 1880, when the marriage rate had begun to fall off, an increasing number of households were headed by women (see Table 18). These statistics indicate that the father-headed, nuclear family based on marriage had not be-

Table 16. Marital Status of St Johnians
20 Years Old and Above, 1846–1901
(in percentages)

	1846		1855	1860	1880	1890	1901
	Free	Unfree					
Single							
Men	57	83	46	37	34	48	46
Women	62	83	46	36	31	33	42
Married							
Men	38	14	50	60	58	45	44
Women	24	12	42	48	51	45	37
Widowed							
Men	5	3	3	4	8	7	10
Women	14	6	13	16	18	22	21

Source: *Statistiske Meddelelser* 1852–1903.

Table 17. Households with Common-law or Married Spouses,
St. John, 1855–1901

	Common-law spouse		Married spouse	
	Number	Percent	Number	Percent
1855	23	13	154	87
1857	23	13	161	87
1860	8	4	181	96
1870	6	5	122	95
1880	13	9	136	91
1901	19	19	79	81

Source: *F* 1855–1901.

Table 18. Headship of Several-person Households,
St. John, 1855–1901

	Male head		Female head	
	Number	Percent	Number	Percent
1855	214	56	167	44
1857	230	57	176	43
1860	229	66	118	34
1870	148	70	63	30
1880	152	78	43	22
1901	115	65	62	35

Source: *F* 1855–1901.

come the only acceptable residential family unit. The reason
seems to be that St. Johnians allowed for several types of affinal
arrangements.

Courtship and the establishment
of a household

The formal system of courtship among St. Johnians emphasized
the role of the woman's parents in the formation of affinal ties:
"When you want to court a young girl, you must first write to her
parents and ask for her. However, before you approach her par-

ents you would first make sure that it was all right with the girl. If the girl told you to write to her parents when you talked to her, then you knew that it was a little lead-off. But if you wrote to her parents, and they objected, there was nothing you could do. The daughter might talk to you on the side, but she couldn't allow her parents to see it. But as long as you kept yourself up as a young man and you applied for the girl, you would generally get a good answer. When you had got that good answer, you had to show up yourself, and you had to go visit her and the parents and sit down with them there. . . . You had to be so particular about what you said, and you had to look decent. If the girl wasn't living with her parents—or if she had been with other men already and had child[ren] for them—then she was on her own, and it wasn't necessary to get the parents' permission. Then you would do the writing with your tongue."

While many St. Johnians insisted that this type of courtship was the most proper way of initiating a sexual relationship, many did not adhere to it. It was not uncommon that a daughter secretly courted a young man and even became pregnant while living at home. The parents would then help to ensure that the father "owned" the child, i.e., acknowledged his fatherhood and contributed support. If the father refused to cooperate, the legal authorities made the man named by the mother legally and economically responsible. Only in rare cases when a woman was known to have engaged in several relationships at the time of conception was it possible for the alleged father to deny paternity, and virtually all children were accorded their father's last name at baptism. In most cases, the father readily accepted the child, and if the relationship was maintained and more children were born, the couple might formalize the union by establishing a household. If the parents did not approve of their daughter's relationship, they would try to convince the daughter to stay with them and cut her ties to the man: "My daughter got together with this guy, and he was no good. He would be drunk a lot of times, and once when I met him, he was so drunk that he didn't even see me, but walked right past me. So I told my daughter that she shouldn't marry him. If she did marry him, she shouldn't come back to us for help, because I would be finished with her then. So she didn't marry him, and she had the child and stayed with us."

It was considered wrong for a couple to have a number of children without establishing their own household: "It was nothing to have an outside child [i.e., child born out of wedlock]. Your parents might fuss a little, but it was forgotten. ... If a man wanted to have children by a woman he should ideally get a house for her. He would go to her father to talk about it, or the father might contact the man, seeing that the two were getting together. If the man had no land of his own, the woman's father might offer some of his land, saying that this is really her portion of his land, and the man can then build a house on this plot of land. The man would usually accept a piece of land like that. ... But it did happen that a man had a lot of children by one woman and never took her out of her parents' house to build a house for her. This was disliked ... because it was the most honorable to get a house for her." An affinal relationship thus was made official when a man built a house for a woman. Such a house was usually located on land that belonged to the man's family, as shown in the census returns from 1901 and 1911 (Table 19). In 1901, of the fifty-six households that could be classified according to the ownership of the land on which they were located, 56 percent were situated on the man's land, 24 percent on the woman's land, and 10 percent on estate land. In 1911, the figures were almost the same.

After a couple established a formal affinal relationship when the man "carried the woman out of her mother's house" to live in a house that he had built for her, this relationship might be cemented further by official marriage. Often this did not occur before the couple felt sure that the relationship was going to be per-

Table 19. Residence of St. Johnian Couples Starting to Live
Together, 1901 and 1911

	1901		1911	
Lived on	Number	Percent	Number	Percent
Man's family's land	35	56	44	54
Woman's family's land	15	24	19	23
Estate land	6	10	7	9
Unclassifiable land	6	10	12	15

Source: *F* 1901, 1911.

manent: "It was common to live together unmarried and get children too. If you had lived together with a common-law spouse for a while and you were sure that it was going to work and didn't want to separate, then it would be time to get married." Marriage was a sign of achievement and showed that the couple were confident that their union would work and that they were able to manage on their own; it was therefore inconceivable to get married without having a house in which to live. Marriage also signified the legal recognition of a relationship that in many cases had existed for a number of years. It was therefore thought to bestow special status on the couple: "I lived with my wife for twelve years, and then we got married. And then we lived thirty years married after that. Many lived common-law at that time. Marriage was only for the rich people, not the poor. But they got married after so many years, when they could afford it. At that time it was honorable to get married. You got married mostly for the children's sake, to make them lawful. If I had no children, I would just have lived common-law and I wouldn't have felt compelled to get married." The wedding ceremony was supposed to be quite elaborate in keeping with the honorable status associated with being married: "Weddings were big occasions at that time. You would kill a cow or a goat or more than that, and everybody was invited and had a good time. The wedding started in the church, where the minister really gave a sermon for the couple. Then there was a party afterwards, where the people came and had a good time."

The European concept of an affinal relationship (marriage) thus may be contrasted to the St. Johnian concept of an affinal relationship: a sexual relationship, to which the woman's parents have consented, between a man and a woman living in their own house or planning to establish a joint household. The *Annual Reports* of the Virgin Islands Department of Health from 1919 to 1931 listed the birth of 271 children on St. John; 154, or 57 percent, were born out of wedlock. Apparently, the Moravian Church had resigned itself to this concept of marriage; by the turn of the century, the church had stopped refusing to baptize children born out of wedlock, although such children were baptized at the entrance to the church—the baptismal font being reserved for "legitimate" children. The church also recognized the importance of the establishment of a new household by participating in a ceremony similar to a wedding; the minister blessed the house and made a little speech wishing the members of the new household good luck. As in the case of a wedding, the ceremony was followed by a party.

Extra-domestic relationships

Most men held the opinion that it was all right to have sexual relationships on the side as long as they didn't interfere in the domestic relationship. A man stated: "If I should come to know a woman, and she would offer me 'a little piece of thing', I would take it, and suppose she would encourage me to come back, if you find it good, then the other wife wouldn't know what is happening." Many men expressed high regard for those who managed to have a large number of children with a number of women and pointed to men who had been particularly successful in this respect: "They called him Kunze ... he was a little fellow, and *kunze* is little in Creole. He was little, but he was big. He had children over there, he had children over here, oh boy! I think it is good he had so many, if a lady likes you, you like her back." The men generally pointed with pride to the example of one man who had managed to maintain a permanent, publicly known relationship with two women at a time, providing adequate support for both of them: "Uncle Joseph had two wives, Anna and Caroline, but they lived at two different places, Anna on Uncle Joseph's land and Caroline on the other side of the road on her land. When Uncle Joseph came back from St. Thomas on his boat, two donkeys were sent down to the boat to pick up groceries and whatever there might be. The one donkey with two *dom* boxes would go to Caroline, the other one to Anna. He supported the two of them, and when he came back from town, he would have to go to the one wife first, and then to the other one. He always went to Caroline first, left her at ten, eleven o'clock and then he would go to Anna, where he slept till morning. Anna was the main wife because he was married to her. There was no reason why she should divorce him, as long as he could satisfy her, as long as she got what she wanted." Some of those who referred to this case noted, however, that the two women were not happy about the situation, never spoke to each other in public, and once got into a violent fight: "One day I was in the gut, where the two women also happened to be. One of the women's children picked a mango and offered it to his half-sister, who took it. The two

women got so vex with one another, seeing that the children accepted each other as brother and sister, that they got into a big
fight, cutting each other up and nearly drowning each other."

Men were more reluctant to accept women's outside relationships. Women had to be discreet about such relationships so that
children resulting from them would not be rejected by their husbands. In many cases, husbands were aware that the wife was
having a child with another man, but not always. One man remembered how his widowed father used to visit married women:
"I remember my father being with other women. He always lived
at home. And then he would go visit the others. But the danger
was that some of them had husbands. I remember one of the
women came up to where we lived. At that time she was living on
an estate, and her husband used to sail a boat belonging to the
owner of the estate, carrying cargo to St. Thomas. And when he
went one day, he didn't come back before the next day or so. Then
she would come to our home, and she would stay there with
Papa." Some men who knew that a child had been fathered
by another man accepted the child and adopted it as their own.
One woman recalled being surprised when she learned that her
mother's husband was not her father: "I used to call him Papi,
and I didn't know that he wasn't my real father before I had
grown up and was big enough to understand about it. I then
learned that it was the man whom I usually called Cousin George
who was my father! I then started to call him Uncle George, but
never Father."

Women were much more confined than men, with children to
care for and a household to run, and were not able to go out very
often. Their responsibilities caused them to be more hesitant
about outside relationships. One woman stated: "There always
was quite a bit of fooling around with other people. Many husbands think that they are losing out if they don't have one on the
side, and some wives think the same way. I think that you could
have your joke, but that you shouldn't do it all the time." Most
women did not tolerate excessive "fooling around" on the part of
the man, preferring to discontinue the relationship. One woman,
for example, decided to call off a planned marriage when she
learned that her husband-to-be was overdoing it: "I was going to
marry him, and he built a house and all like that, but I didn't
marry him. I found out that he had two, three women besides me,
and that I was the youngest, getting my first child. . . . He would

only be home for meals and stay out the rest of the night, coming home very late. I said to him that it was no good, because I was expecting and I would need help, when I was having the child, and with him gone all the time, I wouldn't know who to call. He was just too unreliable."

Affinal relationships were discontinued by moving out of the joint household. Theoretically, the house had been built by the man for the woman, and the man had to move out. However, since the house was usually built on the man's land and thus located near houses inhabited by his relatives, the woman often chose to move out in order to be near her relatives. She might move into her parents' house or her relatives might help build a small house for her. In fact, some men explained that they would build a house only on their own land so that they would not lose it if the union should break up.

Marriage and the domestic family

The changeable affinal relationship and the many children who were born out of wedlock continued to cause consternation among religious and governmental authorities. Though the churches baptized all children, they attempted to pressure unwed parents into marrying—with limited success, as is apparent in this 1911 report by the Lutheran minister of St. Thomas and St. John: "The year was especially disappointing with regard to young girls who had illegitimate children, a particularly sad case was that of a Sunday school teacher. On the reverse side, there are others who have become tired of their life in sin, and they either got married or gave up their old life and asked to come to the Lord's table. It is still very difficult to reach the men" (STP 1: 1911).

The American government, upon assuming control, expressed great shock at the local customs concerning "morals, marriages and domestic relations." A federal commission, investigating the islands in 1924, reported:

Upon the occasion of American occupation there were found age-old customs, many of them dating back to the days of slavery, when the men and women were only chattels and things, called upon to breed children to supply an ever-growing demand for field laborers; the home as an institution was unheard of and unknown, and women were held in the lowest esteem and forced to serve as the chief breadwinners in all domestic relations. Despite American protests these practices have continued, and the problem of morality on the islands presents a problem whose proper solution means so much to the welfare of these people that the Government, the churches, and every social agency are fully occupied and concerned in the endeavor to solve it. .... On the part of the natives themselves, strange to say, there is little sentiment against these [sexual] practices, and yet the people are orderly and law-abiding to a noticeable degree. It is believed when there has been more fully developed a strong and healthy public sentiment, expressed in legal enactments against consensual and other forms of irregular marriage, the people as a whole will quickly rise to an understanding of true American ideals in this direction. (Quoted in Fairchild 1935: 142–43)

It is not surprising that "family instability" was regarded as a main obstacle to successful application of the New Deal programs of the 1930s (Grede 1962: 38).

This attitude toward the "unstable" Afro-Caribbean family has been common throughout the Caribbean. A royal commission appointed by the British Parliament in 1938 to "survey the social and economic conditions" of the British West Indies "to recommend appropriate programmes for action" emphasized "the evident 'disorganization' of family life" (M. G. Smith 1966: iv). This survey led to the initiation of a marriage campaign on Jamaica, intended to prevent the spread of the reported promiscuity (ibid.). The concern of Western society to change the "problematic" West Indian family has led to a great concentration on family studies in Afro-American research by social scientists who have sought to account for the special character of the family (see, for example, Comitas and Lowenthal 1973; Gerber 1973; Marks and Römer 1978). Melville and Frances Herskovits, who were among the first to do fieldwork in the West Indies, investigated the reason why the residential family in the Caribbean was characterized by both marital and common-law relationships. They theorized that the often impermanent sexual unions were caused by the African cultural trait of polygyny being reinterpreted under the conditions of slavery (Herskovits and Herskovits 1973 [1949]). Later anthropologists have stressed the importance of the disruptive effects of slavery in breaking down the normal domestic unit so that a mother-centered matrifocal or consanguineal family was created (see, for example, Frazier 1968 [1939]; Henriques 1973 [1949], 1968 [1953]; M. G. Smith 1962b). Others have emphasized possible economic causes (for example, Gonzalez 1969; Greenfield 1966; R. T. Smith 1956). In these studies one gets the impression that although a smoothly operating household based on a nuclear family is desired by the West Indians, it is often not achieved because of various socioeconomic and historical factors.

In recent years, the methodological and theoretical bases of these West Indian family studies have been questioned. It has been argued that anthropologists have not been concerned with understanding Afro-Caribbean social structure on its own terms as much as with "explaining" the West Indian family, because it departs from established conceptions of normal family structure (Mintz and Price 1976: 50; Tanner 1974). A foremost authority on West Indian family structure, R. T. Smith, has suggested that previous studies of Afro-Caribbean social structure, including his own, have suffered from an "undue concentration on household studies, and the false functionalist assumption that stable co-residential conjugal unions are necessary for the proper upbringing of children—and for the firm establishment of kinship ties" (1978b: 335). This concentration was caused not only by theoretical considerations but by ethnocentric, moral concerns; research has taken its point of departure primarily from the "common-sense, European view of the family . . . [which] is completely misleading in comparative study" (ibid.: 339).

The St. Johnian case reveals that it is not useful to concentrate on household studies when examining social structure, nor is it possible to view "stable co-residential conjugal unions" as basic to the family. It is questionable whether the residential nuclear family was ever an important ideal on St. John, as it has been believed to have been in other Afro-Caribbean communities. Households were important economic units in the peasant economy, and they were centers for the bearing and rearing of children. Creating a new household therefore constituted a major event in the life of an individual. It did not follow, however, that households had to be nuclear families, or that the nuclear family structure that resulted when a couple established its own household was a family ideal. The system of procreation valued the ability of individuals to engage in a variety of relationships, and

Table 20. Composition of Households, St. John, 1901

	Households	
	Number	Percent
Man only	40	16
Woman only	31	13
Couple and possibly others	98	40
Single male head and possibly others	19	8
Single female head and possibly others	60	24

Source: *F* 1901.

the peasant economy was not dependent upon nuclear family households but presented a wide range of economic activities that women as well as men were able to perform. Furthermore, the sexual division of labor was flexible, posing few occupational constraints on men or women. Neither production nor procreation, therefore, was based on the residential nuclear family. The 1901 census shows that only 40 percent of households included a nuclear family (see Table 20).

When St. Johnians spoke about the family, they were not referring to the nuclear family but an entirely different social structure. It was associated with networks of kin relationships encompassing the individual households. These networks had developed during slavery and had helped the slaves maintain life despite the severe social and economic deprivation they suffered. As the peasantry emerged, supported by the marginal resources that were left to it by the colonial society, these networks came to form the basis of the social structure of the peasant society.

6

The Network of Exchanges

WHILE HOUSEHOLDS were important as foci in the daily activities of subsistence production and procreation, they were not the basis of the peasant community. The community's socioeconomic exchanges took place instead within the strong kinship networks that had emerged during slavery and that tied the separate households into an interrelated whole. Mutual aid among the slaves helped them survive despite the rigors of slavery and plantation work; mutual aid fostered the development of an Afro-Caribbean community, which had important cultural and political significance, out of resistance to the extreme repressiveness of the planter class. For the peasant community, the same exchange system provided St. Johnians with a means of subsistence, offered them a sociocultural identity, and helped maintain their community despite the limited resources ceded to them by the plantations. The peasants' exchange system differed from that of the slaves, as did their altered social circumstances.

During slavery, networks of mutual aid were most intense among closely related slaves living on the same estate. On estates with stable populations, the slaves became a large interrelated kinship group, helping and protecting each other. Relatives or spouses living on other estates were important on special occasions, in particular when normal relations within the estate broke down. The Afro-Caribbean community during slavery rested on a structure of kinship that created an obligation to provide support and assistance of various kinds whenever needed. With the establishment of the peasantry, the kinship basis of the Afro-Caribbean community of the estate was projected to the entire island society. Most St. Johnians I interviewed stated that even though they might not be able to trace kinship to certain persons, they felt that all "common folks" were "some kind of a cousin": "I think that all of St. John is related somehow, and I don't feel much different toward a St. Johnian who is an actual relative, and one who isn't. We are all close." This feeling of relatedness was expressed in the terms of address used on the island; all St. Johnians commonly addressed each other using kinship terms. Close relatives were addressed by such specific kinship terms as papa, mama, *tantan* or *tan* ("aunt"), uncle, grandpa, or grandma. Older siblings and cousins were also addressed by kinship terms in order to show them respect, whereas younger relatives were addressed by name only. All unrelated St. Johnian peasants were addressed as cousin if of the same generation, or uncle or *tantan* if older. In cases where children shared godparents, or where one child had a parent who was godparent to another child, the children could refer to each other as godsisters and godbrothers.[1]

The kinship basis of the St. Johnian community was underlined by the attitude that all were "in the same boat" in their common poverty and that they had to help each other in order to "fight their way through life." The configuration of networks of mutual support, which stretched to all peasants, was not uniform or permanent. Relatively permanent clusters of particularly intense relations combined with more fluid clusters that formed and dissolved as the need for them arose. The pattern of the networks thus changed and regrouped, but the network principle itself was the permanent basis of the Afro-Caribbean community.

Close relatives

As during slavery, the most intensive reciprocal socioeconomic aid occurred among close relatives who lived on the same estate. Most St. Johnians lived next to households inhabited by near relatives because they built their houses on land originally purchased by their parents or grandparents. In this way, small settlements of kinsmen arose. Though they lived in separate households, they offered each other various kinds of aid in daily life. One household was often inhabited by members of the elder generation, who were cared for by their younger relatives. To St. Johnians it was a matter of pride to care properly for one's parents: "When my father died, he lived in a house by himself. As he got old, he started to complain and say that he could not go along with the tasks any longer. At that time, I still had my wife, so I told him to rest, and then I would do the working, and my wife would cook and bring meals to him. In this way I could say that I took care of him, until he was no more." Another St. Johnian remembered being sent as a child to her grandmother's house to help her: "On Friday afternoons I used to go to my grandmother's house to clean it for her and to carry water." Later, when the grandmother became too old to manage by herself during the week, she moved in with her daughter, who had settled with her husband on another estate.

The elderly were not just a responsibility but also a resource. They were usually available for child care and whatever other assistance they could manage, which was especially important to persons who lived without a spouse: "When my husband was out sailing, I missed him, but I never missed company. At that time there were elderly people who came around and helped me a little with the washing, house cleaning and so. The men often helped look after the animals. When I started to work for money, I used to leave my small children with my mother. So I really depended a lot on these relatives around me."

Parents sometimes sent children to live with older relatives (see Table 21). The population census of 1901 listed thirty-six children as living with their grandparents, fifteen with aunts,

Table 21. Residence of Children Up to 15 Years Old,
St. John, 1901

	Children	
	Number	Percent
With parents	239	64
With grandparents[a]	36	10
With guardian, godparent, or adoptive parent	10	3
With aunt/uncle[a]	15	4
With others	36	10
On St. Thomas	35	9

a. The category of grandparents includes great-grandparents; that of aunt/uncle includes great-aunt/great-uncle.

Source: F 1901.

uncles, great-aunts, or great-uncles, ten with guardians, adoptive parents, or godparents, and thirty-six with others (*F* 1901). Most children who lived with "others" were staying in the houses of estate owners and were working for their upkeep as servants, much like St. Johnian children living on St. Thomas. The relative importance of child exchange is apparent in the fact that of all children less than sixteen years old, approximately a third lived in a household where no parent was present.

A child was often sent out of the parental household (usually not before being weaned) when another child was born or on the way, so that the mother would have more time to take care of the new baby and do her work. But it was not just the parents who benefited. It was common for one of the first grandchildren to be sent to live with grandparents, and the St. Johnians emphasized that these children provided company for the elderly. As the grandchildren became older, they would be able to help out; a number of tasks such as fetching firewood and water, tracking down straying animals, and helping to pull fish pots were allocated to children. If there were no children in the household, it was sometimes difficult for elderly people to get their daily work done, even if they were physically active. A child would therefore be most welcome in their household.

When a household took in a child, its parents were placed in a position of debt. The household was caring for the child, and even though the child might be of help, it still had to be fed and clothed. The parents often sent foodstuffs and whatever else they could spare to the households in which the children were living (unless the households were headed by estate owners). The exchange of children therefore intensified the relationship between the two households.

Those who were active in the peasant economy also relied on relatives living nearby for certain kinds of assistance in their daily life. One St. Johnian remembered how, because various relatives could be relied on for help, she had had no difficulty managing on her own when she decided to leave her husband and establish her own household: "It wasn't hard to manage by myself, because my father and my uncle used to help me. My uncle was working on a piece of land just above mine, burning coal there. He used to help me saddle up the donkey with the coal and transport it down to the beach. I didn't fish myself, but my father and my uncle were fishermen, and they gave fish to me.

My father had a big round wist basket [basket made of a local vine called wist] and when he came in, it was loaded. My aunt was a real worker, too, and she also helped me picking charcoal and so. They helped me, and I helped them." Although such households were separate entities, they were enveloped by tight networks of exchanges of goods and labor that enabled them to function even if they did not have sufficient resources on their own.

Close relatives were often connected not only through exchanges of various kinds but also through common ownership of the property on which their households were located. In 1902, the tax records showed 156 owners of land in plots of up to fifty acres (*VRR* 1902). The official records do not accurately reflect the actual ownership and use of the land, however.[2] The St. Johnians had a different conception of property than did the colonial authorities. For the government, land was property to be used for various economic pursuits, whether sugarcane cultivation, stock rearing, or small farming; for the St. Johnian peasants, land was also a symbol of freedom and independence and a source of security for the family. Land therefore was not to be held by individual proprietors solely in order for them to earn the most from it, but was rather to be placed in the family's trust for all to enjoy. While 156 persons were listed as owners of peasant lots in 1902, many were really not owners of the land but merely persons in charge of land owned by large families. When land originally was acquired by the St. Johnians, it was purchased by individual persons. When these persons died, the land was passed to all descendants of the first owner so that each had a right to use the land: no descendant owned a particular parcel of the land, but all had a joint claim to all of it. The claim gave all descendants a right to settle on the land and cultivate it, but the family members had to agree on where each person could live and how much land each could use. Since much of the actual farming and stock rearing took place in the hills on land owned by the large estates, this agreement was primarily a matter of deciding where to locate the house. Clearly if two acres of land were inherited by ten children, it would not be practical for all ten children with their spouses and children to live on only two acres. But their joint claim meant that they always had a possibility of settling on the land and a ready refuge should they need a place to stay. Family members did not relinquish their claim by not living on the land, and they passed their claim on to their own children, who might someday settle there. Even though it was not always possible or practical to use the land, the claim system did distribute the potential for its use to a large number of people without dividing it into useless fractions.

Thus the land that had been sold to individuals by the estate owners in the last decades of the nineteenth century had become "family land" by the following generations rather than being split into smaller, individually owned lots. The family land system was part of the general system of sharing and exchange among close relatives. It had the function of redistributing the limited land resources among the different relatives so that they were able to use the land according to their need rather than according to a particular share that they owned.

Flexibility in the exercise of rights to family land is illustrated by the residence pattern of a group of descendants who collectively owned a piece of family land. Insofar as residence implies the most intensive usage of land, it gives some indication of how access to the family land was actually distributed. The case is taken from the population census returns. In 1880, the family was residing on ten acres of land purchased by *A* in 1873. In 1901, all the children had moved out of the household except the youngest child, *I*, who was still living at home. The oldest child, *C*, had moved to St. Thomas, where she was living with her husband in a rented apartment; he was a St. Johnian who had been living on St. Thomas since childhood. *D* was living on land that belonged to him (a little more than eight acres), some distance from his parents' land; it was not possible to ascertain whether he acquired the land through his wife or by purchasing it himself, but it was registered in his name. *E* was living on his father's land with his wife and child. *F* was also living on his father's land with her two outside children. *G* lived with her husband and children on his family land. *H* lived with her common-law husband and their child on his family's land (ten acres).

In 1911 *A* and *B* lived alone, *I* having left home. *C* was still living on St. Thomas, *D* on his own land, *E* on his father's land. *F* now lived with her common-law husband, either on his family's land (twenty-nine acres) or on her father's land; the two families' land was parceled out of the same estate and was not distinguished in the census. *G* had died, *H* lived with her husband and children on his family's land, and *I* was living with her husband and children on his family's land (forty acres).

In this case, the tendency for the daughters to move to their

Residing on A's land in 1880:

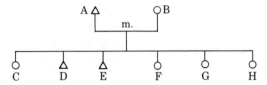

Residing on A's land in 1901:

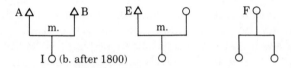

C lives in St. Thomas with her husband. They do not own the
property.
D lives on his own land with wife and child.
G lives on husband's land with him and their children.
H lives on common-law husband's land with him and their
children.

Residing on A's land in 1911:

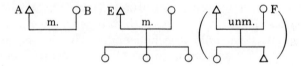

C lives in St. Thomas with husband. They do not own the property.
D lives on his own land with wife and children.
F possibly lives on common-law husband's land with him and
their children.
G has died; her husband continues to live on his family land with
children and new wife.
H lives on husband's family land with him and children.
I lives on husband's family land with him and children.

Figure 4. Residence pattern of a St. Johnian family, 1880, 1901,
and 1911. Source: *F* 1880, 1901, 1911.

husbands' land is apparent. Thus *C*, possibly *F*, and *G*, *H*, and *I* moved to live with their husbands, who all had land; *D*, the eldest son, also moved away from the family land, possibly to land acquired through his wife. As noted, one did not lose a claim to family land by moving away from it (e.g., after marrying). Later, when *I*'s children found it crowded on their father's family land, one child moved to *I*'s family land (*A*'s land) and built his house there. When *F* later married another man, he moved to her residence, because his family did not own much land and it was already settled by several other family members. As the data in Table 19 also indicate, the patrilocal ideal left room for much variation, and a couple who decided to settle down together considered several factors before deciding where to live: the quality of the soil on the family land, the size of the land, the current density of settlement, the location (a sailor or fisherman would, for example, prefer to live fairly close to the sea), and fondness (or lack of it) for the respective families.

Though all the members of a family owning land retained their claim to the use of it even if they didn't live on it, they were able to use the land only if they lived on or within easy walking distance of it. In the prior case, *E* was the only child, with the possible exception of *F*, who was living on the land in 1911. However, *F*, *H*, and *I* lived so close to the land that they could easily ask their father for permission to "make a cultivation on it" or keep a few animals there. It is unlikely that *C* or *D* used the land because they lived so far away that it was impractical. Thus there were at most only five households that used the land in 1911 (unless *G*'s husband used his children's claim on the land, which was unlikely, since his family at this time had enough land of its own); this left two acres to each, if all used the same amount of land. At the same time that the out-marrying daughters maintained a right to use part of their family land, *E*'s wife, who moved to *E*'s family land, also had family land nearby that she could use if she chose to do so.

Though family land was usually not large enough for all children to settle on it comfortably had they chosen to do so, they still appreciated the fact that they had a claim to the land which they could invoke at any time. Many older St. Johnians expressed their close attachment to the land, which their ancestors had bought for their families, and they were strongly opposed to selling the land (which today is extremely valuable), seeing its sale as a sign of disrespect for the family:

My grandfather is very important, because he bought this land for his children and their children. I don't know for sure when he bought the land, but I was born here seventy-nine years ago, so the family had it already then. . . . My grandfather made the deed so that the family owned it, not individuals, and so that the land would be handed down to the family and kept by it. If a person has no children, the land goes to the rest of the family. Everybody has a claim to the land, not to a specific part of it, and we are many who share the land today, although only few actually live on it. . . . If everybody who has a claim to the land actually wants their own piece, I think that there would be very little land to each. . . . It would be very easy to sell the land, because many people would want it, but then the land would be gone forever. It is the old ancestor who made a provision for us, and I will not abuse it.

The joint claim to family land tied relatives together into fairly permanent groups. The common family tie to the land was concretized in the family's cemetery, located on the land. The original buyer of the land was buried here together with descendants who had died. Even if family members had not been interested in keeping the land for its own sake—if there was, for example, better and more easily accessible land available elsewhere within the family—the presence of this cemetery on the land would prevent them from selling it. Even family land that had not been used by the end of the peasant period was not sold but remained in the family. Although the St. Johnian population could be divided into groups associated with certain areas of the island where they owned land, these groups were not mutually exclusive. Many St. Johnians had claims in several properties, having inherited them through both parents. Thus an extensive kinship network tied these "land families" together.

The peasant community as "one big family"

Exchange of goods and services was a moral obligation among relatives, and it was a sign of "givishness" and responsibility toward the community when extended to others. While free or "generalized" among close relatives, exchange often was a reciprocal social or economic transaction between nonrelatives. Island-wide, exchanges were associated with moral values that defined what was considered good about life on St. John and thus about peasant society. The exchanges involved a variety of elements, which may be grouped into two basic categories: goods and labor.

Exchange of goods

Though there was some specialization in the peasant economy, most households either produced vegetables or fished or both. Even so, few households produced a surplus large enough to be worth shipping to St. Thomas; and some households occasionally needed to purchase vegetables and fish, whereas others had somewhat more than they could use. There was thus a limited basis for the trading of produce on St. John, but there was no central marketplace on the island. People who needed "groundfood," for example, could go to others who were known to have large provision grounds (hence the name "ground" food) and "ask to buy for five or ten cents produce." The procedure was explained by an elderly St. Johnian:

> My father used to have a lot of groundfood, and he did sell some of it. A huge basket could hold ten cents of potatoes, a big one five cents worth. He would sell to anybody who wanted to buy from him. He also gave away, he was the kind of man who would give away anything. To me, it seems that they used to cultivate to give away. If you planted a ground, you did not just plant a little bit, you planted a whole section. so you would take out a section of potatoes, and it would be too much for your home. Then you would give to anybody who wanted. There were no special people that you gave. . . . Anybody could come up from Cruz Bay to Cousin Isaac, as they called my father, and they would say that they wanted ten cents potatoes or five cents potatoes, and he would go out and gravel the amount for his house, and then he would give the balance to the people. More than ten cents worth. Plenty more. You couldn't sell anybody by the pound.

In this description it is apparent that there was much more to the selling of produce than a mere commercial transaction. It sounds almost as if the selling of produce was incidental to growing provisions for home consumption and giving away. This provision farmer did not actively seek to sell his produce; he sold only to people who came to him and asked to buy something from his ground. Cousin Isaac lived on a parceled-out estate not far from Cruz Bay. Cruz Bay people came to buy from him, perhaps because space for provision grounds was limited in that village and it was difficult to cultivate fields just outside it. Since Cousin Isaac was not a commercial farmer but merely a provision farmer like many other St. Johnians, it was not always certain that he had groundfood to spare, and it was almost as if he did the buyers a favor by selling them potatoes.

The selling procedure indicates that the exchange was not strictly a commercial transaction. For example, the buyer asked for "five or ten cents potatoes," but this did not mean a fixed quantity of potatoes (except that they were roughly measured in baskets). St. Johnians had a fair idea of how much provision food one could buy in a market for that much money, and they would then give a very generous amount of potatoes in relation to the stated price. This "giving over," i.e., not selling potatoes by the pound but in approximate bulks that exceeded the amount one should get for the price at a market, was called *neappe*.[3] The seller who did not give *neappe* was thought to be cheap and would fall in the esteem of St. Johnians; conversely, the farmer who had a provision ground and was very generous with *neappe* would be highly regarded among fellow St. Johnians. St. Johnian generosity did not reach far enough, however, unless it went beyond *neappe*, sometimes as far as giving produce away outright.

Fish, the other major food on St. John, was also partly sold, partly shared. Since many people were not able to fish, they were ready to buy fish either on the beach, when the fishing boat came in, or delivered to their houses. After tending their fish pots, the fishermen pulled their boats up onto the shore, arranged the larger fish on strings, and carried them to homes where they regularly sold their catch. These strings, as long as a man's arm, were sold for five or ten cents. It was important that the fisherman was generous and put only large fish on the string. Small fish were not sold, and nobody would think of selling fish by the pound. After the fisherman had sold a string of fish to a householder, he often gave over, i.e., gave an extra fish or a few smaller fish. Some fishermen also gave these smaller fish away to the poorer people who could not afford to buy fish. One fisherman remembered being met by a group of women every time he came in from the sea. They would help him pull up the boat, and he gave them the little fish he did not feel were large enough to sell.

Though there was some direct exchange of fish for groundfood in certain areas of St. John, there was no bargaining and no direct exchange of so much fish for so many vegetables. Rather, a child might be sent off with some fish to "give" to a farmer. This farmer would then in return "give" the child some vegetables— whatever he thought was reasonable in relation to the first "gift." The farmer would never reject the fish but would accept whatever was given, and likewise the fisherman would receive whatever was given in return and would not refuse or complain that the quantity was too little. Thus, even when direct exchange took place, the people maintained the illusion that they were giving each other things and not actually bartering. The act of giving in this way was very important in St. Johnian life. People were judged for their "givishness," and someone who never shared with others was thought to be mean or low and something of a social outcast. Though some households could produce most of the food they needed, it was considered essential that such households be generous and give away whenever possible so that members of these households did not isolate themselves from the rest of the community. Thus the reason behind much of this giving seems to have been not so much economic as social. One of the old fishermen on the island told of having given fish to fishermen as skilled as he because the fish was a type particularly well-liked by the other men or by members of their households. Some St. Johnians explained that they gave because they "felt like" giving this fish to that household.

Many social occasions also involved gift giving. When someone paid a visit to a house, it was customary that the visitor was given something—groundfood, fish, or whatever the household could find to give. Indeed, many householders would have felt ashamed if they had nothing to give to a visitor. The giving of foodstuffs was highlighted at large festivities, such as weddings. One St. Johnian described her wedding, which took place during the early part of the century:

> The wedding was held in a house owned by my husband's sister, because she had a large house. We were all baking and cooking, preparing the wedding feast for days. Though we prepared

our own food, other people also sent us gifts of food. Mr. Thomas, whom I had worked for, sent a big pig, Cousin Alma sent some tarts, and other people sent bread. We had invited a lot of people, and they came from Cruz Bay, Coral Bay, all about. When the feast began, I and my husband, together with the minister and the older people, were first served. Then the other guests were served, and when I saw they needed somebody to serve the food, I started to do this, with my train and everything. We had plenty of food, I had never before seen so much food at one time: many different cakes, goat meat, bull soup, and so.

The importance of gifts is indicated in several ways in this description. It was very important for the families of the couple to be able to stage a large feast, where all could eat and drink as much as they liked, to show that the couple's families were not "mean" (i.e., cheap) or low. Former employers, friends, and relatives showed their high esteem for the couple by sending gifts of food for the wedding feast and by helping prepare the food; the people who helped prepare were the ones with whom the couple and the families had had the most intense exchange relationships during the years. The couple's families invited many islanders to the festivities, so many that they could not all be served at one time. The groom's sister gave the use of her house, the largest in the family, so that the feast could be held properly.

Because charcoal, baskets, and animals were produced primarily for export to St. Thomas so that the provision farmers could import necessary goods, these items were not given freely, as was domestic produce, but they were traded. Around 1900, most St. Johnians cooked with wood and had no need for charcoal. Later, the coal pot became popular, and by 1930 most St. Johnians probably used coal for cooking. Those who had no means to acquire charcoal were often single women, possibly with children, who could not manage the strenuous work associated with the burning of charcoal. If they wanted coal, they could offer to help a charcoal burner with his lighter tasks in return for some of the coal. As in the exchange of groundfood and fish, there was no initial bartering about how much coal for how many hours of work.

Though most animals kept by the provision farmer were intended for home use, occasionally one would be slaughtered for sale on St. John. Since there was no regular market on this island for selling meat, and since the meat had to be used before it spoiled, the person who was going to butcher an animal first made sure that all the meat was "engaged out." Meat was not a staple in the daily diet, as were fish and groundfood, and, apart from the immediate family, it was not given away freely. Yet it was customary to give *neappe* in the sale of beef, just as in the sale of fish and groundfood, even though beef was sold by the pound, being more valuable because it could readily be sold for cash on St. Thomas.

The exchange of goods also tied the peasants and the plantation owners together, though for rather different reasons. The estate owners were not regarded as part of the global St. Johnian family. They were not poor like the peasants, and few were tied to the peasants by kinship. The peasants emphasized the superior social and economic status of estate owners and addressed them with the titles "Mr.," "Mistress," or "Miss" preceding their last name. The estate owners were not thought to be without social responsibility toward the peasant community, however, and St. Johnians generally believed that the landowners should share the natural resources they owned. The estates' marginal land contained bush for charcoal burning, hillsides where cattle and goats could graze, and vines from which baskets could be woven. In return, the plantation owners had the right to demand a certain fee for the use of these resources; some, for example, asked for a third of the charcoal that was burned from estate wood.

Most owners, however, did not have such a "commercial" relationship with the users of their marginal land but chose to view its use as part of a system of social as well as economic exchange relations. These owners therefore did not permit the peasants to use their resources in exchange for a specific rent, but rather chose to "give" freely of resources they did not need. In exchange for the right to use the estate's resources because they were poor, the peasants were expected to show great respect and gratitude toward the owners, which they usually did by giving them produce. The peasants also preferred this social relationship to the owners, believing that it accorded them economic privileges not to be had otherwise. Many St. Johnians asked estate owners to be godparents for their children. The generous planter's relationship to the peasants had a strong patriarchal character. By not demanding anything, the planters placed the peasants in a posi-

tion of obligation. On the other hand, by treating the estate owners as patriarchs, the peasants pressured them to be as generous
as possible.

A St. Johnian described the situation on one estate:

> The owners of the estate didn't rule the people with an iron
> hand, but yet the people had respect for them. They were a
> very nice family, especially the old man. The big estate was his,
> but he just knew that it was there and his, everybody could use
> it, as if it were their own. We could make our own garden on
> the land, we got vines for making our fish traps, we burned our
> charcoal from the land, we could find employment cutting pas-
> ture for the cattle, and if someone needed milk, it was all right
> to milk one of the cows. You would then take the calf away from
> the cow overnight and milk the cow in the morning. If you
> needed a horse to go to the other end of the island, you could
> also borrow a horse. If you wanted to, you could give the old
> man one or two bags of your charcoal, but this was not some-
> thing which he demanded.

The view of plantation owners was clearly expressed by a descendant of a former estate owner:

> Though we used some of the property for pasture and other
> cultivation, there was plenty which was unused, and this we
> let the laborers use. We did not take anything from them for
> this, but if they wanted to give something we did not refuse. In
> fact, almost all of them offered us coal, which was the only thing
> that we did not have ourselves, and they also gave us the best
> of their provision foods. At the same time, as we received these
> things from them, we knew that they would do whatever work
> we asked them to do—usually for wages, of course—and they
> knew that we would help them, if there was any way we could
> do this.

Not all estate owners were as well liked as this one: some were
more calculating in their relationships with the small farmer. An
owner might require that the charcoal burner cut wood only
where the estate needed pasture, so the owner got the pasture
area cleared and at the same time demanded one of every three

bags of charcoal. The estate owner had a right to make such demands, but the relationship thereby became formal and the peasants would not go out of their way to help such an owner. Since
the owner was dependent upon cheap labor to tend the cattle, cut
the pasture, or pick the bay leaves, it probably paid off in the long
run to follow the more generous and popular course.

Exchange of labor

The exchange of cooperative work took three main forms: in partnership, by a club, and by lending a helping hand. Of these three
forms of cooperation, the club and the helping hand were the
most common.

In partnership, two men or more worked steadily together and
shared the proceeds from the goods they could produce, or they
sometimes simply took turns working for each other. There were
few tasks in provision farming that could not be done by the
household alone; individual members of households were usually
able to clear land and build terraces, till the garden, cut wood,
and burn wood for charcoal on their own. Most agricultural tasks
in particular were not dependent upon teamwork, so regular
partnerships most commonly occurred in fishing and sailing. It
was usually not difficult for a man who owned a rowboat to find a
partner, because many St. Johnians could not afford a boat and
would be able to fish only by entering into informal partnership
with someone who had one. If the partners were long-time friends,
they might divide the fish equally, or each would keep whatever
was caught in his own pots, without taking into consideration
that only one person owned the boat. Partners might also have a
formal relationship, owning and operating a boat together, sharing the proceeds.[4]

Most St. Johnians did not like formal partnership because it
bound them together with a certain person in ownership. The local saying "Partnership is leaky ship" expresses the problem
with common ownership very well. When several persons own a
boat in common, none of them takes the responsibility for the upkeep of the boat, so that none of them will stop a leak, which then
goes from bad to worse. Moreover, many did not like the idea of
commitment to working with the same person all the time, and
there were no special social activities associated with partner-

ship. Since one man could do most of the daily work himself, there were thus neither economic nor social reasons for working in partnership. Most St. Johnians therefore chose to work on their own and to depend on the club when they needed help with their work.

Most cooperative work involving a group of men was done in a single event called the club. These men worked together to help a person complete a task, such as clearing bush for a garden or pasture, cutting wood for charcoal, or constructing terraces for a garden. The person who arranged the club would in turn supply the workers with a meal and drinks and implicitly promise to return the favor. The person who arranged the club would begin to plan it several weeks ahead; and about a week before it was to be held, he would ask his friends and relatives whether they were able to work for him on a certain day, usually on a Saturday. The size of the club varied considerably from three or four up to thirty men; most common seems to have been a group of ten to fifteen. The person who held the club had to take into consideration that he would be expected to work in turn for all the people who worked for him, and therefore it might not be advantageous to invite a large number. Most St. Johnians characterized their fellow club workers as people with whom they got along well, including relatives, friends, young and old people. Most participants in the club system were small farmers or fishermen, but people with more special skills also participated in some clubs.

Though only men could participate in clubs, it is accurate to say that the household held the clubs, because the participants were friends or relatives of the household, not only of the man in charge of the club. Thus several participants might be related to an adult woman in the house and not to the man. When a household invited men to work in a club, these men would therefore be different from the men working in other clubs. The clubs were not closed groups consisting of the same persons taking turns for each other, as was the case in partnership. Rather, they centered around each household; since no two households had exactly the same social ties, no two clubs were alike.

When the club workers arrived in the morning they usually were given tea before they started to work. Around noon, they paused to eat a big meal provided by the household, and toward the end of the afternoon they stopped working. Throughout the day, rum was offered freely by the club holder, to keep up workers' spirits. It was very important to a St. Johnian to hold a good club, i.e., offer plenty of food and drink and not ask the workers to do an unreasonable amount of work during the day. Goats, hogs, and sheep were often slaughtered by the farmer to feed his club at work. Preparation of the meal could stretch over several days, and the woman in charge of the preparations often asked a friend to help her. Otherwise she did not participate in the club.

Although club work was understood to be reciprocal, the exchange value of the work performed was not formally measured and the work done in return could be of an entirely different kind. Even if a man participating in a club brought along two grown sons who lived in his household, he did not earn three days of club work from the man holding the club. The initial club holder was expected to "work back" just once per household. But if a man and his two sons, living apart, each with their own fields, participated in a club, all three could ask for return work from the initial club holder. This clearly illustrates that the households were central in the club system, not the individuals who did the club work.

Households that depended mostly on provision farming and fishing had the most need to hold clubs; households on the estates, which relied primarily on wage laborers, had less need for club work because their provision grounds were much smaller and they had little time for charcoal burning. Yet when they needed extra money—around Christmastime, for example— households on the estates would hold clubs to burn charcoal to sell for cash. Many male estate workers were active participants in clubs—so in economic terms they gave more labor than they received. They enjoyed the club work as a social occasion. When a task for the estate involved a great deal of heavy work, estate workers would ask the estate manager to hold a club. Many workers' club mates were more than willing to help with the estate work because they knew there would be plenty of good food and drink. The estate owner, though sponsoring the club, did not help with the work; he held the club mostly for the benefit of his workers. He would not be expected to "work back" when participants in the estate's club work later held their own clubs.[5]

Though most St. Johnians described the club system as being loosely organized and not dependent on a strict accounting of who

owed whom how many days' work for what, one could not continue to hold clubs without working in the clubs of others. As
long as there was a feeling of fairness, the system operated
smoothly; but if one person started to take advantage of it, soon
there would be dissatisfaction and refusals to participate. Not all
St. Johnians felt that it was fair for estates to hold clubs; they
refused to do work for estate owners. They reasoned that clubs
should be reserved for people who did not have the means to hire
others to get their work done. One St. Johnian, for example, decided to stop working in clubs because his club mates worked in a
club for a man who was well situated financially and ought
therefore to have paid for labor.

Clubs were mostly associated with farming and charcoal burning, but some clubs built houses, especially in the early period
when houses were still made of wattle and daub. (By the 1930s,
most St. John houses were made of wood; many older houses had
been destroyed by hurricanes in 1916, 1924, 1928, and 1932. In
the *House and Sanitary Survey* of 1935, only six wattle and daub
houses are listed [*EMB* 1].) Building a wattle house with a roof
made of sugarcane tops did not require specialized skills, and
several men could put up such a house quickly. Many households
first settled in a wattle house and remained there until the members could invest in a board house. Most houses were enlarged
as new members arrived in the household and more room was
needed. Many houses consisted of one room divided in two by a
partition, around which various additions were erected. Many St.
Johnians learned enough carpentry in their youth to help put up
a simple board house. Many such houses were therefore built by
club workers supervised by a carpenter, who did only the more
intricate work and got paid for it. Because the carpenter was
skilled and worked at his trade for a living, he was not expected
to join in the club with the unskilled workers. The club workers
had to be equals, so that they were capable of doing the same
work for each other. So a carpenter could not be invited to give
his labor to building a house but he could be invited to do gardening work.

The St. Johnians I interviewed emphasized that only men
could do club work; women could participate only indirectly by
cooking the food for the workers. But a woman could organize a
work group that functioned just like a club even if it could not be

called a club but instead was known as "lending a helping hand."
A single woman who headed her own household often organized
work parties to get help with the heaviest work. One woman explained:

> When I was alone and wanted to burn charcoal, I could pack
> and burn the wood myself, but I needed men to cut the wood for
> me. That was no problem, I could get up to fifteen men to work
> for me, all I had to do was to cook some food, and when I had
> the fifteen, I cooked a whole goat, a kerosene tin full. I usually
> cooked alone, but I could also get help from another woman.
> But the people who worked for me were only men. . . . I might
> then later help the men who had worked for me, for example,
> picking coal out of their charcoal pits if they needed to get some
> coal ready for a boat that was leaving for St. Thomas.

When the men had lent a helping hand, return help was not formally required; on the other hand, it would be advisable, if the
woman wished to organize more work parties. The ready availability of work parties was an important precondition for many
farm activities of the female-headed households that included no
adult men.

Lending a helping hand was a feature of everyday life. It was
especially important when small jobs had to be done in a hurry
and one or two extra persons were needed, as in the case of getting charcoal ready for shipment to St. Thomas. It was common
when small favors were asked of people with skills. Though all
major work requiring special skills had to be paid for, small jobs
often were requested of skilled persons as favors. Thus a carpenter might be asked to lend a helping hand with minor repair
work, or a seamstress might be asked to help make a dress, as in
this case:

> My mother did the sewing in the area. If people came to her
> and said: "I would like to have a dress sewed" and left the ma-
> terial there, she would sew it and charge them money for it.
> But if they came with the material and said "Cousin Doris,
> please help cut out this dress for me," and they sat down and
> worked on it with her, then she wouldn't charge them. And
> when they sat down and worked on it with her, she even had to

feed them in addition to helping them sew their dresses! But things were cheap, so nobody thought too much about that. We didn't think in terms of money at all.

Thus when exchange of labor included a social occasion, it did not involve money.

The exchange of goods and labor was regarded as part of the essence of life. It embodied the values that St. Johnians esteemed the most, such as "givishness," "generosity," and "cooperation." Persons who shared their produce with others, joined in the clubs, and gave a helping hand showed that they were the "common folks," ready to extend help and receive it from others. Those who did not were "mean" or "low." They did not want to share with anybody and were afraid to owe anybody anything:

There was a lot of giving in those days, there wasn't much sell-ing. It was a kind of exchange but there was no direct ex-change; that we call lowness. If you come with a pin and give it to the house that you are visiting, we call it lowness if the per-son who got the pin feels that she must give you a needle, be-fore you leave that house. Lowness is being exact; because you give me that, I must give you this on the dot. It didn't work that way. When I have something, I will give you. It wasn't so that because I have received something, I must give back right away, not at all. My mother couldn't give anybody any fish. Where would she get it from? My father didn't fish, so maybe my mother would cut up a dress for them or fix something for them, and then they brought fish for her. But you never had the feeling that this was direct payment for the dress or any-thing like that. If you wanted something sewn but had no fish, you would bring the things to get sewn anyway and not worry about having no fish. Another time, you would have the fish and nothing to be sewn. So it was whenever you needed some-thing or whenever you had something to give.

St. Johnians were well aware that the system of exchange as it was known on St. John functioned within a subsistence econ-omy: they did not give charcoal or meat freely. They also knew that generous sharing did not characterize market-oriented St. Thomas, whose competitive trading practices some St. Johnians called robbery. They realized that trading was necessary to earn cash, but they preferred to commission others to sell their produce because they disliked rough bargaining and feared that they would be cheated by the shrewd St. Thomians. One St. Johnian laughed loudly at the thought of having his wife sell his fish on St. Thomas instead of engaging a St. Thomian market woman: "That would have been impossible, she would have given it all away!"

Social sanctions: positive and negative

Though commercial trade was necessary, informal exchange transactions predominated on St. John and were regarded as its distinctive difference from St. Thomian society. The social signifi-cance of these relationships was apparent in rituals such as the wake held immediately following a death. As soon as St. Johnians were notified of a death, friends and relatives rallied around the bereaved family to help prepare for the funeral. Like a club, the wake involved collective work (many people compared it to the club when describing it). A work group dug the grave and made a coffin under the direction of a carpenter, who often charged little or nothing for this service. Women prepared the body by washing it, dressing it in proper clothes, and rubbing it with a mixture of lime, alcohol, and water. The wake was held through the night so that the bereaved family was not left alone. This was not a solemn occasion. As in club work, food, rum, and coffee were served. Dur-ing the night, as the people waited together for the dawn and the burial of the dead, many stories were told, often about the legend-ary spider Anansi, who had many powers and could get out of any situation (see Emmanuel 1974). Spooky stories about *jumbies*, which were spirits of people who "didn't die good" and therefore "haunted around bothering people," were also entertaining. When people left the house, they never said goodbye but left quietly so as to go unnoticed by the living or the dead, thus to ensure their safe passage home.

The following morning the deceased was buried on family land or, if there was none, in the Moravian or Lutheran cemetery. The "club" helped carry the body to the grave and bury it. Though there was no special invitation to attend the wake and help with the burial, the news that a friend or relative had died was enough reason to go to the home of the bereaved.

There were several social controls for St. Johnians who did not conform to the ideals of givishness and cooperation. St. Johnians appealed to the Danish *landfoged*/American administrator and to the Moravian minister to help them when they felt they had been wronged, and quarrels were quickly settled, usually before developing into major disputes. One case from the American period illustrates the role of the administrator as the guardian of the peasant social order: *A* used *B*'s net without *B*'s permission, and was then accused by *B* of having stolen the net. *A* explained that he had not stolen the net but had merely borrowed it, which he had felt free to do because he and *B* were very close friends and therefore could use each other's things as they wished. *A* elaborated on this, noting that about three months earlier he had brought sugarcane from Reef Bay, and as he had passed *B*'s house *B* had taken one of the canes, saying that "they were one," meaning that they as friends could do as they liked with each other's property. *B* confirmed this, adding that he had gotten angry at *A* only because *A* had returned the net in poor condition. It was agreed that *A* had to repair it and pay a fine of one dollar for future caution (*EMB* 3: 1921). When this conflict was discussed before the administrator, the source of the problem was brought out and settled in a way that the two parties could agree on. The St. Johnians often brought seemingly minor cases to be settled out of court—for example, a complaint about being told to go to hell.[6] Some of the most common conflicts in the peasant society are illustrated in the cases brought before the American administrator in the years 1921–30 (*EMB* 3). Eighteen cases were brought for stealing, which accounted for 20 percent of the total; fifteen for fighting (17 percent); fourteen for quarreling (15 percent); thirteen for slander (14 percent); eleven for failure to contribute child support (12 percent); ten for animals trespassing (11 percent); and ten for various other reasons (11 percent).

Although the administrator (and minister) could enforce the law and discourage conflicts of various kinds, they could not force people to be generous and givish in their daily social intercourse. Against persons who were mean or standoffish, there were less formal sanctions, which are revealed in beliefs about witchcraft and life after death. A common reason for imposing such sanctions was improper behavior by a person who had achieved material success. St. Johnians accepted two categories of people: the rich and the poor. The rich were the large estate owners, who could afford to employ others and owned extensive properties. The poor were common folks, who relied on clubs when they needed extra help, and who owned an acre or two and practiced small farming and fishing. These two categories were fixed, and people who attempted to behave like the rich were frowned upon, because such behavior included keeping things to themselves and not sharing as they should. People who prospered too much were not popular. The general social sanction against such mean, low, selfish persons was to make them social outcasts and exclude them from the exchange network. More serious sanctions against persons who continued to keep to themselves or were simply too successful often involved accusations of witchcraft, or *obeah*.[7]

The following story demonstrates how a successful person could be condemned by the community as a practitioner of *obeah*.

> Since I became big and left my family, my father started to work out at an estate nearby, because he couldn't do anything on his own land. This was because a woman had done *obeah* to his land. His garden would bear nothing; the potatoes would grow to long vines and nothing else, and the bananas just grew to become little ones, which then dropped to the ground. So my father decided to give up the ground and started to work on an estate. My father knew that this woman had set *obeah* on him, because everyone knew the kind she was. She had several people in that condition and ruined many people's crops, and she also killed people. There were at least three people that she killed: my *nin* [godmother], my cousin's mother, and my husband's grandfather. One she gave rum, and the other *deku* [a dish of cornmeal]. The one who drank the rum coughed it up and couldn't walk and died. And the one who ate the *deku* tried to leave the house, and by the time she got to the door, she fell down. This woman did *obeah* to others, because she wanted to have everything herself and nobody else to have. In this way, everybody must be a beggar at her house.

The woman accused of *obeah* had a large garden with fine provision crops, whereas her neighbors' gardens failed miserably for unknown reasons. The woman did not share her produce but kept it to herself, so that the people in need had to come to her and actually beg her for food. At about the same time, a number of people died, and the woman, already suspected of having used shady methods in gaining wealth and power, was accused of having "set *obeah* on" her neighbors.

The belief in *obeah* thus excused the envy or jealousy provoked by other persons' success. In order not to be suspected of *obeah*, most St. Johnians were wary of displaying any wealth that they might have. Most St. Johnians lived in modest houses and wore simple, often ragged clothes except on Sundays, when they went to church in their best outfit. By being inconspicuous, givish, and amiable in social intercourse, a St. Johnian could thus keep clear of accusations of *obeah*. Though it was probably more common to accuse a questionable person—for example, a social outcast—of having "set *obeah* on others" than it was to practice *obeah*, there was no doubt that some people did use *obeah* or gave the appearance of using it as a way of keeping others in line. Chicken entrails on someone's doorstep, for example, might be enough to remind them that they were not sharing their groundfood.[8]

Another form of social control related to the supernatural was the generally accepted belief that low persons would never find rest after death. Past sinners were thought to turn into *jumbies*, the spirits of people "who didn't die good" and were forced to haunt the earth at night. A *jumbie* story was told by a woman who, as a child, was surprised by a huge crab while walking along an estate boundary. When she came home, after barely escaping being pinched, she was told by her parents that this was the *jumbie* of a man who had stolen other people's land by moving the property boundary posts. Even after death he was forced to continuously guard the boundary of his estate, visible at night either as a man in black or as a big crab. The prospect of having to guard one's riches after death, though it probably did not by itself prevent anyone from taking advantage of others, was an important part of the belief system and social sanctions that furthered the spirit of cooperation and sharing rather than of individual acquisitiveness and competition.

St. Johnians recognized two basic reasons for engaging in exchanges with one another. Exchanges signaled that they were all poor people who had to help each other, a sentiment expressed in a St. Johnian proverb: "Changie for changie, black dog for black dog." Exchanges also symbolized that, though they were poor, they were not equally poor and therefore some persons would have a surplus to share that others might need. The young and strong would have an easier time providing for themselves than would the old and weak, just as those with few children had relatively more material resources to share than did those with many children. Though some peasants were better off than others, their situations were not permanent, and everyone had to work to subsist. The economic foundation of any household could be removed in one stroke of bad luck, leaving its members destitute. It was therefore regarded as important to share whenever possible so that others would be willing to share when the situation was reversed, as in the following case:

> I was for many years a fisherman, and I always used to give small fish to the women who waited for me on the beach, after I had tended my fish pots. A number of years ago, I was in an accident which made me an invalid, so that I was no longer able to fish. A few days after I had returned from the hospital I received a letter from one of the women that I had given fish for many years. In it was a five-dollar bill and a note which read: "This is for the bread you have cast on the water!" When I read it, I said to myself: "Well, I cast in good time!"

Receiving help therefore was not shameful but a reason to be proud because it was the result of many years of good citizenship in the St. Johnian community.

Networks and family structure

If this study of St. John had focused on household structure alone, a most significant aspect of the family would have been left out. Households were important entities. They constituted formal declarations of affinal relationships, and they were the basic units of production. They were, however, enveloped in a network of social and economic exchanges of goods and labor. Among close relatives this network was so tight that it overrode, to a large degree, the pooling of resources that has been described as a characteristic feature of households (Sahlins 1972: 94–95). If the households pooled anything, it was exchange relations rather than the resources they owned or produced themselves. Households were most important as nuclei in the network of exchange and were not regarded as separate families like the European or American nuclear family. The family was that network of relatives who exchanged freely with each other, and it could be extended almost indefinitely as the need arose. A St. Johnian, reflecting on the difference between the traditional local family and the American family, noted: "In the United States they think of husband, wife, and children, when they talk about the family. It is not so here, our family includes all known relatives, and it can go as far as second, third, fourth, or maybe even fifth cousin. . . ."

Given the obvious importance of the interconnection of exchange networks and households, it makes sense to view them both as central to Afro-Caribbean family structure. Many elements found in the St. Johnian social structure have been noted elsewhere by other researchers. Family land and large kin networks solidified in common proprietorship have been found to exist widely in the Caribbean, just as the exchange of labor, goods, and even children has been reported in varying forms (see, for example, Clarke 1953, 1957; Besson 1979, 1981; Cumper 1958; M. G. Smith 1973; Wilson 1973; Sanford 1975; Goossen 1972). The importance of the exchange network to the interpretation of the "problematic" family has been largely neglected. The Afro-Caribbean family has been interpreted primarily as a response to social and economic deprivation, as a consequence of slavery, as an atavistic African inheritance, or as a consequence of some other single causative factor.

Because social scientists have tended to fix on the nuclear family or corporate descent groups as established norms, the Afro-Caribbean family has come to be perceived negatively—in the sense that it is seen as an anomaly, a residue, a product of deprivation of some sort rather than as a positive expression of a given social order (Olwig 1981a). R. T. Smith, in reevaluating his earlier research, has come to see that the family system of the lower classes, who constitute the bulk of the Afro-Caribbean population, may rather be a different sort of social organization. He views the "lower classes" as displaying "a tendency to keep open as many possible kinship links as is feasible, a tendency which is in sharp contrast to the middle-class practice of stressing the self-sufficiency of the husband-wife team" (1970: 68). He concludes that since such kin ties are important to the family, it must be understood in this light (see also Smith 1978b). A few recent studies have similarly emphasized the link between the exchange network and kinship, but they still interpret this family form in terms of lower-class status or poverty (Stack 1970, 1974; S. E. Brown 1977; Gussler 1980). The basis of these studies— purely synchronic field data—may be the cause of their difficulty in seeing the family network system as part of an Afro-Caribbean tradition. As noted by Helms, "the functional concept of adaptation must be accorded a temporal dimension of some depth if cultural processes are to be properly recognized" (1981: 77).

In the present study, I have sought to take a historical approach to the family networks to uncover the "cultural processes" behind their formation. During the period when the plantation society predominated, kin networks were important elements in the slaves' system of social reproduction; they developed both as part of and in opposition to the system of slavery and plantation cultivation within which St. Johnian culture first emerged. When the plantation society collapsed after emancipation, the slaves' system of reproduction became the basis of a peasant society. The exchange networks, based on a perception of St. Johnians as members of "one big family," became the organizing principle of the peasant society, gradually developing into institutions known throughout the Caribbean peasant communities originally established by freed slaves. These institutions—family land, clubs, the lending of children—were built on exchange relationships among real or fictive kinsmen. Just as during slavery, these exchange relationships provided the means for the social reproduction of the peasantry—for its physical survival and the preservation of its unique way of life. They were, like their antecedent forms, mechanisms of adaptation as well as resistance to the repressiveness of the colonial order. Family land, clubs, and loaning of children could not emerge as formalized institutions during slavery. Structural antecedents of these practices can be seen, however, in the slaves' system of social reproduction, which included such customs as common access to land resources, mutual help in farming, and temporary placement of children in the homes of relatives or godparents.

The particular characteristics of exchange and land distribution described in this study were observed mainly in peasant communities similar to each other. This does not mean, however, that we are dealing with a peasant phenomenon unencountered in more complex societies having wage economies. The networks of exchange found in urban areas (see Stack 1970, 1974) or in plantation societies (see Gussler 1980), though expressed in different ways, may in fact be part of a general Afro-American sociocultural system with long historic roots inasmuch as West Indians and American blacks share a similar history as plantation slaves in the Americas and a common African background. Furthermore, though they retain distinctive differences, West Indian societies are strikingly fluid and mobile populations. West Indians are world citizens who have traveled widely, have contacts throughout the Caribbean, and whose communities absorb a flow of migrants from many places.

St. John's history has documented the development of the link between community exchange systems and family forms. The St. Johnian conditions were not "ideal," however, in any "idyllic" sense, though they may have seemed so to some nostalgic St. Johnians. Poverty has stalked the island, and strict societal controls have created many hardships. In modern St. John, as elsewhere in the West Indies, the special role of the family is by no means as clear as it used to be. Against the background of the society's history, the exchange network is readily discernible as important in maintaining the identity of a community now being transformed by the introduction of a tourism industry. At the same time, this exchange network can be viewed as part of the reason the St. Johnians have found it difficult to take advantage of the newly introduced market economy.

7

The Tourism Society

AFTER THE collapse of the sugar plantations, St. John by and large remained outside the sphere of major economic interests. During the 1950s, almost a hundred years later, the island along with St. Thomas and St. Croix reemerged as a focus of economic investment—this time as a vacation paradise for tourists from Western countries. While traveling for pleasure dates back several centuries, tourism was dominated by a small upper class until World War I. During the 1930s and 1940s, a growing number of wage earners received vacation with pay, providing a major impetus for the development of vacation centers. After World War II, with rising wages and improved large-scale commercial air travel, mass tourism to distant locations like the tropics became reality. In 1961, international tourism counted 72 million tourist arrivals; in 1970, 168 million tourist arrivals (Popovic 1972: 10, 13); and for the 1980s, a projected 300 million per year (Kitaj 1981: 1). In 1978, the West Indies received more than 5 million tourists, originating primarily from the United States (64 percent), Europe (10 percent), and Canada (7 percent) (Holder 1981: 31). The American Virgin Islands account for over a million tourists every year (Moore 1979). Tourism involves massive economic investments, primarily by large multinational corporations. Taking both national and international tourism into account, in 1976, for example, the industry contributed an estimated 80 billion dollars to the total world economy (V. Smith 1978: 1).

Tourism inflicts enormous changes on local populations, who must adapt to the large-scale developments built to house, feed, and entertain the tourists. On St. John, the social and economic

changes that have occurred since the early 1950s have completely changed the peasant society.

Throughout the history of the Danish/American West Indies,
the islands have been praised for their scenic beauty and pleasant climate, St. John not the least of these. In the 1790s, the
Danish schoolmaster Hans West delighted in the views, bays,
and even the rocks on St. John, describing the cliffs at Mary's
Point as filled with "glimmer which in the sunshine exhibit a
glorious halo" (1793: 338). The Danish botanist A. S. Ørsted,
who visited the West Indian islands in the 1840s, depicted St.
John as an island of "exceptional richness of natural beauty"
with its steep hillsides and deep valleys, mountaintops with wide
views over forests to the "deep blue of the ocean and the count-
less dark quays and islands" (Bergsøe 1853: 569–70). In the early
American period, an article in the New York *Herald-Tribune*
reported that "St. Thomas is one of the most beautiful islands
imaginable, but the views from the heights of St. John are almost
lovelier. Every new summit brought its fresh arrangement of
bold headlands, white beaches, blue water above coral reefs, and
a sea so clear that as the big cumulus clouds rolled slowly over-
head, one could see their shadows traveling across the ocean bot-
tom. ... The swimming is nothing short of heavenly—crystal
clear water, white sand beaches and little reef-protected bays so
clear, generally, that in a small boat you seem suspended in air"
(quoted in *Saint Thomas Mail Notes*, December 4, 1933).

In the Danish period the islands were described as a delightful
backdrop incidental to other pursuits, but in the American period, the economic value of nature began to be noted. Particularly
in St. John, where there was little activity outside the subsistence sphere, tourism was quickly perceived as a means of induc-
ing economic development on the island. In his report to the U.S.
Congress in 1930, Herbert D. Brown suggested that "If tourists
come to other islands, they would make the acquaintance of St.
John and see how beautiful it is and in time villas and possibly
hotels would rise up there. Good roads and good gardens would
be demanded" (1930: 464). The first small tourism development
took place on St. John in the 1940s, when the cattle estate Caneel
Bay was purchased by the Danish West Indian Company to be
converted into a small hotel. The company sold this St. John
property within a few years, because few visitors were coming to

the island at the time. The hotel continued under new ownership, and it offered virtually the only possibility of regular wage employment on the island.

In the 1950s, St. Thomas became a popular destination for Caribbean cruise ships sailing from Miami. Hotels and condominiums began to dot the landscape of St. Thomas and St. Croix as well. On St. John tourist development took a rather different turn, when the Virgin Islands National Park was created in 1956 by an act of Congress (Hatch 1972: 103). The man responsible was Laurance Rockefeller, who by the mid-1950s had purchased a number of cattle estates, covering almost half of the island's total acreage. He gave the estate land to the federal government with the stipulation that it be turned into a national park. He also acquired the modest resort on Caneel Bay, which, with its grounds, was to be kept as private property (an "inholding") within the park and developed into an exclusive hotel to be operated by Rock Resorts.

The national park at first was welcomed on the island. During the 1930s, St. John had received economic relief from the "make work" programs of the New Deal. With the advent of the Second World War and the revival of the mainland economy, these programs had been cut; while the United States proper returned to full employment, the St. Johnians were again faced with having to emigrate for work or to rely on the uncertainties of subsistence farming and fishing. The introduction of a national park administered by the federal government, which had also been responsible for the economic aid of the 1930s, appeared to offer new opportunities to the islanders. The *National Geographic* magazine quoted an assistant to the island's administrator: "Most everybody likes the idea. . . . Park development would bring increased employment and a better standard of living, and yet our hills would not be defaced with billboards and hot-dog stands" (Scofield 1956: 227).

Surveying St. John today, more than twenty-five years later, one sees the economic promise of the park seemingly fulfilled. The island—which once harbored fewer than 800 peasants and fishermen, often dependent upon cash remittances from relatives working abroad, living mostly in two-room wooden cottages without indoor plumbing, electricity, or telephones, their only means of transportation a donkey or a horse—has undergone a dramatic transformation. The population of almost 2,500 persons is now sustained by wage employment that allows many of them to live in modern housing and own cars. Affluence finally seems to have come to St. John. On the surface, the establishment of the park and the growth of tourism have been a great benefit to the island society. The old plantations have become public property to be enjoyed by all, while many new economic opportunities brought by tourism have carried the peasants into the mainstream of modern Western life.

However, the new developments have not been of unquestionable benefit to St. Johnians. The park has been developed as a "nature area" park, following American concepts of nature which are quite foreign on St. John. St. Johnians' access to the economic resources of the park lands has been restricted, indirectly limiting severely their traditional use of the environment. Furthermore, the tourist industry has created only limited economic opportunities for St. Johnians. It is symptomatic of negative local attitudes toward the park that, even though the American government called for the original park of approximately 5,000 acres to be expanded to 9,500 acres, by the late 1970s the park area had increased to only slightly more than 6,500 acres. There is a great deal of private property (owned both by native St. Johnians and others) inside the park boundaries that the owners will not sell. The Park Service has not succeeded in acquiring this land after twenty-five years of trying, despite the fact that millions of dollars have been appropriated for land acquisition. It is questionable whether the park will ever attain the projected 9,500 acres (more than three-quarters of the island's 12,000 acres) approved by Congress.[1]

When the park was established in 1956, many St. Johnians were already employed at Caneel Bay estate, working on the expansion and remodeling of the original hotel into an exclusive resort. A large number of them continued to work for the new management. Some St. Johnians, however, still were at least partly dependent upon the resources of the estate land that had become the park, and they soon discovered that their traditional informal rights to these resources had been severely curtailed by the Park Service. The general policy adopted by the Service dictated that the land was to be "managed 'back' toward the pristine condition" (Robinson 1974: 44–48) that had prevailed "when the area was first visited by the white man" (*Administrative Policies* 1970: 101, 111).

The Park Service on the island was following established American conceptions of nature area parks. The first American national park had been founded in 1872 at Yellowstone in the Rocky Mountains. According to William Everhart of the National Park Service's Department of Interpretation, the concept of the nature area park arose with the loss of the American frontier. As the pioneers were exploring and settling the last areas of the West, says Everhart, the American public began to realize the great loss in natural resources that had been the result of the continental conquest. They became interested in establishing national parks where these original resources could be preserved and shown to the American people (Everhart 1972: 3–13). National parks are thus basically intended to be "islands within a civilized world where the visitor can be primarily imbued and influenced by the forces and components of nature . . ." (*Final Report* 1973: 116). Or, in the words of one of the original leaders of the conservation movement, John Muir, parks are areas to which the "nerve-shaken" and "over-civilized" American urban sector can return to find the true "fountains of life" (1976 [1901, 1912]: 71–72).

When the park was formally established on St. John, the Park Service undertook the great task of undoing the effect of almost 250 years of cultivation. Further agricultural usage of park land was prohibited. If a St. Johnian had a garden plot under cultivation on land acquired by the Park Service, the plot could continue to be cultivated; however, no more land could be cleared for new plots. The St. Johnian system of extensive swidden agriculture was thus rendered untenable, because the soil in the operating garden plots was depleted within a few years, and new areas could not be cleared. Cattle grazing was also outlawed. Previously, during periods of drought farmers could turn their cattle loose on nearby estate land and thus manage to feed the cattle through the dry months. Now this was forbidden, and when drought set in the St. Johnians were forced to slaughter their cattle.

Even though hunting and trapping had never been part of the local economic pattern (except for the occasional killing of wild pigs and mongooses, which kill domestic fowl), the park set up large signs prohibiting hunting, trapping, carrying "unsealed firearms," allowing dogs to run loose on park property, etc. There was a fine of $500 or six months in prison for any person violating park rules. Signs were posted on beaches that were "otherwise unspoilt and deserted" (Eggleston 1959). One visitor to St. John compared this practice to putting "a barbed wire fence around the peak of Mt. Everest" (ibid.: 35).

The Park Service did not prohibit all economic activity in the park area, believing it necessary to provide visitors to the park with modern facilities, since "urban society ... [is] not prepared to cope with wilderness camping" (*Administrative Policies for the Historical Areas* 1973: 100). Trails have been cut in the park area on St. John, and there are trailside exhibits explaining the natural surroundings to the visitors. A paved road has been constructed through the most scenic area of the park. At one beach, Cinnamon Bay, there is a camping complex with tents and concrete block cottages, dining facilities, and a commissary. Facilities have been established for swimmers at all the beaches held by the Park Service.

Tourist facilities have also been developed by private businesses on inholdings within the park. The largest, Caneel Bay Plantation, contains some of the best beaches on the island and has its own ferry service, laundry facilities, power plant, and desalination plant. This development is a permanent inholding within the park, offering the most exclusive services to those who are not satisfied with a tent at the Cinnamon Bay Campground, which is also run by Caneel Bay Plantation. A few years ago a private campground appeared on another inholding, at Maho Bay. It is more modern than the campground owned by the Park Service but not as expensive as Caneel Bay Plantation.

A large number of St. Johnians worked at Caneel Bay in the mid-fifties, and it is difficult to find many St. Johnians over forty-five years of age today who have not at some point in their lives worked at the resort. The great rush to find employment at Caneel Bay Plantation (located near Cruz Bay) and the final abandonment of extensive farming are clearly reflected in the population census returns from the period (see Table 22). The total population of the four rural districts—Coral Bay, East End, Maho Bay, and Reef Bay—thus declined from 470 in 1950 to 326 in 1960, to 232 in 1970. The great increase in population in Cruz Bay is not accounted for entirely by St. Johnians moving into the Cruz Bay area, but is also attributable to the fact that there has been a significant immigration to the island, as will be discussed later.

The economic impact of the national park and Caneel Bay Plantation on the local population is indicated by the statistics on the types of visitor-days the tourists spent in the park in 1977, compiled by park officials (see Table 23). More than 50,000, or about one-sixth, of the visitor-days are accounted for by guests at the Caneel Bay Plantation. Caneel Bay Plantation was the first economic opportunity presented to the St. Johnians in connection with the park development. Transforming a small hotel into an exclusive resort on the 178-acre plantation entailed the building of a large complex of modern buildings and thus a considerable work force. Even though a great many St. Johnians (including some who had formerly had to leave the island to find work) sought construction jobs at Caneel Bay Plantation, the development was so extensive that it was necessary to recruit workers from other West Indian islands to complete it. When the hotel

Table 22. Population Movements on St. John, 1940–70

	1940	1950	1960	1970
Coral Bay	316	305	260	172
Cruz Bay	263	279	599	1,497
East End	77	65	32	26
Maho Bay	52	39	16	15
Reef Bay	14	61	18	19

Source: *Census of the U.S. Virgin Islands*, 1970.

Table 23. Number and Type of Visitor-days, St. John, 1977

Caneel Bay Plantation registered guests	43,529
Caneel Bay Plantation day visitors	8,032
Cinnamon Bay Campground	30,390
Maho Bay Campground	4,862
Organized land tours	61,424
Organized boat tours	6,669
Beach users	48,855
Boat users	85,297
Virgin Islands Ecological Research Station	53
Total	289,111

Source: Virgin Islands National Park, *Visitor Usage of the Park,* 1977.

was finished, a large number of St. Johnians and British Virgin Islanders found work there as maids, maintenance men, kitchen helpers, guards, and so on. Others worked for the ferry service that runs from St. Thomas, where the nearest airport is located, directly to Caneel Bay.

During the years since the resort opened, most St. Johnians have left Caneel Bay Plantation because of dissatisfaction with the hotel's working conditions and the growing competitive opportunities for employment elsewhere (particularly in the government sector). Of the Caneel Bay Plantation work force of about 400 in February 1978, only about 50, or 12½ percent, were native Virgin Islanders. St. Johnians who have left complain that they were confined to the lower-echelon jobs at the hotel and were offered only minimal wages, no matter how much experience they had acquired during the years of work at the hotel. As St. Johnians left the hotel, they were replaced primarily by West Indians from the Lesser Antilles. To them the American wages seem high, and they are eager to accept working conditions that were unacceptable to the St. Johnians. The United States Immigration Service obliged by issuing temporary work and residence permits until the foreign workers could achieve status as permanent residents. Consequently, many British West Indians have entered St. John as "certified workers" or "bonded workers," as they are widely known, because they are only able to stay on the island as long as they work for the person or firm that has employed or "bonded" them. Most of the 350 nonnative employees at Caneel Bay Plantation originally came from the British West Indies on bonds. Until the late 1970s, they lived in specially constructed barracks, isolated from the remaining population of the island. In February 1978, about 40 were still "certified aliens," some of whom had been employed by Caneel Bay Plantation for more than fifteen years. The labor certification system has since been abandoned and the remaining bonded aliens issued permanent immigration visas. Since a large number of British West Indians are still willing to take work at Caneel Bay Plantation for low wages, it has not been possible for St. Johnians to pressure the hotel into offering them better conditions. The hotel is therefore no longer an important employer for the native population.

More than 30,000 of the visitor-days shown in Table 23 were spent at the Cinnamon Bay Campground, which is owned by the Park Service. This facility is concessioned out to be run by

Caneel Bay Plantation, which sets the working conditions and wages; the campground employees are included in the statistics on the Caneel Bay work force. Maho Bay Campground, which accounted for nearly 5,000 visitor-days in the park, is owned and developed by Americans and employs few local people.

The native population derives the most benefit from the organized land tours and the beach users, who totaled about 110,000, or more than one-third, of the visitor-days in 1977. Most organized land tours are by American day visitors to St. John, who come from St. Thomas, a popular destination for Caribbean cruises. Visitors are either booked on a tour of the island by a bus or they engage a taxi driver when they arrive in Cruz Bay, the main settlement on St. John. In 1978, more than 120 licensed taxi drivers chauffeured these visitors around the island; slightly more than a quarter were full-time taxi drivers, while the remainder had other primary employment. Taxi driving is economically viable only between the end of November and the beginning of April, the northern winter, when most tourists are on the island. It is an important source of supplementary income, for both the native population and immigrants who have attained permanent resident status.

Some tourist beach users live in rented cottages or houses outside the park and drive a rented vehicle. There are two major rental agencies, one owned by Americans, the other by a British West Indian. Vehicle rental businesses employ only a handful of persons full time, and it is important largely as a supplement to other economic activities, such as taxi driving or wage employment. A number of beach users are not tourists but part-time residents, primarily retired Americans who have built winter houses on the island. The construction of these houses has employed mostly British West Indian workers.

Many organized boat tours are run by Caneel Bay Plantation, which, as the park's concessionaire, has the right to supply boating services within park waters. Some boat services are run by local boats; they do most of their business transporting people between St. Thomas and Cruz Bay, which is outside the park. The boat users listed in Table 23 were largely Americans either sailing their own boats or chartering or renting a sailboat from American residents on St. John. Persons staying at the Virgin Islands Ecological Research Station, which is located on park land, add little to the local economy; the research station employs only one or two St. Johnians full time.

Apart from about 100 full-time jobs provided by the park-related economic activities, approximately 70 jobs have been created by the Park Service itself, "technician" jobs in park maintenance and tourist guidance. While 80 percent of the present Park Service work force is recruited in the Virgin Islands, these park employees occupy the lower positions. They have little influence on decision making, which is in the hands of professional rangers, all but two of whom are Americans who normally spend only a few years on St. John before they are promoted and assigned to another park. This system, which makes promotion contingent upon transferral to another park (Everhart 1972: 52), means that native Virgin Islanders cannot, as a rule, achieve supervisory park positions on St. John.

Some St. Johnians are involved in tourist-related activities outside the park such as renting cottages or running stores and restaurants. Most rentals of vacation houses are administered by an agency run by American residents on the island; it rents mostly American-owned homes. Most stores catering to tourists are also run by American residents. Native-run stores and restaurants are supported largely by the local population, not by tourism. In general, tourists make relatively little use of the few commercial facilities that have emerged outside the park, though economic activity is increasing in the Cruz Bay area. They come to St. John primarily to use the park's beaches or lodging facilities, which are completely self-sufficient and do not encourage them to visit areas outside the park. Most guests at Caneel Bay Plantation, for example, rarely venture outside the entrance gates but spend virtually their entire stay within the resort. They do not even have to pass through Cruz Bay, since the resort has direct ferry service from St. Thomas to Caneel Bay. It is not unusual to meet Americans who have spent several days at Caneel Bay Plantation without knowing that there is a community of local people on the island outside the park. Campers or day visitors only pass briefly through Cruz Bay en route between St. Thomas and their destination in the park, and usually spend little time outside the park.

While the National Park has thus created a great deal of economic activity on St. John and provides the main income for about 150 American Virgin Islanders (including a number of St. Thomians and Crucians), most jobs are under the supervision of Americans and islanders are not involved as private entrepreneurs. Transportation of tourists is the main exception; it is the tourist-related economic activity in which St. Johnians are most active. Most, however, have sought work outside the tourist sector in the local government, which expanded rapidly during the 1960s on all three American islands. During the early 1960s about 2,700 people were employed by the Virgin Islands government; by the late 1960s, this had increased to over 7,000, perhaps 75 percent of the native-born adult Virgin Islanders (O'Neill 1972: 72). During the 1970s, this figure continued to increase, though not as dramatically. The growing number of government employees was a function of the more extensive infrastructure that developed as tourism increased. On St. John, for example, it was necessary to transform donkey paths into paved roads; expand the electrical power system, which was introduced in Cruz Bay just before tourism set in; and establish a telephone system (part of the infrastructure but not owned by the government). The police force of two full-time constables was increased considerably; a fire department, a health clinic, and a day-care center for preschool children were created. These developments were paid for partly by increases in local taxes and partly through arrangements with the federal government, which returned federal taxes to the islands, including excise taxes "collected on Virgin Islands products [rum] to the mainland" (Lewis 1972: 140). The Virgin Islands were also able to benefit from a number of special grants and loans available to American states, and from federal social service programs designed to assist minority groups and the economically underprivileged.

A steady influx of foreign workers, largely from the British West Indian islands, have entered the job market in the past three decades. From 1950 to 1954, 14 legal immigrants arrived in St. John; from 1955 to 1959, when Caneel Bay Plantation and the park were developed, 52 moved to the island; from 1960 to 1970, 373 entered (*Census of the Virgin Islands* 1970).[2] During the 1970s, this immigration continued, as resident aliens sent for relatives back home. Today, most manual labor is performed by foreign-born persons, and an increasing number of government jobs and white-collar jobs are held by permanent residents of British West Indian origin.

St. Johnian attitudes toward Caneel Bay Plantation, the park, and tourism in general are rather mixed. Most St. Johnians emphasize that the park has brought about positive changes. One St. Johnian summed up these feelings: "There is no question that

the island has benefited from the park. The park attracts a lot of
tourists who bring money to the island. The park has also taught
us to be more appreciative of the natural beauty and peacefulness of the island. We now know that we don't want to cover
St. John with hotels and housing projects, whereas formerly we
were embarrassed to admit that we came from the jungle on St.
John." There is also general agreement, however, that the park
has not been managed or developed in the best interest of the native population. Most conflicts have arisen because the Park Service, in the words of one St. Johnian, assumes that "what is good
for Yellowstone is good for St. John!" In other words, the park is
administered and developed as if it were a large tract of "wilderness" situated in a sparsely populated western American state,
despite the fact that it is located on a tiny, relatively densely populated island.

One local leader noted: "I am convinced that sooner or later
the park must give some of its land back. The island has a total of
12,000 acres, and there is less than 3,000 that is left undeveloped
and accessible to use. But it is available only at thirty to forty
thousand dollars an acre. The millionaires are virtually outbid-
ding each other buying the land, and so the locals can't purchase
any. I think that the local government will have to ask the park
for land for a school, for public facilities, and for roads. The Virgin Islands government has only fifty-five acres of the total of
twelve thousand acres on the island. The park has almost seven
thousand acres at this point, and most cannot be touched or even
seen, as it is not possible to get to it." The local people are also
beginning to experience difficulty obtaining house lots. A young
man complained that "there is a lot of resentment among the locals because the park occupies so much land, as there is a great
deal of pressure to get land to build houses, and so on, and the
result is that people live crowded in small areas and pay exorbi-
tant prices for tiny lots. I think that in a few years there may be a
big explosion among the locals against the park!"

Many also expressed serious reservations about the "wilderness" landscape the Park Service is developing. They did not accept the idea that a park must emphasize preservation of undisturbed nature. As one person interviewed expressed it, "I
don't see what kind of nature it is the park wants to preserve.
There are no redwood trees or any vegetation that is of significance in itself. As it is now, the park is just preserving bush,

mongooses, and jackasses!" They would like to see various kinds of land usage represented in the park. One person explained, "I like wilderness in certain areas, so that I can sit on a rock in peace and quiet. But I also like to see cows and I love the smell of mangoes." Another said, "The park should understand that the land is not just to look at, but that it provides, and that the locals appreciate land as a source of food. The natives lived in harmony with nature before the Park Service arrived. They didn't have to be taught by the Park Service about ecology. The island was beautiful when it was filled with cows and grass."

In recent years, the Park Service has begun to provide "living history" programs at an old sugar plantation, Annaberg, showing how the peasant population used the natural resources on the island. Though the program is supervised by the Park Service, it is financed by the Eastern National Park and Monument Association, a nonprofit corporation. Some St. Johnians wish the park would expand this program, while others do not like it. One person explained, "The living history program is artificial and condescending toward the local population. I cannot identify with the little garden they have at Annaberg."

In some ways, the presence of the park has meant that the whole island effectively has been set aside as a "nature island." Even though the island's infrastructure was improved with the advent of tourism during the 1950s, it is totally inadequate to accommodate any major new developments. The electrical power system breaks down regularly; the paved roads are constantly washed out after heavy downpours, and many new roads remain unpaved.[3] There is no piped water system, each building relying on rainwater collected in its own cistern. There is no public transportation, and most business has to be conducted on St. Thomas; there is, for example, no supermarket on the island. Classifying St. John as a nature island seems to include the assumption that major expenditures on the part of the government to improve the infrastructure are not necessary. Any major new tourist development either must convince the local government to expand services before it is constructed or it must be able to provide its own, as Caneel Bay does. It is no wonder that after twenty-five years Caneel Bay remains the only large hotel on the island. Furthermore, the "natural" look of the island has attracted a large number of continentals, i.e., Americans who have chosen to reside on St. John, either permanently or during the northern winter months. Most have built their own houses, and this has given rise to a construction industry, mostly controlled by whites and employing people of British West Indian origin. These residents actively promote the "natural" appearance of the island and resist most attempts by the local population to "modernize" the island. Most of the Americans have fled from the hectic urban life of industrial America to enjoy a more leisurely life in the tropics and are not interested in an increase in tourism on the island. The local people, however, are trying to make their living and enjoy some of the material benefits of the tourism economy that has descended on them.

In summary, today the island has three population groups who have more or less divergent interests. The largest segment is made up of aliens, numbering from about 1,000 and up. They have migrated to find wage employment and most are satisfied with the income they can earn from manual work within the tourist industry. An increasing number are settling more permanently on the island, however, and merging with the local population. The second largest group, the continentals, varies widely in number depending on the time of year. The resident continental population numbers several hundred, and to this figure may be added the many tourists visiting daily. Most continentals are concerned with preserving the peacefulness and "natural" appearance of St. John, even at the expense of the local economy. The smallest group of people today is the native population, which numbers barely 1,000 and has grown little since the early 1950s. The major source of income among the St. Johnians is governmental employment.

In many ways, the establishment of the Virgin Islands National Park and Caneel Bay Plantation and the general rise of tourism on St. John have turned everything upside down. Still, the long history of struggle to establish and preserve an Afro-Caribbean community on the island has not been defeated by the introduction of tourism on the island. It continues in full force, though its structure and content have changed.

8

St. Johnian Culture and
Community Today

IN VIEW of developments that have taken place in St. John within the past forty years, the socioeconomic basis for the traditional exchange system appears to have been removed entirely. The majority of St. Johnians are wage employees working for the government. There is little need for club work to help with such chores as gardening, charcoal burning, or clearing pasture. Most produce is purchased in stores on St. John or even St. Thomas, and there is not much to exchange. After the establishment of a day-care center and the initiation of Head Start teaching programs for young children, parents were able to take jobs outside the home, so there seems to be little need for exchanging children. Welfare allowances help to support single mothers who have trouble making ends meet. Food stamps are supplied to the families where the provider/consumer ratio is not favorable, and social security checks and pensions from the government help out the elderly. The modern welfare system seems to have taken over the role formerly played by the exchange system.

The exchange system no longer dominates land ownership. As land became more valuable with the introduction of the tourism economy and as peasant farming decreased in importance, family land began to be divided into individually owned lots that could be sold. Two factors especially prompted St. Johnians to divide their land. During the 1930s all land became taxable; previously, only cultivated land had been taxed. This presented the person in charge of the family land with a serious economic problem. The entire family was expected to contribute to paying the taxes, but it was difficult to collect taxes from relatives who lived elsewhere and had never used the land. The problem was aggravated as the taxes rose from a few cents per cultivated acre during the Danish period to more than a hundred dollars per acre in the 1970s. Furthermore, as St. Johnians began to build more substantial houses, they often needed to borrow money from a bank. But a bank would not accept family land as security for a loan because the land could not be sold.

A person who had a part in family land therefore was at a financial disadvantage. By 1975, much family land had been divided, and that which remained had not been parceled out, in many cases, only because the family could not agree on how to divide it. In some cases, disagreements over family land led to court cases between relatives. Though most of the original land acquisitions date back to the late nineteenth century, a few go as far back as the early nineteenth, even the late eighteenth century; in these cases it is virtually impossible to find a suitable way to divide up the land. With present land prices as high as they are, no one wants to lose any land that is rightfully theirs. Land disputes have caused cleavages within families that have led to considerable unpleasantness for other St. Johnians, who are often related to both parties.

The great unity characteristic of the religious community on St. John has also disappeared. Beginning with the introduction of a Baptist church in the 1950s, a host of different religions have appeared on the island. In 1975, the following churches were active on St. John: Moravian, Lutheran, Catholic, Anglican, Methodist, Baptist, Seventh-Day Adventist, and Jehovah's Witnesses. Though the Moravian and Lutheran congregations remain large and are dominated by natives, the Baptists have won many local supporters and have established two churches on the island. The Catholic, Anglican, and Methodist churches are operated almost exclusively for alien workers and continentals; however, the Seventh-Day Adventists and Jehovah's Witnesses actively seek new followers among all populations, including St. Johnians. Some island congregations are in keen competition with each other. Today's situation presents a definite contrast to those of earlier times—for example, in 1909 a Seventh-Day Adventist missionary "nearly received a beating because he criticized the Moravian minister who is dearly beloved" (*Den vestindiske Kirkesag* 1909: 102).

Despite the changes in the economy, there are indications that the framework of St. Johnian social and economic activities is still defined by a concern with the St. Johnian community and not by individualism and competing business relations. It is remarkable that the vast majority of St. Johnians have avoided engaging directly in the tourism economy but rather have opted for government employment. The St. Johnians who do make a living by driving a taxi or renting out cottages or jeeps are very relaxed about it. Most taxi drivers charge full price to tourists only and frequently offer free rides to St. Johnian friends. They studiously refuse to engage in any sort of aggressive business relations with one another; rather, in their everyday behavior they continually make a point of expressing social and economic alliance. A St. Johnian who had returned after living in the United States for several years noted: "St. Johnians have accepted that material things are good and important, but they have not accepted the competitive spirit which in the States goes with these material goods. So they want good-paying jobs instead, like government jobs, where they can earn good money and feel secure."

St. Johnians have not abandoned their system of cooperation and sharing, but rather have redefined its social role. It is tempting to suggest that St. Johnians still operate within the parameters of a subsistence economy, though the basis for subsistence has been changed. The households are not primarily units of production any longer, but rather groups of co-residential people who pool economic resources received through wage employment, taxi driving, or pensions; they also seem to play a different economic role today. I shall first offer a microview of contemporary St. Johnian society through a description of three representative households. I shall then analyze the reproductive functions of these households by examining their composition and structure. Finally, I shall attempt to elucidate the character of the exchange system that still operates on the island and the role it plays in the social reproduction of St. Johnian society today.

The three case studies of St. Johnian households are composite types based on a study of forty-five households in 1974–75.[1] They are not actual households. I have chosen to present fictive rather than real units in order to preserve the anonymity of the persons I interviewed. The three households described here represent three types: a household recently established by a couple in their twenties who have known almost only the "modern" period; that of a somewhat older couple, in their forties, who were born toward the end of the peasant society period; and a household headed by a woman in her eighties, who lived through much of the peasant period and supplied much of the information about the peasant society presented in chapters 4, 5, and 6.

Household and exchange: three cases

Case 1: The young couple's household

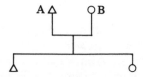

The household consists of a young couple, A and B, and their two children, aged four and one. A was born in the Coral Bay area and moved to the Cruz Bay area when he was in his late teens. B was born in the Cruz Bay area, where she has lived most of her life. Both have been in the United States several times to visit relatives, and B lived there for two years with an elder sister after she finished high school. A drives a taxi and also owns a jeep, which he rents out to tourists. B works as a secretary in a government office on the island. They lived in a rented apartment after they were married, about five years ago, but they just moved into a house which they recently finished building. The house was built by A with help from hired alien construction workers and from his friends and relatives on weekends. A few regulars helped a lot; when concrete was poured for the cistern and the floors, A held clubs to finish whole sections in one day. He held the clubs on Saturdays, and B's mother came to help B prepare food and offer drinks for the friends and relatives who came to work. A would mention to his friends that he needed help on a particular Saturday, and as many as thirteen would come. A few of these were paid because they were skilled. The land on which the house was located belonged to B and was inherited through her mother's family.

Because A has been busy building the house, he has not had time to fish, and they have had to buy most of their fish from acquaintances. Now that the house is done, *A* will start fishing again in order to supply his family, and also because he likes fishing. When he catches a lot of fish, he gives them to *B*'s brother, sister, mother, and close friends. *A*'s family, since they live at the other end of the island, do not receive fish so often. *A* and *B* do not get fish from anybody. They buy almost all the vegetables they eat, and it is very seldom that someone sends them any. They buy some from the stores and some from a market woman who brings vegetables from the other islands. *B* plans to start a garden, however, now that they have moved to their own house and have enough land.

They buy some fruit from various grocery stores, and they regularly receive soursop, guava, sugar apples, and mangoes from friends and relatives. Almost all other food is bought in the supermarket on St. Thomas, though two to three times a year goat meat is given them by relatives who keep goats. *B* does all the major shopping on St. Thomas and sometimes goes with her sister with whom she makes purchases in bulk, which they afterward divide. Cooked food is sometimes shared out only within the close family. One day, for example, *B* cooked soup in a huge pot and sent some to her mother, brother, and sister. They in turn send her baked goods and other specialties of theirs. *B* is responsible for the housework, but *A* helps quite often. The two children are sent out during the day for child care, the older to the government's day-care center in Cruz Bay, the younger to a private person, a distant relative of *B*'s who looks after children.

A, who is skilled as an amateur carpenter, often repairs things for his friends, and *B*'s brother, who is a mechanic, helps *A* keep his jeep in working condition. They never charge each other anything. *A* also gives many people free rides in his taxi. He charges tourists the government's established fares; however, if he meets a friend on his way home, he will offer him a free ride. Likewise, he may pick up somebody going in the same direction when he has a paying passenger. If a St. Johnian asks to be driven some place, *A* may charge a lower price than the official fare. He especially does this for friends and relatives from Coral Bay who need a ride home from Cruz Bay, because the official taxi rate is quite high by native income standards and he would not want to charge them the full amount. *A* also helps his friends through club work; in particular, he is asked to help build houses. *A* has many

friends, and he sees them almost every day when they meet in a
Cruz Bay bar to drink and talk. They often see each other after
6:00, when most of the men have stopped working; *A* has usually
finished driving by this time unless he decides to wait for the last
ferry from St. Thomas at 7:00. *B* does not go out much during the
week and goes directly home from work, but she does stop on the
street to chat with friends. She likes to visit others on Sundays
and to receive visits. She also participates in women's groups
such as the Business and Professional Women (the BPW), and
she is active in church activities. She goes to the Lutheran church
every Sunday morning, with or without her husband, who is less
enthusiastic about it. Both of them sometimes go to fish fries, social gatherings where fried fish, johnnycake (an unleavened fried
bread), and drinks are sold, usually to make money for some social cause such as scholarships for island youth or funds for a
school excursion. These fish fries are arranged by organizations
such as the PTA, the BPW, or the Lions Club.

Though *A* and *B* are too young to remember the period when
there was only provision farming and cattle estates on St. John,
they expressed their awareness that there is less exchange today
than formerly, and that the most significant change is that people
used to exchange generally with anybody, whereas nowadays
they exchange primarily with the close family.

Case 2: The household of a
well-established couple

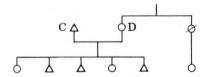

This household consists of eight persons: *C*, who is in his mid-
forties and works for the Department of Public Works; *D*, who is
about forty and works as a cleaner of government offices in Cruz
Bay; and six children, one of whom is a twelve-year-old niece of
D's and is living with them because her mother died a number of

years ago. The other children are between six and fourteen years old, and they all go to school. *D* had two children from a previous relationship who are now grown and live in the United States. Both *C* and *D* were born in Coral Bay but as a child *C* lived on St. Thomas, where his parents worked for a number of years before they returned to St. John. *D* has lived on St. John all her life, but she has visited relatives and her two children in the United States.

The family lives in a house that *C* built largely on his own, with some help from his friends and a few hired hands. In 1962, when *C* began to live with *D*, the house started out as a one-room board house divided into two rooms by a partition. In 1967, after they had married and had had two children of their own and *D*'s extramarital children were living with them, they needed more space and added a kitchen and bedroom to the house. The partition between the first two rooms was then taken down, so that the house consisted of three rooms. In 1970, they decided to add two more bedrooms, because they had two more children. When *C* made a cistern under the second addition, he held a club to pour the concrete. In 1972, they added another bedroom to the house and a bathroom to replace the outhouse. Despite the fact that the house was built in so many sections, it was well built and is neatly painted. The house is located in Coral Bay on *C*'s family land, which means that *C* has no title to the land, which would have made it very difficult for him to get a bank loan to build the house all at one time. Furthermore, *C* did not like the idea of borrowing money.

They get their fish mostly from their fish pots. *C* does not enjoy fishing, but his uncle, who lives on the same family land, also has fish pots, and he tends *C*'s fish pots once a week together with *C*'s cousin, who also lives on the family land. Since not all the fish pots provide the same amount of fish every week, they usually "share the fish around" so that there is fish in everyone's bucket. *C* and *D* get many of the vegetables they eat from their own ground, such as tomatoes, okra, pumpkins, and sweet potatoes, and they grow some fruits—soursop, limes, and bananas. They often share their vegetables and fruits with friends and relatives. Because they live on family land, they are surrounded by relatives, and quite a lot of sharing takes place. *D*'s family also lives fairly close by; they too are provided with fish and vegetables regularly, and they reciprocate. *C* and *D* raise chickens and when they have enough eggs they give *C*'s mother and sister some; they also sell to several continentals (Americans) who live nearby. They always try to keep a goat or a pig; at the time of this study they had four goats. They kill the ram goats for meat, which they share with their parents, brothers, and sisters. Sometimes dogs attack the goats, once killing two at one time; then there is enough extra goat meat to sell, and the neighbors buy it at about 80 cents a pound. *C* sometimes buys beef from men who slaughter cattle in Coral Bay regularly. *D* sometimes sends cooked food to her mother and her mother-in-law, but not often—only when she has cooked something special, such as *kallaloo*, a soup of greens, pork, fish, and various shellfish.

Even though they have a provision ground and keep a few animals, *C* and *D* still do not supply themselves with most of the food they eat but must buy it in the supermarket on St. Thomas. *D* does most of the shopping. She often goes to St. Thomas with her mother so that they can split the cost of going by taxi.

C works primarily in the Coral Bay area with public works, and he is picked up every morning by the public works truck. *D* usually travels on the school bus to Cruz Bay in the morning, but she sometimes gets a ride with her cousin, who works at the National Park in the Cruz Bay area. She usually pays the school bus or her cousin a dollar for the ride. In the afternoon she sometimes gets a lift home with people going to Coral Bay by waiting at a corner that, by local custom, is a pick-up point. When she comes home from shopping on St. Thomas, she must often rely on taxis; if they charge her the full fare, she has to pay about ten dollars. If she can arrange it, she asks her husband's cousin, who drives a taxi, to come for her because he will charge her only three dollars.

As in Case 1, *C* likes to stop at a local bar for a chat after work, whereas *D* goes straight home. *C* likes to go to fish fries every once in a while; *D* confines her external social activity to going to the Baptist church on most Sundays, usually without *C*. *D* likes receiving visitors, and she chats with her husband's relatives and her mother, who lives nearby, almost every day.

Though *C* and *D* try to be self-sufficient by growing their own provisions and having a few animals and fish pots, they do not succeed. However, the provisions enable them to exchange things with their family and friends, from whom they in turn receive something. They nevertheless did not think the amount of sharing which they managed to do was very significant, and believed that it was much more widespread at the time of their adolescence.

Case 3: The old woman's household

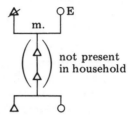

This household is occupied by three persons: *E*, who is in her eighties, and two of her great-grandchildren, ten and twelve years old. They are staying with *E* because both of their parents work, and it was felt that *E* could do a better job of taking care of the children. These children are the fourth generation of children *E* has reared. When she was seventeen her mother died, and she then reared her youngest sisters while she lived at home with her father. Later she reared her own children, and when they started having children she brought up several of those as well. *E* is not unhappy with her lot and seems rather satisfied that she has played such a key role in the family. *E* has never married, and the house she lives in was built for her by her children and grandchildren, who paid for the construction materials themselves. The house was built in two sections—in 1955 a one-room board house partitioned in two, then in 1957 a two-room addition. It is located on land in Cruz Bay Town that *E* bought in the early 1950s through a homesteading program. *E* had formerly lived in the Cruz Bay countryside, where her family has land. However, when the rest of the family moved to the town of Cruz Bay, she did not like to remain in the country alone and also moved to the town.

E lives on Social Security. She grows no vegetables but has a few fruit trees. She picks the fruit and makes tarts, which she gives to her grandchildren or sells to neighboring children. Her son regularly gives her fish, which he buys in Cruz Bay, and her granddaughter on St. Thomas sometimes sends fish that her friends have pulled in their fish pots. She regularly gets fresh eggs from her grandson, who lives nearby and raises poultry. This grandson also gives her goat meat, which he infrequently buys from his neighbors. Almost all the food E's household eats is therefore bought in the supermarket. E doesn't like to "worry with going backwards and forwards" to St. Thomas or even Cruz Bay Town, so almost all her shopping is done by her granddaughter, who lives on St. Thomas. E endorses her food stamps to her granddaughter and sends her a list of what she needs. The granddaughter then purchases the things, takes them to one of the ferries, and calls E to tell her when the groceries are coming and in how many boxes so that E can ask her son or grandchildren to pick them up for her. The ferry does not charge for this service. Though E has a modern gas stove, she has recently returned to making her johnnycake on a coal pot, a less expensive cooking method. She has no trouble getting coal for the pot because her brother, who is retired from public works, has begun to burn charcoal again and will sell her some at a very low price. E cooks for herself and the two children who live with her, and if her son or grandchildren stop by at lunchtime they are invited to eat. E rarely cooks food to send out. If she has cooked something that the children do not like, she will call her grandchildren to come and pick it up so that it will not be wasted. E does not like to take food from others because she would not know whether it was clean. She does accept food from relatives, however, and sometimes her children or grandchildren send something to her.

E is active in the women's fellowship organization in the Moravian church, and she likes to go to senior citizen picnics. If she needs to go somewhere, her son or grandsons will drive her, and she never has any problems with transportation. E does not visit people often in their homes, but her close family stops by her house almost every day, and she chats with her friends at church and senior citizen gatherings. E seemed to think it only reasonable that her children and grandchildren help her by sending her fish, meat, and other provisions, that they had built a house for her, and that her grandchild did all her shopping. This was natural and nothing one needed to be grateful for, just as it was natural that she should take care of some of the children and still be the center of much family activity.

The traditional system of social reproduction reinterpreted

These three case studies show how the St. Johnian households function today. Small farming and fishing and the exchange system continue to play an important role in the St. Johnian system of social reproduction, despite the fact that wage employment has become the predominant source of income on the island. Wherever the households have land around their houses, they almost invariably grow some provisions or at the very least have some fruit trees. If they have access to a boat, they often keep a few fish pots, which supply them with fish much of the time. A fish pot costs about forty-five dollars, an investment which will be paid off within a few weeks (fish sells for about one dollar a pound).

Today's high cost of gas and petroleum has led some St. Johnians to begin burning charcoal again, although during the 1950s and 1960s virtually all of them acquired modern cooking stoves. At the time of this study, at least six men were burning charcoal regularly and selling it to other St. Johnians and to continentals, who use it in their barbecue grills. One charcoal burner noted that in the old days it was a lot of trouble to ship the coal to St. Thomas, where he would most likely get no more than twenty cents a bag; whereas now he could ask for six dollars and also require the buyers to come to his house—or even to the charcoal pit—to purchase the coal.

The high cost of living, which is geared to tourism and the standard of living of fairly well-to-do continentals (which St. Johnians in modern times have attempted to emulate to a certain extent), is in many ways forcing St. Johnians to fall back on the subsistence economy they depended on formerly. Even though all employed St. Johnians make enormously high salaries compared with the daily wages their grandparents received for plantation work, the money does not stretch very far today; and the old subsistence methods are beginning to provide an important subsidy to wages. Though some young St. Johnians have no interest in subsistence farming or fishing, many seem to develop an interest in these things as they begin to settle down in their own households and have children. Even though the households are not units of production as far as their main income is concerned, they are nevertheless important in the supplementary subsistence economy.

The traditional system of reproduction is also apparent in the composition and structure of the households. This was revealed in the data collected from the questionnaire administered to forty-five households on St. John. Though the sample is small, the households to which the questionnaire was administered represented a cross-section of St. Johnian households. There is no certainty that the statistics are fully representative for the entire St. Johnian population, but they do show certain characteristics of the households that are probably indicative of developmental trends in St. Johnian household structure.

Now, as before, most households are or have been based upon a conjugal relationship and the parent-child tie. Of the forty-five households, twenty-nine (64 percent) were headed by conjugal couples, thirteen (29 percent) by women, three (7 percent) by men. Of the thirteen female-headed households, eleven had originally included a male but had changed headship, seven because the conjugal partners were divorced or separated, four because the head had died. Two households were occupied by single women who had inherited their parents' house and had never lived in a conjugal union. Of the three male-headed households, one was occupied by a man separated from his partner, two by single men. It is notable that, while the percentage of female headship has remained rather stable, the basis for female headship has changed somewhat. During the peasant period, female headship was based upon extra-residential relations, the breakup of common-law unions, or the death of a spouse; today the basis of female headship is primarily separation (or divorce) or the death of the spouse. While informal common-law unions used to be very frequent and easily broken, the statistics on the conjugal households show that these unions are now based on marriage. The marital tie is not as permanent as it was formerly; marital unions seem to be easily broken by separation, as evidenced by the seven households thus affected. Furthermore, five of the twenty-nine conjugal unions were based upon the remarriage of at least one partner. Thus thirteen, or 29 percent, of the households had experienced a period when the conjugal unit was dissolved. While the common-law institution seems to have disappeared (or at least did not appear in my sample), many marriages, in fact, have the character of common-law unions in that they are entered into at an early age and are frequently dissolved, as were the common-law unions previously. Marriage, therefore, today subsumes the early co-residential common-law unions as well as the later permanent marriages, so that, while the form of conjugal ties has changed, the developmental structure of the unions has remained the same. It involves first a period of courtship, during which extra-residential sexual relations may occur, followed in most cases by the establishment of a household based upon marriage. Such a marriage may be terminated by divorce, however, followed by later marriages.

This developmental structure of the households indicates that children often do not grow up with both parents. Ninety-five children (eighteen years old and younger) were living in the households interviewed.[2] Of these, fifty (53 percent) were living with both parents, eighteen (19 percent) were living with one parent, twenty-four (26 percent) were living with relatives, and three (3 percent) were living with others. Of the eighteen living with one parent, one case was attributed to the father having died, the others to parents' separation or divorce.

Most children who were not living with both parents were staying with relatives. Of these twenty-four children, nineteen were living with grandparents or great-grandparents, five with aunts/uncles or great-aunts/uncles. It was sometime difficult to discern exactly why these children did not grow up with their parents. Most guardians mentioned that, since the parents worked or went to school full time, it was not convenient for them to look after the child, especially if the parents lived on St. Thomas or in the United States. The day-care center on St. John did not accept infants, and it was open only between certain daytime hours. The relatives had offered to help by taking in the children, and the parents visited their children on weekends or during holidays, when they had time. In other cases, especially when the guardian was a grandparent, the child was supposed to keep the relative company and help with errands. It was apparent that some children lived with relatives because the parents were separated and a lone parent was not able to care for the child. The impermanence of early marriage unions thus contributes to the high number of children living with relatives. The mating relationships of young St. Johnians and the necessity for both parents to work outside the household are therefore important in the exchange of children from young households to older ones, where the residents are retired and able to spend more time with the children.

Even though marriage has become more important, perhaps in accord with American ideology, it is apparent that the old structural relationships within and between the households have been largely maintained. The developmental cycle of the households is similar to what it was in the peasant period, except that marriage and divorce have now replaced the residential common-law unions. There is still a substantial number of female-headed households throughout the life cycle of the households. More than a fourth of the children live with neither parent, slightly more than half with both parents.

Although most St. Johnians are gainfully employed and make relatively good salaries, not all households are equally well off. Some contain a large number of children, and some have only one provider. Others must rely largely on limited pensions. The government, as noted, has taken over some burdens formerly alleviated through the exchange system. Welfare and food stamps are available to households that lack cash resources; lunch programs assure that all children receive a nutritious meal every day, and Head Start and the day-care center help teach and care for young children. The case studies and the statistics on household composition nevertheless show that the exchange system continues to function, and certain socioeconomic problems are still best handled by the exchange system.

A St. Johnian consciousness

St. Johnians are not just engaging in economic activities when they cultivate a small garden, tend a fish pot, or help in club work. Many are also making a statement about their place in St. Johnian society. A household that has no garden or fish pots, whose members work only for pay and do not visit with neighbors or join the men at the bar, is saying that it does not wish to be part of the St. John community. By engaging in one or several of the subsistence-related activities, a household is expressing its desire to be part of the community, with all the pleasures and restrictions this brings. Participating in the subsistence economy is a declaration of solidarity with the St. Johnian past and dissociation from the new American way of life. St. Johnians to a certain extent idealize their former social system and contrast it with the modern one, using the ideology of the old system to create an identity for themselves. Many St. Johnians stated, for example, that they wanted to have their own little garden and to fish regularly because this enabled them to give things to friends and relatives. Some quoted the Bible, saying that all should "unite and live like one," and others said that they were proud to give something because this was how a real St. Johnian acted.

This emphasis on cooperative and generous behavior has had not only the positive effect of forming a sense of identity; it also has had the negative effect of making St. Johnians resistant to the economic opportunities available in the tourism industry. As already noted, St. Johnians have chosen government jobs to avoid the competitive interactions and risks associated with business. The few St. Johnians who run businesses generally compromise between St. Johnian ideals and the economic reality of the tourism industry. Owners of local businesses who have a sizable income, including some continentals who have become or would like to become part of the local society, feel obligated to share some of their profits with the island's population. On New Year's Eve, bars serve free drinks, and during the Christmas season a number of businesses serve meals and drinks to their customers, which actually means anybody who would like to come.

The exchange system has become an important way in which a sense of community is maintained among the St. Johnians amid the introduction of the tourism economy and the numerous foreign residents. St. Johnians recognize that there are two ways of doing things—the official American way and the unofficial St. Johnian way—and they choose one or the other depending on whom they are dealing with. One St. Johnian explained how the two ways work:

> On many holidays you will find many of us working together on something. At carnival, for example, we didn't go to St. Thomas, but stayed right here working together doing something. This kind of helping one another is like the common-law marriage. You have the legal work, which is official and paid for, and you have your legal marriage, which is organized like the paid work and is official. Then you have your club work, which is

less organized and unofficial, and you have your common-law
marriage, which likewise is less organized and unofficial.

The "common-law" socioeconomic system has been an important
factor in preserving the St. Johnian community, which would
otherwise be overwhelmed by the large continental and alien
populations who live on the island. These two groups are not nec-
essarily excluded from the St. Johnian society but are included
only if they accept the premises of the system and thereby become "St. Johnian." Some continentals who have lived on St.
John for a number of years have become integrated into the system to a great extent. They participate in the clubs, drink in the
local bars, and cultivate little gardens or keep fish pots from
which they share the products. They have realized that even if
they give a lot, they will in the long run receive just as much as
they have given. An increasing number of aliens have also been
incorporated into the St. Johnian community. In many cases they
have come from island societies similar to the St. Johnian peasant society and are sometimes shocked that St. Johnians do not
have a more open, welcoming attitude. Some of them eventually
realize that the introduction of a large-scale tourism economy to
the island led the St. Johnians to close their exchange system in
order to establish a defense against being overrun by American
businessmen looking for profitable investments or West Indian
laborers seeking work no matter how poorly paid. Both the continentals and the aliens are perceived as being on the island
largely in order to make money; it is only when they learn to sup-
press their competitive behavior that they are welcomed into the
St. Johnian socioeconomic system.

In summary, there are two main reasons why the exchange
system continues to function today. First, some St. Johnian households have much greater incomes than others. In particular,
households headed by elderly people, single mothers, and couples
with many young children are at a clear economic disadvantage
despite the welfare programs introduced by the local and federal
governments. The economic difficulties of such households are
alleviated through the exchange system. Second, St. Johnians today—like their ancestors, who were united against the estate
owners—live in common resistance against the individualistic,
competitive socioeconomic system of the tourist industry, repre-

sented by the continentals and the alien workers. The two groups threaten the St. Johnians from above and below. Through the exchange system the St. Johnians protect themselves from the encroachment of both groups. The exchanges form the social as well as the economic basis for the survival of the St. Johnian community. I do not mean to imply, however, that the St. Johnians have consciously organized their exchange system for this purpose. Rather, the system has worked completely informally and on the basis of tacit agreement. In this double role, as adaptation and resistance to the tourist economy and to socioeconomic deprivation, modern St. Johnian culture carries out the same dual function it did in the slave period.

Toward a historical anthropology of the family

The historical continuity and the present-day ideological importance attached to the St. Johnian exchange networks, as evidenced in the social and economic transactions taking place outside the household, may provide some insights into the current debate on Afro-American family structure. As already noted, Afro-American kin networks have been associated largely with lower-class segments and viewed as functional because of the mutual support that they offer (S. E. Brown 1975; Gussler 1980; Stack 1974; Whitehead 1978). The St. Johnian research suggests that these networks have an important cultural component, having developed since slavery as part of a movement of resistance against the oppression of Western society and its denigration of Afro-American culture. It is difficult to discern this element of resistance and continuity in analyses that are based almost entirely on the ethnographic present. A historical anthropological perspective, on the other hand, sets the ideological and cultural aspect of the present-day community in relief.

The emphasis on fieldwork as a research tool has made it difficult for anthropologists to view Afro-American culture as the product of a long historical development, which can be elucidated through particular historical-anthropological case studies. The discipline, therefore, has seen the emergence of a host of interpretations of Afro-American culture, few of which rely upon historical research, but almost all of which nevertheless invoke the past as an explanatory factor (Herskovits and Herskovits 1973 [1947]; Greenfield 1966; Henriques 1973 [1949], 1968 [1953]; Clarke 1957). Mintz (1974: 243), in a discussion of Caribbean household composition, concluded that "the importance of specific historical circumstances for particular forms of domestic organization has not yet been properly assessed for Caribbean societies."

In recent years historians have completed a number of investigations of the slave family in order to uncover the first family forms among Afro-Americans and thus the basis for their later social organization. This research has led to the general conclusion that, contrary to previously held views, stable nuclear families existed in substantial numbers among slaves, African as well as Creole (Gutman 1976; Higman 1973, 1975; Craton 1978a, 1978b). Thus, at the very time that anthropologists have begun to point to networks of exchange and mutual cooperation as the basic element of Afro-American social structure, historical research is pointing to the historic importance of the nuclear family.

The primary reason for the gap between the anthropological and the historical findings seems to be that while anthropologists through their field research have studied interacting people and their social and economic relationships, historians working with archival sources have based their research on socioeconomic units such as households and marriages that are recorded in the official documents. Historian Barry Higman has pointed out some of the problems this historical approach has created—for example, while historians have been successful in mapping out various household and kinship groups among slaves on a number of plantations, the meaning of these groups remains unclear. Higman sees this to be largely a methodological problem caused by the paucity of empirical data describing the social and economic function of these units (Higman 1977).

The approach taken in this study suggests that research on the history of the Afro-American family should concentrate not primarily on reconstituting family units as such, but rather on delineating the systems of social reproduction within which family relations and households must be understood. In this way, it is possible to document not just the presence of households but also the wider social framework within which they exist, and thus the significance of family networks.

Historical anthropological case studies of the development of particular communities thus may help reconcile some of the divergent conclusions reached by anthropologists and historians. More important, such case studies may also help provide a research framework relevant to the developing Afro-American social context, rather than a framework derived primarily from Western academic or social concerns.

In the case of St. John, social structure involves three levels of organization: (1) the household, (2) networks of exchange centered on individual households, and (3) the total mesh of networks constituting the St. Johnian community. Some of the households correspond to the nuclear family, yet this unit has never been the basic building block of social organization. The St. Johnian notion of family is that of a large network of kin ties, which embody rights and responsibilities of mutual aid and support. These ties tend to be most intensive and enduring among close and coresidential kin, but they can be extended geographically and biologically. Though the character and relative importance of the three elements of St. Johnian social structure have varied through time as historical circumstances have changed, the St. Johnian notion of the family has remained remarkably stable.

Notes

Chapter 1: The Historical Anthropology of St. John

1. The concept of social reproduction originally emerged in the context of Marxist scholarship as a counterpole to the sphere of production in industrial society (see, for example, the collection of essays in Seddon 1978). The concept has since become the common property of social scientists in the general sense I have defined here. It is particularly useful in the study of slave society because of the clear separation that emerged, as in the case of industrial society, between productive and reproductive activity.

Chapter 2: The Plantation Society

1. The *landfoged* transcribed the following English text of the song: "The lady tells him to take him thing and go to Tortola land, Mr. Edwards says: no we stay for 2–3 weeks more. The lady lays in the window and cries out for her dear John; Mr. Edwards! didn't I tell you so? You wouldn't take care of Jonis Gang—Jonis Gang has carried you to livis land. Little Maria has confessed upon the bad woman and Manager! You wouldn't hear—The cup of tea sent him to livis land." Maria was a house servant in Mr. Edwards's house and supposedly watched "the bad woman" Nanny, the senior house servant, mix poison in Mr. Edwards's cup of tea (*LA* 41: December 31, 1839).

Chapter 3: The Emergence of
an Afro-Caribbean Culture

1. The explanatory text has no author, but it is almost identical with passages in a description of the Danish West Indies, credited to Ørsted, in Bergsøe's *Den danske Stats Statistik* (1853).
2. The *stadshauptmand* was "the leader of the St. John civil militia and the free corps (*jægerkorpset*); was treasurer for St. John civil council and supervised the island's artillery. In addition to this, he was engaged in such activities as the procurement of statistical information, the establishment of roads and the control of labor power on the plantations" (Rigsarkivet 1981: 9).
3. The religious beliefs and ritual practices in connection with childbirth on St. John were probably similar to those described for St. Croix in the eighteenth century: "The female childbirth attendants burn candles during the first eight days throughout the night; the eighth night the newborn baby is especially guarded by more than twenty Negroes to prevent it from being stolen or eaten by witches. . . . This is superstition, which one cannot, even with the help of every sort of religious argument, preach out of their heads. They thus believe that if a witch during the first eight days (thereafter she has no power) is able to get so close to the newborn child that she can look into its eyes, she will be capable of inhaling the child's breath in such a way that it must die" (Schmidt 1788: 260).
4. Gutman's study of the American black family (1976) is a typical example. It was inspired by a desire to challenge the conclusions of the controversial Moynihan report of 1965, which was interpreted to suggest that Afro-American social problems stemmed from the relative lack of stable nuclear families, which, in turn, was seen as a legacy of slavery. Gutman sought to prove that the two-parent family actually was widespread among the American slaves, but in the process he also discovered the presence and importance of extended kin groups in slave family structure. The work of Higman (1973, 1975, 1978) and Craton (1978a, 1978b, 1978c) has paralleled Gutman's in this respect. However, the fact that these historians have been primarily concerned with the presence or the absence of the nuclear family has meant that the central role of the kin networks has not been fully explored. In the present study, the lack of emphasis upon the nuclear family as a basic element in the slaves' socioeconomic system is not due to a difference in the general situation of the St. John slaves from

that of other Afro-Caribbean slaves. It is due, rather, to the fact that the family has been approached within the context of a larger socioeconomic whole. The family has not been studied primarily in terms of residential groups and sexual units, but in terms of the relationships that the slaves recognized and utilized in their everyday living. It is therefore important that the empirical data used have been qualitative as well as quantitative in nature (cf. Rawick 1972).

5. This dual character of the slaves in the Danish West Indies was noticed by contemporary observers. J. C. Schmidt, who was on St. Croix in the late eighteenth century, noted that the slaves "are far from being stupid or ignorant. Many times I have been in their plantations in the evening and heard them among one another carry on quite reasonable conversations and reasonings over the whites' behaviour and moral character; but towards the latter they are withdrawn, and pretend to be very ignorant" (1788: 232).

Chapter 4: The Peasant Society

1. The Danish islands, along with other West Indian colonial areas, were visited by representatives from the English *Anti-Slavery Reporter*, who severely criticized the Danish labor contracts imposed on the freed. The conditions on St. John were described as follows: "The labouring population have nearly the same low wages, and are under the same coercive regulation, which, in some late instances, had been exercised with greater severity than the law, severe as it is, could ever have contemplated. Some well-disposed people, helpers in the Moravian Church, had been flogged for slight transgressions of discipline, who had never been flogged as slaves; and we hear of one well-authenticated case, in which a young man, for stealing canes, had been so severely flogged as to die of the lacerations, four days after. The labourers, generally speaking, are abject and crouching, and unwilling to give evidence of the wrongs that come under their notice. We did not visit St. John's through want of time, but these facts were communicated to us by trustworthy persons. No such wrongs can be practiced with impunity in British colonies, where the people are free. Emancipation, entire and unconditional, will be found the only remedy for them in the dependencies of Denmark" (*Anti-Slavery Reporter*, 1851, pp. 45–46). This report was

reprinted in the Danish magazine *Fædrelandet*, which was received by the *landfoged* on St. John in May of the same year. He wrote a letter to the editor of the magazine, dismissing the report as hearsay: "I have admittedly heard that it is customary here on St. John to make boots out of the Negroes' skin. I really haven't seen this myself; in any case, it must have happened before my time; but 'trustworthy persons' have told about it. . . ." He added that "trustworthy persons" also had told him that it was common to "hang Negro children in a hook in order to catch sharks on the coast of Guinea" (*LA* 7: May 31, 1851).

2. The Lutheran church baptized children born out of wedlock but refused to let unmarried parents become godparents or go to communion (Hoffmeyer 1905: 69–71).

3. The *landfoged* position was subsumed under that of the assistant judge and clerk on St. Thomas in 1906 (Rigsarkivet 1981). On St. John a Danish doctor took over the official status of the former *landfoged* as "head" of the community on the island. The transfer ceremonies on St. John and the other two Danish islands are described in Konow (1966: 80).

Chapter 5: The Households

1. Hereafter, quotes from interviews with St. Johnians, unless otherwise noted, are from my field notes.

2. In *Kreole Ketch'n' Keep*, Arona Petersen, a native of St. Thomas, describes the economic difficulties of a boatman when there are few ships in the harbor. The book depicts life on St. Thomas at this time in a series of short stories (Petersen 1975).

3. St. Johnians spoke Dutch Creole until the end of the nineteenth century, when English became the major language. When I did fieldwork on St. John in 1974–75, there still were two St. Johnians who knew Dutch Creole, and many nicknames were Dutch Creole. For a dictionary on the special English Creole spoken on the Virgin Islands, see Valls (1981).

Chapter 6: The Network of Exchanges

1. The extension of kin terms to nonrelatives within the community is common in the Caribbean; see, for example, R. T. Smith 1956; Henriques 1981 [1953]; M. G. Smith 1962a.

2. The Danish land records were not inaccurate only with regard to ownership of the land; they were also questionable concerning acreage. When the land records stated that a lot was ten acres, the deed itself might read "ten acres more or less." When these lots were parceled out from the plantations, the acreage was estimated as closely as possible, and the area itself was marked out very informally. The boundary posts for many lots were a large stone, a tree, a cactus, or a wooden pole placed in the ground. During the past thirty years the Virgin Islands courts system has been inundated with lawsuits because the original land buyers did not give serious consideration to the fact that stones and wooden poles are easily moved and that trees and cacti disappear sooner or later. For a discussion of the Danish land records and the St. Johnian conception of landownership and usage, see Olwig 1984.

3. *Neappe* probably derives from the Spanish word *llapa*, or *yapa* ("more").

4. During the seining season, two or more people also worked together catching fish in seines. However, since they worked together only during the short seining season of a certain fish species, such an arrangement was scarcely a true partnership, and apparently the crew changed according to which men were available to do the fishing. During the seining an account was kept of how much fish was sent to St. Thomas; and when the seining was over, the members of the crew received a percentage of the money. Since this was commercial fishing, the accounts were strictly compiled, and a larger share was reserved for the owner of the boat.

5. Not all the work on estates was paid with daily wages, although this was the most common method. A worker could also make a contract with an estate to complete a certain task (such as clearing a hillside for bush) for a certain sum of money. The full amount would not be paid before the work was complete; however, the worker could ask for an advance before beginning the work, so that he could buy liquor or food to hold a club. The club might then do most of this contract work in a single day, but the participants would not get a share of the pay, except for the meat and liquor provided for them by the estate worker who held the club, and the implicit promise of a day's work in return.

6. There were very few serious conflicts on St. John brought formally to the courts. *Saint Thomas Mail Notes* observed: "The people in St. John are law-abiding. Less than a dozen minor cases

have been brought to the Police Court during the year, and no case has been taken to the District Court" (December 4, 1933).

7. Many St. Johnians I interviewed were hesitant to speak openly about *obeah* and pretended not to know about it. Two admitted to having consulted an *obeah* woman on St. Thomas, when they became ill and suspected that the cause might have been *obeah*. They were, of course, confirmed in their belief and had to pay her a fair amount of money for this service. Most St. Johnians emphasized that the best *obeah* practitioners lived on St. Thomas, Tortola, or on such Caribbean islands as Haiti and Dominica. In his book *The Virgin Islands and Their People*, J. Antonio Jarvis, a St. Thomian, devotes a chapter to witchcraft and superstition. He describes several cases of the practice of *obeah*, condemning it as "undermining health and morals." The book was not popular when it was first published in 1944 because of the openness with which it discussed clandestine affairs on the islands, and Mr. Jarvis was nearly ostracized from the islands community. The book was quickly banned from sale, and it was not reprinted until twenty-seven years later (Jarvis 1971 [1944]). For a discussion of the Jarvis case, see Hill 1975: 86–90.

8. The large-estate owners were also included in the supernatural belief system of the islands. Most of the estate owners were colored, i.e., fairly light-skinned, having white as well as black ancestors. A few of these light-skinned (and white) estate owners of the past were pointed out to me as having been werewolves. A werewolf is believed to be the child of a white woman, who, to avoid pain in childbirth, gives birth to a werewolf. During the day, the werewolf is like a normal person, but at night it turns into an animal—for example, a donkey—goes to the houses of pregnant women, and sucks the blood out of the fetus through the woman's toe so that the children are stillborn. There were few St. Johnians who had much knowledge of werewolves, which were apparently more feared on St. Thomas, where there were more white and colored people; I was therefore not able to learn about many cases. The case most referred to in my interviews concerned an American who was much disliked for his refusal to let St. Johnians pick fruit on his estate, as was customary elsewhere. It is possible that mean estate owners were branded as werewolves; I doubt that this made much impression on American estate owners, though it might have had some effect on Creole owners. Women werewolves were called *desoto*. Jarvis has a vivid description of some of the beliefs concerning werewolves on St.

Thomas (1971 [1944]: 129–34). Valls is of the opinion that the concept of werewolves originally was introduced by the Danish colonists "to keep the slaves in line" (1981: 134).

Chapter 7: The Tourism Society

1. In 1962, 5,560 acres of "submerged land off the northern and southern coasts of the island" were transferred to the "supervision of the National Park Service" (Robinson 1974: 48). This transfer was relatively simple since both the Virgin Islands and the National Park Service are administered by the Department of the Interior. For further discussion of the establishment of the park on St. John and the concept of nature associated with it, see Olwig 1977, 1980; Olwig and Olwig 1979.
2. These statistics do not include the large number of immigrants who have entered the American territory "through the window," i.e., through unofficial routes without visas. This number may have increased in the 1980s, when it has become virtually impossible to obtain temporary visas.
3. Motor vehicles came to St. John within a very short period. In 1953, fourteen jeeps were registered on the island, which represents an increase of eight within six months. The administrator, who was not used to such traffic on the island, expressed concern that the automobile traffic would destroy the peace and quiet. He proposed that the peaceful life of the island be preserved by "limiting the number and size of motor vehicles on the island" (*Annual Report of the Administrator for St. John* 1953: 3). Apparently this was not done, and in 1956 no fewer than fifty-six jeeps, thirty-one trucks, and five station wagons were registered (*Annual Report* 1956: 92).

Chapter 8: St. Johnian Culture and Community Today

1. This study is based primarily on questionnaire interviews carried out toward the end of my fieldwork on the island in 1974–75. The questionnaire covered 177 natives, 8 aliens, and 2 continentals. A native population of less than 1,000 is listed in the 1970 census; thus the survey covers approximately 20 percent of the total native population.

2. Individuals in this study are designated as children up to age fifteen during the Danish/early American period (when children left school for employment at that age), and up to age eighteen during the present period (when most children are kept in school until they graduate from high school).

References Cited

Books, Articles, and Documents

Administrative Policies for the Historical Areas of the National Park System.
  1973   U.S. Department of the Interior, National Park Service. Washington: Government Printing Office.
Administrative Policies for the National Parks and National Monuments of Scientific Significance.
  1970   U.S. Department of the Interior, National Park Service. Washington: Government Printing Office.
Annual Reports.
  1931–35   Department of Health of the Virgin Islands. St. Thomas Library microfilm collection, Charlotte Amalie.
Annual Report of the Administrator for St. John.
  1952–70   Enid M. Baa Library, Documents Division, Charlotte Amalie, St. Thomas. (Certain years are missing.)
The Anti-Slavery Reporter.
  1851   "The Danish Colonies," March 1, pp. 43–46.
Bergsøe, Adolph Frederik.
  1853   *Den danske Stats Statistik.* Vol. 4. Copenhagen: Forfatterens Forlag.
Besson, Jean.
  1979   Symbolic Aspects of Land in the Caribbean: The Tenure and Transmission of Land Rights among Caribbean Peasantries. In *Peasants, Plantations and Rural Communities in the Caribbean,* edited by M. Cross and A. Marks. Department of Sociology, University of Surrey; Department of Caribbean Studies, Leiden.
  1981   Plantations, Peasants and Kinship in the Caribbean: Towards an Ethnography of Afro-Caribbean Peasantries. Paper presented at the Fifth Conference of the Society for Caribbean Studies, High Leigh Conference Centre, Hoddeston, England, May 26–28.

Bloch, Marc.
1953   *The Historian's Craft*. New York: Vintage Books.
Boyer, William Walter, Jr.
1949   Civil Liberties in the Virgin Islands of the United States. Master's thesis, University of Wisconsin, Madison.
Bro-Jørgensen, J. O.
1966   *Dansk Vestindien indtil 1755*. Vol. 1, *Vore Gamle Tropekolonier*, edited by J. Brøndsted. Denmark: Fremad.
Brown, Herbert D.
1930   Report on the Political, Social and Economic Conditions in the U.S. Virgin Islands. House Committee on Insular Affairs. U.S. Congress.
Brown, Susan E.
1975   Love Unites Them and Hunger Separates Them: Poor Women in the Dominican Republic. In *Towards an Anthropology of Women*, edited by R. R. Reiter. New York: Monthly Review Press.
1977   Household Composition and Variation in a Rural Dominican Village. *Journal of Comparative Family Studies* 8 (2): 257–67.
Børgesen, F., and F. P. Uldall.
1900   *Vore vestindiske Øer*. Copenhagen: G. E. C. Gad.
Caron, Aimery P., and Arnold R. Highfield.
1983   Nov. 23, 1733, St. John Slave Revolt: A Look 250 Years Later. *Virgin Islands Education Review* 1 (8): 9–20.
Carstens, J. L.
1981   [1840s]. *En Almindelig Beskrivelse om alle de Danske, Americanske eller West-Indiske Ey-Lande*. Dansk Vestindien for 250 år siden. Copenhagen: Dansk Vestindisk Forlag.
Carstensen, A. Riis.
1897   *Over Viden Strand*. Copenhagen: G. E. C. Gad.
Cavling, Henrik.
1894   *Det danske Vestindien*. Copenhagen: Det Reitzelske Forlag.
Census of the Virgin Islands of the United States.
1917   Prepared by E. F. Hartley. Washington: Government Printing Office, 1918.
1950   U.S. Bureau of the Census. Washington: Government Printing Office.
1970   U.S. Bureau of the Census. Washington: Government Printing Office.
Christmas, W.
1923   *Krydstogt gennem Livet*. Copenhagen: H. Aschehoug.

Clarke, Edith.
1953   Land Tenure and the Family. *Social and Economic Studies* 1 (4): 81–118.
1957   *My Mother Who Fathered Me*. London: George Allen & Unwin.
Comitas, Lambros.
1973   [1964]. Occupational Multiplicity in Rural Jamaica. In *Work and Family Life*, edited by L. Comitas & D. Lowenthal. Garden City, N.Y.: Anchor Press/Doubleday.
Comitas, Lambros, and David Lowenthal, eds.
1973   *Work and Family Life*. Garden City: Anchor Press/ Doubleday.
Craton, Michael.
1978a   Hobbesian or Panglossian? The Two Extremes of Slave Conditions in the British Caribbean, 1783 to 1834. *William and Mary Quarterly* 3d ser. 35 (2): 324–56.
1978b   Changing Patterns of Slave Family in the British West Indies. Paper presented at the Organization of American Historians Conference, New York City, April 15.
1978c   *Searching for the Invisible Man: Slaves and Plantation Life in Jamaica*. Cambridge: Harvard University Press.
1979   Proto-peasant Revolts? The Late Slave Rebellions in the British West Indies 1816–1832. *Past and Present* 85: 99–125.
Cumper, G. E.
1958   The Jamaican Family: Village and Estate. *Social and Economic Studies* 7 (1): 76–108.
Danmark.
1855   Em. Baerentzen & Co. Lith. Inst.
Degn, Christian.
1974   *Die Schimmelmanns im Atlantischen Dreieckshandel: Gewinn und Gewissen*. Neumünster: Karl Wachholtz Verlag.
Eggleston, William C.
1959   *Virgin Islands*. Princeton: Van Nostrand Company.
Emmanuel, Lezmore E.
1974   *Broo 'nansi: A Selection of Anansi Stories*. Washington: General Learning Corporation.
Everhart, William C.
1972   *The National Park Service*. New York: Praeger.
Fairchild, Pauline.
1935   Sociological Aspects of Negro Life in the Virgin Islands. Master's thesis, Western Reserve University.
Final Report to the President and the Congress of the National Parks Centennial Commission.
1973   Washington: Government Printing Office.

Finley, M. I.
  1980   Slavery and Historians. *Social History* 12 (24): 247–61.
Frazier, E. Franklin.
  1968   [1939]. *The Negro Family in the United States*. Chicago: University of Chicago Press.
Frucht, Richard.
  1968   Emigration, Remittances and Social Change: Aspects of the Social Field of Nevis, West Indies. *Anthropologica* 10 (2): 193–208.
Gerber, Stanford N., ed.
  1973   *The Family in the Caribbean*. Puerto Rico: University of Puerto Rico Press.
Gonzalez, Nancie L. Solien.
  1969   *Black Carib Household Structure*. Seattle: University of Washington Press.
  1970   Towards a Definition of Matrifocality. In *Afro-American Anthropology*, edited by N. E. Whitten and J. F. Szwed. New York: The Free Press.
Goossen, Jean.
  1972   Child Sharing and Foster Parenthood in the French West Indies. Paper presented at the American Anthropological Association, New York City, November.
Goveia, Elsa V.
  1969   [1965]. *Slave Society in the British Leeward Islands at the End of the Eighteenth Century*. New Haven: Yale University Press.
Grede, John Frederick.
  1962   The New Deal in the Virgin Islands, 1931–1941. Ph.D. diss., University of Chicago.
Green-Pedersen, Svend Erik.
  1976   Den danske negerslavehandels historie 1733–1807. In *Från medeltid til välfärdssamhälle, Nordiska Historikermötet i Uppsala 1974*. Uppsala: Almqvist & Wiksell.
  1978   The Abolition of the Slave Trade and the Slave Demography of the Danish West Indies. Paper presented at the Symposium on the Abolition of the Atlantic Slave Trade, University of Aarhus, October 16–19.
  1979   The Economic Considerations behind the Danish Abolition of the Negro Slave Trade. In *The Uncommon Market: Essays in the Economic History of the Atlantic Slave Trade*, edited by H. A. Gemery and J. S. Hogendom. New York: Academic Press.
Greenfield, Sidney M.
  1966   *English Rustics in Black Skin*. New Haven: College and University Publishers.
Gussler, Judith D.

1980   Adaptive Strategies and Social Networks of Women in St. Kitts. In *A World of Women*, edited by E. Bourguignon. New York: Praeger.

Gutman, Herbert G.
1976   *The Black Family in Slavery and Freedom, 1750–1925.* Oxford: Basil Blackwell.

Haagensen, Richard.
1758a   *Beskrivelse over Eylandet St. Croix i America i Westindien.* Copenhagen: Lillies Enke.
1978b   *Om de på Øen St. Croix værende sorte Hedninge eller Slaver.* Copenhagen: Lillies Enke.

Hall, Douglas.
1971   *Five of the Leewards 1834–1870.* Barbados: Caribbean Universities Press.

Hall, Gwendolyn Midlo.
1971   *Social Control in Slave Plantation Societies: A Comparison of St. Domingue and Cuba.* Johns Hopkins University Studies in Historical and Political Science 89[1]. Baltimore: Johns Hopkins Press.

Hall, Neville.
1976   Anna Heegaard: Enigma. *Caribbean Quarterly* 22 (2, 3): 76–79.
1977   Slave Laws of the Danish Virgin Islands in the Later Eighteenth Century. In *Comparative Perspectives on Slavery in New World Plantation Societies*, edited by V. Rubin and A. Tuden. Annals of the New York Academy of Sciences, 292: 174–86.
1979   Establishing a Public Elementary School System for Slaves in the Danish Virgin Islands, 1732–1846. *Caribbean Journal of Education* 6 (1): 1–45.
1980   Slaves' Use of Their "Free" Time in the Danish Virgin Is-. lands in the Late Eighteenth and Early Nineteenth Century. *Journal of Caribbean History* 13: 21–43.
1983   Slavery in Three West Indian Towns: Christiansted, Fredericksted and Charlotte Amalie in the Late Eighteenth and Early Nineteenth Century. In *Trade, Government and Society in Caribbean History, 1700–1920*, essays presented to Douglas Hall, edited by B. W. Higman. Pp. 21–38. Kingston: Heinemann Educational Books Caribbean.

Handler, Jerome S., and Frederick W. Lange.
1978   *Plantation Slavery in Barbados: An Archaeological and Historical Investigation.* Cambridge: Harvard University Press.

Hatch, Charles E.
1972   *Virgin Islands National Park.* Washington: National Park Service.

Helms, Mary W.
  1981   Black Carib Domestic Organization in Historical Perspective: Traditional Origins of Contemporary Patterns. *Ethnology* 20 (1): 77–86.
Henriques, Fernando.
  1973 [1949]   West Indian Family Organisation. In *Work and
  Family Life*, edited by L. Comitas and D. Lowenthal. Garden City,
  N.Y.: Anchor Press/Doubleday.
  1968 [1953]   *Family and Colour in Jamaica*. London: MacGib-
  bon & Kee.
Herskovits, Melville J., and Frances S. Herskovits.
  1973 [1949]   Retentions and Reinterpretations in Rural Trinidad. In *Work and Family Life*, edited by L. Comitas and D. Lowenthal. Pp. 287–93. Garden City, N.Y.: Anchor Press/Doubleday.
Higman, B. W.
  1973   Household Structure and Fertility on Jamaican Slave
  Plantations: A Nineteenth-Century Example. *Population Studies*
  27 (3): 527–50.
  1975   The Slave Family and Household in the British West Indies, 1800–1834. *Journal of Interdisciplinary History* 6 (2):
  261–87
  1977   Methodological Problems in the Study of the Slave Family. In *Comparative Perspectives on Slavery in New World Plantation Societies*, edited by V. Rubin and A. Tuden. Annals of the New
  York Academy of Sciences, 292: 591–96.
  1978   African and Creole Slave Family Patterns in Trinidad.
  Journal of Family History 3 (2): 163–80.
Hill, Valdemar A.
  1975   *Rise to Recognition*. St. Thomas: Valdemar A. Hill.
Hindness, Barry, and Paul Q. Hirst.
  1975   *Pre-Capitalist Modes of Production*. London: Routledge
  and Kegan Paul.
Hoffmeyer, H.
  1905   *Vor Kirke i Vestindien*. Copenhagen: Bethesdas Boghandel.
Holder, Jean S.
  1981   Turismens rolle i Caribien. *Kontakt* 33 (5): 31.
James, C. L. R.
  1980 [1938].   *The Black Jacobins: Toussaint L'Ouverture and
  the San Domingo Revolution*. London: Allison and Busby.
Jarvis, J. Antonio.
  1971 [1944].   *The Virgin Islands and Their People*. New York:
  Farlyn Enterprises.

Johansen, Hans Chr.
1981   Slave Demography of the Danish West Indian Islands. *Scandinavian Economic History Review* 29 (1): 1–20.
Jørgensen, Andreas.
1953   Et dansk imperialistisk eksperiment. Plantageselskabet "Dansk-Vestindien." *Erhvervshistorisk Aarbog* 5: 52–99.
Kitaj, Torben.
1981   Bag turismens kulisser. *Kontakt* 33 (5): 1.
Knap, Henning Højlund.
1983   Danskerne og Slaveriet. Negerslavedebatten i Danmark indtil 1792. In *Dansk kolonihistorie. Indføring og studier*, edited by P. Hoxcer et al. Pp. 153–174. Aarhus: Forlaget Historia.
Knight, Franklin W.
1970   *Slave Society in Cuba during the Nineteenth Century*. Madison: University of Wisconsin Press.
Konow, Henri.
1966   *Erindringer* ved Tage Kaarsted. Jysk Selskab for Historie, Skrift no. 16. 2 vols. Aarhus: Universitetsforlaget.
Lassen, H.
1895–96   Momenter af Vestindiens Geografi (slutningen). *Geografisk Tidsskrift* 13: 60–85.
Lawaetz, H.
1902   *Brødremenighedens Mission i Dansk-Vestindien 1769–1848*. Copenhagen: Otto B. Wroblewski.
1916   Hvad skylder Danmark den indfødte Befolkning i Vestindien? In *Sandheden om Dansk Vestindien, Dansk Vestindisk Samfunds Skrifter*. Copenhagen: Hagerup.
1940   *Peter v. Scholten*. Copenhagen: Gyldendalske Boghandel.
Lewis, Gordon K.
1972   *The Virgin Islands*. Evanston: Northwestern University Press.
Manners, Robert A.
1965   Remittances and the Unit of Analysis in Anthropological Research. *Southwestern Journal of Anthropology* 21 (3): 179–95.
Marks, Arnaud F., and René A. Römer, eds.
1978   *Family and Kinship in Middle America and the Caribbean*. Co-publication of the University of the Netherlands Antilles Studies and the Royal Institute of Linguistics and Anthropology, Leiden, Netherlands.
Mathurin, Lucille.
1975   *The Rebel Woman in the British West Indies during Slavery*. Kingston: Institute of Jamaica for the African Caribbean Institute of Jamaica.

Mintz, Sidney W.
    1973   A Note on the Definition of Peasantries. *Journal of Peasant Studies* 1: 91–105.
    1974   *Caribbean Transformations*. Chicago: Aldine.
Mintz, Sidney, and Douglas Hall.
    1960   The Origins of the Jamaican Internal Marketing System. *Yale University Publications in Anthropology* 57: 1–26.
Mintz, Sidney, and Richard Price.
    1976   An Anthropological Approach to the Afro-American Past: A Caribbean Perspective. Institute for the Study of Human Issues Occasional Papers, no. 2. Philadelphia.
Moore, James E.
    1979   *Everybody's Virgin Islands*. New York: J. B. Lippincott Co.
Morton, Henry.
    1975   *St. Croix, St. Thomas, St. John: Danish West Indian Sketchbook and Diary, 1843–44*. Copenhagen: Dansk Vestindisk Selskab and St. Croix Landmarks Society.
Muir, John.
    1976   [1901, 1912]. A Voice for Wilderness. In *The American Environment: Readings in the History of Conservation*, edited by R. Nash. Pp. 71–74. Reading, Mass.: Addison-Wesley.
Nørregaard, Georg.
    1966   *Dansk Vestindien 1880–1917*. Vol. 4, *Vore Gamle Tropekolonier*, edited by J. Brøndsted. Denmark: Fremad.
Oldendorp, Christian George A.
    1786   *Historiska Beskrifting över Evangeliska Brødernas missionsarbeta paa Caraibiske öerne St. Thomas, St. Croix och St. Jan*. Stockholm: P. A. Brodin.
Olsen, Poul Erik.
    1980   Dansk-vestindisk koloniadministration. En undersøgelse af tilstande og forandringer i forvaltningens institutionelle opbygning o. 1800–1865. Cand. phil. diss., University of Copenhagen.
    1983   Danske Lov på de vestindiske øer. In *Danske og Norske Lov i 300 år*. Pp. 289–321. Copenhagen: Jurist og Økonomforbundets Forlag.
Olwig, Karen Fog.
    1977   National Parks, Tourism and the Culture of Imperialism. In *Cultural Imperialism, Cultural Identity*. Transactions of the Finnish Anthropological Society 2: 243–56.
    1980   National Parks, Tourism and Local Development: A West Indian Case. *Human Organization* 39 (1): 22–31.

1981a Women, "Matrifocality" and Systems of Exchange: An Ethnohistorical Study of the Afro-American Family on St. John, Danish West Indies. *Ethnohistory* 28 (1): 59–78.
1981b Finding a Place for the Slave Family: Historical Anthropological Perspectives. *Folk* 23: 345–58.
1984 "Witnesses in Spite of Themselves": Reconstructing Afro–Caribbean Culture in the Danish West Indian Archives. *Scandinavian Economic History Review* 32: 61–76.
1985 Slaves and Masters on Eighteenth Century St. John. *Ethnos* 50: 3–4.
Olwig, Karen Fog, and Kenneth Olwig.
1979 Underdevelopment and the Development of "Natural" Park Ideology. *Antipode* 11 (2): 16–25.
O'Neill, Edward.
1972 *Rape of the American Virgins*. New York: Praeger.
Padgug, Robert A.
1976 Problems in the Theory of Slavery and Slave Society. *Science and Society* 40 (1): 3–27.
Paludan, C. F.
1894 Blade af de dansk-vestindiske Øers Historie. *Museum: Tidsskrift for Historie og Geografi* 3: 341–65.
Petersen, Arona.
1975 *Kreole Ketch 'n' Keep*. Charlotte Amalie: St. Thomas Graphics.
Philpott, Stuart B.
1973 *West Indian Migration: The Montserrat Case*. London School of Economics Monograph on Social Anthropology, no. 47. University of London: Athlone Press.
Popovic, Vojislav.
1972 *Tourism in Eastern Africa*. Munich: Weltforum Verlag.
Price, Richard.
1966 Caribbean Fishing and Fishermen: A Historical Sketch. *American Anthropologist* 68 (1): 1363–83.
Proceedings of the Colonial Council for St. Thomas and St. John.
1865–93.
Ramløv, Preben.
1968 *Brødrene og Slaverne*. Copenhagen: Kristeligt Dagblads Forlag.
Rawick, George P.
1972 *From Sundown to Sunup: the Making of the Black Community*. Contributions in Afro-American and African Studies, no. 11. Westport, Conn.: Greenwood.

Rigsarkivet.
    1981   *Landfogeden på St. Jan 1741–1910.* Rigsarkivets 1. afdeling.
Robinson, Alan H.
    1974   *Virgin Islands National Parks: the Story Behind the Scenery.* Las Vegas: KC Publications.
Rodney, Walter.
    1981   Plantation Society in Guyana. *Review* 4 (4): 643–66.
Rubin, Gayle.
    1975   The Traffic in Women: Notes on the "Political Economy" of Sex. In *Towards an Anthropology of Women,* edited by R. R. Reiter. New York: Monthly Review Press.
Sahlins, Marshall.
    1972   *Stone Age Economics.* Chicago: Aldine.
Saint Thomas Mail Notes.
    1933   St. John, December 4.
St. Thomas Tidende.
    1848   Government Placard, August 2.
Sanford, Margaret.
    1975   To Be Treated as a Child of the Home: Black Carib Child Lending in a British West Indian Society. In *Socialization and Communication in Primary Groups,* edited by Thomas R. Williams. The Hague: Mouton Publishers.
Saul, John S., and Roger Woods.
    1975   [1971]. African Peasantries. In *Peasants and Peasant Societies,* edited by T. Shanin. Harmondsworth: Penguin.
Scofield, John.
    1956   Virgin Islands: Tropical Playland, U.S.A. *National Geographic* 109: 201–32.
Seddon, David.
    1978   *Relations of Production: Marxist Approaches to Economic Anthropology.* London: Frank Cass.
Shaw, Earl.
    1934   The Bay Oil Industry of St. John. *Economic Geography* 10: 143–46.
Schmidt, J. C.
    1788   Blandede Anmærkninger, Samlede paa Ejlandet St. Kroix i Amerika. *Samleren* 41: 225–49; 43: 259–63.
Schifflett, Crandall A.
    1975   The Household Composition of Rural Black Families: Luisa County, Virginia, 1880. *Journal of Interdisciplinary History* 6 (2): 235–60.

Smith, M. G.
1962a   *Kinship and Community in Carriacou.* New Haven: Yale University Press.
1962b.   *West Indian Family Structure.* Seattle: University of Washington Press.
1966   Introduction. In *My Mother Who Fathered Me*, by Edith Clarke. London: George Allen and Unwin.
1973   [1956]. Patterns of Rural Labor. In *Work and Family Life*, edited by L. Comitas and D. Lowenthal. Garden City, N.Y.: Doubleday/Anchor Press.
Smith, Raymond T.
1956   *The Negro Family in British Guiana.* London: Routledge and Kegan Paul.
1970   The Nuclear Family in Afro-American Kinship. *Journal of Comparative Family Studies* 1: 55–70.
1973   The Matrifocal Family. In *The Character of Kinship*, edited by J. Goody. Cambridge: Cambridge University Press.
1978a   The Family and the Modern World System: Some Observations from the Caribbean. *Journal of Family History* 3 (4): 337–60.
1978b   Class Differences in West Indian Kinship: A Genealogical Exploration. In *Family and Kinship in Middle America and the Caribbean*, edited by A. F. Marks and R. A. Römer. Copublication of the University of the Netherlands Antilles and the Department of Caribbean Studies of the Royal Institute of Linguistics and Anthropology, Leiden.
1982   Family, Social Change and Social Policy in the West Indies. *Nieuwe West-Indische Gids* 56 (3, 4): 111–42.
Smith, Valene.
1978   Introduction. In *Hosts and Guests: The Anthropology of Tourism*, edited by V. Smith. Oxford: Basil Blackwell.
Stack, Carol B.
1970   The Kindred of Viola Jackson: Residence and Family Organization of an Urban Black American Family. In *Afro-American Anthropology: Contemporary Perspectives*, edited by N. E. Whitten and J. F. Szwed. New York: Free Press.
1974   *All Our Kin: Strategies for Survival in a Black Community.* New York: Harper and Row.
Statistiske Meddelelser.
1852   Folketællingen paa de dansk-vestindiske Øer den 1. October 1846. Series I, 1 (2): 163–95.
1865   Folketællingen paa de dansk-vestindiske Øer den 9[de]

October 1860. Series II, 4: 141–204
1883 Folketællingen paa de dansk-vestindiske Øer den 9de October 1880. Series III, 6: 127–97.
1903 Folketællingen paa de dansk-vestindiske Øer den 1. Februar 1901. Series IV, 12 (5): 5–45.
Sveistrup, P. P.
1942 Bidrag til de tidligere Dansk-Vestindiske Øers økonomiske Historie, med særligt henblik paa sukkerproduktion og sukkerhandel. *Nationaløkonomisk Tidsskrift* 80 (2).
Tanner, Nancy.
1974 Matrifocality in Indonesia and Africa and among Black Americans. In *Woman, Culture and Society*, edited by M. Z. Rosaldo and L. Lamphere. Stanford: Stanford University Press.
Thomas-Hope, Elizabeth M.
1978 The Establishment of a Migration Tradition: British West Indian Movements to the Hispanic Caribbean in the Century after Emancipation. In *Caribbean Social Relations*, edited by C. G. Clarke. Centre for Latin-American Studies, University of Liverpool Monograph Series, no. 8.
Valls, Lito.
1981 *What a Pistarckle! A Dictionary of Virgin Islands English Creole*. St. John: Environmental Studies Program.
Vestindiske Kirkesag, Den.
1909 No. 7, May.
Vibæk, Jens.
1966 Dansk Vestindien 1755–1848. Vol 2, *Vore Gamle Tropekolonier*, edited by J. Brøndsted. Denmark: Fremad.
Virgin Islands National Park Service.
1977 *Visitor Usage of the Park, 1977*. Statistics prepared by James E. Ray, chief ranger, St. John.
West, Hans.
1793 *Bidrag til Beskrivelse over St. Croix med en kort Udsigt over St. Thomas, Tortola, Spanishtown og Crabeneiland.* Copenhagen: Friderik Wilhelm Thiele.
Whitehead, Tony L.
1978 Residence, Kinship, and Mating as Survival Strategies: A West Indian Example. *Journal of Marriage and the Family* 40 (4): 817–28.
Wilson, Peter.
1973 *Crab Antics*. New Haven: Yale University Press.

Archival Sources

Rigsarkivet, Copenhagen

Danske Kancelli, 3. Dept. Abbreviated herein: *DK*.

Breve 1844: 11. May–21. May, Nr. 2041–2300: Brev fra Konstitueret Landfoged Brahde, 6. November 1841, til Det kongelige Raad, St. Thomas.

Generaltoldkammeret. Vestindiske (og guineiske) sager. Abbreviated herein: *G* (my numbering).

1. 1873–1806 Diverse Dokumenter. Dokumenter vedk. Kommissionen for Negerhandelens bedre indretning og ophævelse m.m.
2. Etatsråd Martfelds samlinger over de dansk vestindiske øer. 6 vols.

Folketællingerne. Dansk Vestindien. Det statistiske Departement. Abbreviated herein: *F*.

Folketællingslisterne for St. Jan: 1835, 1841, 1846, 1850, 1855, 1857, 1860, 1870, 1880, 1901, 1911.
Folketællingslisterne for St. Thomas: 1846, 1850, 1855, 1857, 1860, 1870, 1880, 1901, 1911.

Haandskriftsamlingen. Danske Bilande og Kolonier. Abbreviated herein: *H* (my numbering).

1. E. V. Loses Historiske Samlinger om den lutherske Kirke. VII D7-8, n.d.

Landfogeden på St. Jan. Vestindiske Lokalarkiver. Abbreviated herein: *LA*.

1. Kopier af/koncepter til udgåede skrivelser, 1857–69.
2. Kopier af/koncepter til udgåede skrivelser, 1869–88.
5. Kopier af/koncepter til skrivelser til guvernementet, St. Thomas, 1824–45.
6. Kopier af/koncepter til skrivelser til guvernementet/præsidentskabet, St. Thomas (1846–56) og til rådet, St. Thomas (1824–37).
7. Kopier af/koncepter til skrivelser til rådet, St. Thomas, og til (general) guvernementet, St. Croix, 1838–55.
15. Indkomne skrivelser fra kommandanten/guvernøren, St. Thomas, 1815–27.
17. Indkomne skrivelser fra kommandanten/guvernøren, St.

Thomas, 1834–45.
   28. Sager ang. politi- og pasvæsen, 1837–48.
   29. Sager ang. politi- og pasvæsen, 1843–48.
   30. Politisager, 1844–50.
   31. Politijournal, 1829–36.
   32. Politijournal, 1836–40.
   33. Politijournal, 1840–44.
   34. Politijournal, 1845–47.
   35. Politijournal, 1847–60.
   39. Politiretsprotokol, 1818–25.
   40. Politiretsprotokol, 1825–32.
   41. Politiretsprotokol, 1832–41.
   42. Politiretsprotokol, 1841–51.
   43. Politiretsprotokol, 1851–55.
   44. Politiretsprotokol, 1855–62.
   45. Politiretsprotokol, 1862–65.
   46. Politiretsprotokol, 1865–67.
   47. Politiretsprotokol, 1867–68.
   48. Politiretsprotokol, 1868–71.
   58. Politiretssager, 1788–1832.
   59. Politiretssager, 1829–36.
   64. Landretsprotokol, 1752–59.
   65. Landretsprotokol, 1760–71.
   66. Landretsprotokol, 1772–77.
   67. Landretsprotokol, 1777–82.
   68. Landretsprotokol, 1783–86.
   69. Landretsprotokol, 1786–87.
   70. Landretsprotokol, 1787–90.
   72. Landretsprotokol, 1802–7.
   73. Landretsprotokol, 1807–20.
   76. Landretsprotokol, 1837–44.
   77. Landretsprotokol, 1844–56.
   81. Landretssager, 1811–20.
   83. Landretssager, 1827–32.
   85. Landretssager, 1832–45.
   86. Fogedprotokol, 1748–74.
   87. Fogedprotokol, 1789–1813.
   86. Fogedprotokol, 1789–1866.
   89. Sager vedr. fogedforretninger, 1790–1845.
   107. Testament- og skifteretssessionsprotokol, 1836–59.
   109. Skiftedokumenter, 1778–1824.
   117. Skiftedokumenter, 1841.
   120. Skiftedokumenter, 1848–49.

149. Sporteljournaler, 1822–26.
150. Sporteljournaler, 1839–53.
159. Sager vedr. stadshauptmanden, 1830–56.
160. Sager vedr. stadshauptmanden, 1840–58.

St. Thomas guvernement/Kommandantskab. Vestindiske Lokalar-
kiv. Diverse Sager. Abbreviated herein: *STG* (my numbering).

1. Sag angaaende administrationen af plantagen Bordeaux. TB
35 th, fag 1 hylde 2.
2. Privat-Correspondence Protokoll for Vicegouverneur H. H.
Berg 1848–52. TB 35 th, fag 1 hylde 2.

Privatarkiver. Abbreviated herein: *SP.*

Schimmelmanske Privatarkiv. Dokumenter vedr. de Schimmel-
mannske Plantager. Vestindien 1757–1869. No. 33.

Sundhedskollegiet/Sundhedsstyrelsen. Abbreviated herein: *SS.*

1854, Medicinal Indberetning fra St. Thomas og St. Jan Land-
physicat.
1856, Medicinal Indberetning fra St. Thomas og St. Jan Land-
physicat.

Den Vestindiske Kommission af 18. November 1902. F 04-1199/35.
Abbreviated herein: *VK.*

8. Journalsager 91: Adresse til den Kongelige Kommission fra
Indbyggerne paa St. Jan; 132: Landejendomme paa St. Jan.

Vestindisk Revideret Regnskab. Abbreviated herein: *VRR.*

1755–1917, Matriklen for St. Jan. Fag B, reol 40–41, tv.

Landsarkivet, Copenhagen

St. Thomas Pastoratsarkiv. Abbreviated herein: *STP* (my numbering).

1. Brevkopibog over indkommende og udgaaende Sager,
1901–17.
2. Kirkebog for St. Jan, 1861–1917.
3. Skolekommisionen for St. Jan, 1862–1918.

Landesarchiv, Schleswig

Schimmelmann Archiv Ahrensburg (Familienarchiv). Abbreviated
herein: *SAA.*

216   *References Cited*

62. Carolina Plantagenjournal 1766–67, Westindische Besitzungen (Carolina, La Grange, Princesse) 1767–1863.

National Archives, Washington

Records of the Danish Government of the Virgin Islands, 1672–1917

Records of the Office of the Sheriff on St. John, Record Group 55. Abbreviated herein: *RD*.
Box 1904, list of slave owners and former slaves, 1853–54.

Moravian Archives, Bethlehem, Pennsylvania

J.1 Emmaus Church Register, 1833–81. On microfilm, Enid M. Baa Library, St. Thomas. Abbreviated herein: *M*.

Enid M. Baa Library

Archives Division, Charlotte Amalie, St. Thomas. Abbreviated herein: *EMB* (my numbering).
   1. House and Sanitary Survey, 1935.
   2. Heste- og Baadskat, 1912–19.
   3. St. John police records, 1921–30.

Index

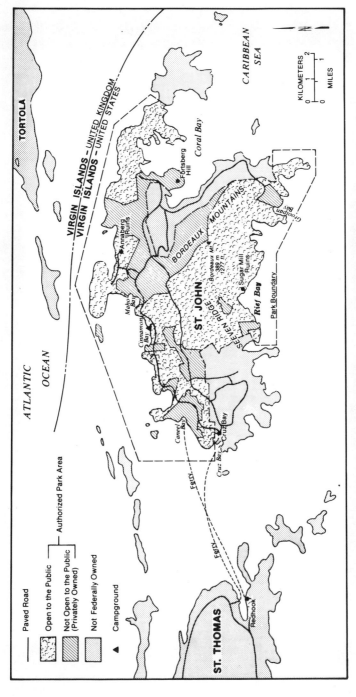

Map of St. John, 1975, showing national park areas and private property within the park boundary.